More
The ^ Complete
Second Verse

BY

CHARLES B. COOPER III, PhD

ELIZABETH RIVER
PRESS

THE MORE COMPLETE SECOND VERSE

By Charles Cooper, PhD

Publication of Elizabeth River Press
First Edition, First Printing

Catalog in publication data is on file with the Library of Congress.

Author: Dr. Charles B. Cooper III
Foreword by Dr. Daniel Ford, PhD
Editors: Michel Mealo, Stella Samuel, Amy Lloyd
Art: Becky Kiper, JM Stegar, Charles Cooper, Martin Hill, Remedios Varo, Lana Radovich, Tammera Cooper
All art used by Permission

Cover Design by Rae Merritt Design, raemerritt.com

ISBN: 978-1-952818-00-4

Printed in the United States of America.

Poetry

FOREWORD

By Dr. Daniel Ford, PhD

I almost asked Archibald MacLeish the wrong question one time, namely, "What did you mean in 'Ars Poetica' when you wrote that a 'poem should not mean but be'?" I caught myself before making the foolish query and I am glad, for now, over a half-century later, I see quite clearly what the poet was getting at as I digest this present volume.

Dr. Charles Cooper's work epitomizes the mysterious ways poetry gives substance to what is often ineffable. Cooper's methodology does not come from linguistic trickery as is common in contemporary verse, but from a profound gift that takes many forms. Its quintessence is sensory language hovering over universal truths.

A strong example of this gift resides in "Forget the Sun." Here, the poet admits the insufficiency of language: justice itself prevents mere words from capturing the beauty he sees. It is as if the limitation of language causes him to want more of what cannot be expressed. Thus, Cooper's poem hints at a deep secret hidden in all our hearts. In wanting more than language can yield, Cooper reaches the realm of what Emily Dickenson named telling it "slant." The main way Cooper tells it "slant" resides in his rejection of anything artificial, along with his desire to ameliorate man's persistent tendency to go through life mindlessly. In such rejection and its concomitant desire, I find a singular connection with Robert Frost.

Speaking of how people are prone to go mindlessly about their affairs, Amy, in Frost's "Home Burial," says, "I'll not have grief so / If I can change it." Cooper makes a similar outcry in this volume. But his artistic wail is not only about the transitoriness of grief, but many other emotional pulls on the human psyche. In his well-structured poem, "God and Man," for example, Cooper identifies the complex heart of the human condition. Citing the multiple paintings at St. Peter's, he depicts destruction as sin and production as virtue. This seemingly endless cycle of destruction and production is repugnant to the poet. The words "Give me more," with which Cooper concludes the poem is his way of saying "slant" what Frost's Amy utters, "I won't have it so / If I can change it." There is no way to encapsulate Cooper's overriding theme of "Give me more" in this space, but I can report the joy I feel in seeing Dr. Charles Cooper's potentiality fulfilled. He has, indeed, given me more. Twenty-plus years ago, Chuck enriched my English classroom at Palm Beach Atlantic University with wit and clear-eyed commentary. He also favored me with friendship and visits to my academic study. He was more my colleague than my student and I see that his drive to ask hard questions with grace has not burned up in the sun, but gelled. This fine collection shows that solidity while somehow giving utterance to a beauty beyond mere words.

DR. DANIEL G. FORD, PHD

"ALL YE WHO ENTER HERE"

ART BY BECKY KIPER

TABLE OF CONTENTS

13

INDEX OF ARTWORK

BOOK 1: OPEN WOUNDS & FAIRY TALES

"DRUID TOWER"

ART BY UNKNOWN

"FAIRY TALES ARE TRUE
NOT BECAUSE THEY TELL US
DRAGONS ARE REAL,
BUT BECAUSE THEY TELL US
DRAGONS CAN BE DEFEATED."

- NEAL GAIMAN MASQUERADING AS G.K. CHESTERTON

"DRAGON SLAYER"

ART BY BECKY KIPER

I WAS YOUNG

You know your name.
I will not write it here.
This is dedicated to you:
To what I remember of you,
Being young,
Radiant, righteous, patient, poised, and beautiful

I burned night and day with passion.
Sleep was a mortal companion.
What I mean to say is,
I will sleep when I'm dead.
When I was young,
I was a fan of fire.
It was the only thing
Which burned
as hot
as me,
Until I met you.
For that woman,
and the woman you became,
and every iteration in between,
Each of these words, chosen in time
For you, by truth itself.
These are the words I tried to pen
So long ago,
In so many ways
So you could know.
Read the words,
Perhaps to see why,
I never could say goodbye.

As much as I knew you then,
There was still too much
I did not understand.
I had left to learn…
To learn to live.

Open Wounds & Fairy Tales
Chuck Cooper

Now, I have sliced
From my whole heart,
These ink stains on this page,
Written for you,
In long, loving cuts.

With this apology,
With a lifetime behind,
I give you ink,
paper,
and poems,
And the life I've led.

A life lived white hot.
Burning pain,
scarred remains of memories,
A fire that vanquished the night,
Brought you into my life
and my love,
A love that burns for you,
Casting divine truths.
Expel the wind and waning dawn.
I cast my lot with this song
And cry out in joy;
It won't be long now…

Yours in verse,

Chuck Cooper

"SPILLED INK"

ART BY BECKY KIPER

JOURNAL

Fine, leather-bound journal,
Brown, suede with creamy white page,
Fine paper, with true lines of blue,
Each says, what a fine fellow are you
To me and my pen.

I raise my pen and violate
Those pages.
Day after day;
Night after night;

Jet black ink,
Which paints my rage with love,
Which stains the creamy page.
I watch as it evolves,
Growing with each new word,
Better than it was,
But am I better, is life,
For having spoken those words out loud?

Open Wounds & Fairy Tales
Chuck Cooper

Truth without regard for others is so loud
And painful.
It hurts too much not to say
Something.
Something, which hurts so many when said.
Sticks and stones, broken bones,
But we all end up dead.
So be it. So let it be.
A day and night in reverie.
In the ink there is no retreat.

Given what is said,
Once read,
Will anyone who counts these words…
In their lexicon of knowledge,
Ever be able to recall
What it meant to be
Before they *knew* me.

I hope not.

GIFT

I was given life,
So I have tried to live
By building, solving, creating.
But I do not know when I will simply live,
Given wage, and ink, and page,
And a chance to decide my own fate.

This I asked of the Creator…
"Must I wage war against fate,
So I can love and not hate
People who labor to decide
what is right for me?
Fools one and all
Who cannot see the way I see.
When will the past let me be.
I am tortured by duty
to always do what I must.
When will I be free?"
Even desire is bound by reason
Sometimes. We call this wisdom.
But what if wisdom,
stole the desires of my heart,
In a periodic, pragmatic, lark
And left me with nothing,
Again?

When I think I'm not enough,
I find myself looking up,
Into the infinite space over my head.
I take a breath and know the potential
Of creation is infinite.
I know it because I feel it…
As I dance on the Astral plane...
I live it. I breath it.
I take that next step.
No, it is not always wise or right.
But I can never, ever stop,

Open Wounds & Fairy Tales
Chuck Cooper

Because of who I am.

What moves men to be wise?
How would I know?
There is no greater man than a builder;
No greater person than a mother;
There is only one thing more,
The Architect of us all,
Because all creation begins and ends with love.
I have been, done, and seen,
But I am not wise.
What would wisdom mean to me,
If I create?
In those creations, I live,
But life is denied to me.

Every day seems further away
Through the eyes of age.
Those eyes that see less,
But reveal more,
And that is experience.

With my experience,
I choose love.
Divine maker, must I ask...
"God, please,
Let me choose love?
Let me dance naked on a parquet floor,
As a gift for you...
my joy...
This dance...
Let me live and create
And find romance."

If there is a chance,
If I have this choice,
To display truth and beauty in love
Painting holy ground,
With sweat and blood

The Complete Second Verse
Charles Cooper, PhD

Drained from my open wounds onto the floor.
I will give you all,
And when there is no more.
I will rest with
No regrets.
No regrets, Not thinking how much or how long,
No matter what beats in my chest.
What I have made, what I have done,
Is my gift to you."

"ELIZABETH"

ART BY CHUCK COOPER

The Complete Second Verse
Charles Cooper, PhD

ELIZABETH

Elizabeth River,
Caress the ground,
Through bend and turn, your rushing sound.
Not wanting less, you saved your kiss.
Each breath, each look,
Nothing was frivolous.

Every heartbeat had meaning.
Every step, every sound,
Embracing life and living;
Experience unbound.
A gentler soul then,
Not laden with experience
Life without doubt.

I called to the river, not dressed
In finery or vapid prose
I wanted that kiss,
Sometimes a child knows.
That you are the beginning,
The journey, the home,
The key, the love,
Tender mercy in silent nights,
The river from which all good grows.

Eyes open wide into the light
To shout from high
To all who hear, "The beauty of today,
A sight that brought me tears."

What love, what love, what love, of man
Beckons him to this fallen land
Guided by his own deft hand

On a journey to finally say, "I am."

Flow gently River of light:

Open Wounds & Fairy Tales
Chuck Cooper

Elizabeth,
the guide,
through curves and strife,
past valley's unseen
to perilous peaks,
On this journey to be
        more.

Until the day
        we two lay down
Embracing life,
        beneath the ground.
Finally,
        in each other's arms
Finally,
        free from harm.

HAUNTED

I lay and watched your final breath,
Lay in a pool of steel, blood, and gnashing teeth.
Everyone knew that smile and laugh,
As you saw the life you had lived
Replay before your eyes,
I Watched the life you were to live
Play in front of mine.

So many people, so much love,
So much you left behind.
So much more you had to give,
So the responsibility became mine.

Every breath I took was fire, not desire.
No repose to be had
The life I was given back
was given to chasing ghosts.
No action, no deed, nothing ever was my own;
From beginning to end,
Whether hidden or exposed
It was a life spent chasing a ghost.

In times such as these,
What is the gift?
Death gives birth to mourning
And mourning to life and living.
The breath in my lungs,
The blood on my hands
Gave life to the man I am.
Achievements you will never see
Tears, monuments, and poetry.
You gave your life,
I gave you those.
I've lived this life chasing a ghost.

QUANTUM LOVE

What is this madness?
I am changed, simply by your existence.
Not in a Shrodinger's Cat Way,
But a very real, visceral way.
Even with you locked away in a grave,
You changed me,
And I changed the world,
For you.
What else could I do?

You changed the way I thought,
With words.
You changed the way I walked,
With direction.
You changed the way I lived,
With a feral desire to be better than I was,
And I was, for the memory of you.

I never wanted to tell you as much as today.
I whisper it to the wind,
For you have gone away.
Your ears will never hear the sound
And eyes will never see the ground
That I tread to be here
So I could spread these tears
In this hallowed place.
They don't say what I want to anyway,
But they come all the same.
Along with all the desire
That will not go away.
I whisper to the wind, wipe my face free of feelings,
Until Tomorrow,
When I will do this all again.

The Complete Second Verse
Charles Cooper, PhD

FIRST LOVE

A lifetime ago,
I glimpsed you for the first time.

Dark eyes,
      black hair,
            ruby lips.

I didn't know what it meant to love,
But I loved you.
Before the days turned to night
Before death came from life
I loved you.

Every day, I walked you to class,
Snuck a kiss, shared a laugh.
When I looked at you, I saw life,
My life, the way it should be,
What we could achieve as you and me.

I saw you and knew I could be what you deserved,
But to be him, I had to leave.
The blow to my head notwithstanding,
Wandering eye and brain damage, I walked away.

Through days and nights of struggle,
I worked to become a man.
The one that you deserved
I lived and fought, failed to succeed
I learned from every circumstance, learned humility.
In a tunnel of turmoil, tortured hell and hail
Your vision was my breath.
In all my learning and long experience
You beat within my chest.
At night when my eyes closed
I would see you before I would rest.

Forever and a day has passed.

Open Wounds & Fairy Tales
Chuck Cooper

I have returned to the place of my birth.
More clear than ever,
the life that awaited me here.
Driven to be the man you deserve,
I have achieved so much;
In the words of Mercédès to her beloved Dantès,
"I have nothing left to ask of God;
I have seen you again."

So much has come and gone since then,
So I will only say,
"I have some power in this world and
I stand ready to use that power for those I love.
I love you."

The Complete Second Verse
Charles Cooper, PhD

WHAT IT TAKES

Yesterday felt
Like the quarter arcade
From so long ago…
It was long and lonely.
Filled with vacant sounds
Someone said something
But it my memory, all I heard was
Beep, Boop, Bop.
Sad… Hollow, seeping, sound.
Something, rolling across the floor
Slippery… Sliding.
"Grab ahold," says every instinct
And I do, holding firm,
Wanting so much more,
I kissed a girl.
And she liked it…
Enough to do it again,
But not enough to make it mean,
Not enough to value me.

It doesn't matter anyway.
The sun came up today
In a lackadaisical parade of purpose
You could almost hear Apollo say,
"If I must" or "I suppose."

Modern men,
And women,
Wearing black and white,
Having earned the right to be free
Do Not Even Vote…

Even… *Today*
Is so near to meaningless.
People who used to smoke and laugh
Count calories and eat broccoli
Because they fear

Open Wounds & Fairy Tales
Chuck Cooper

The inevitable.
The same people
Look down their noses, judging…
Pumping smug
onto those,
Who create smog
With their breathing
Brought on by embraced, raptured life.
Pretending at victimhood,
Like a pedestrian
At the running of the bulls
in Spain,
Gored to death on TV.
It's not fame,
But it feels like it.

For me, another day
Turns into a long night.
I play both sides of the fence
Against each other.
I sell prosperity to the rich
Who didn't know they needed nothing
So very much.
For me, it's time to give this up.
Doing something right
Matters, this time.
A burden I should have never known
was too large to be carried,
But I did it anyway.
It's time to put it down.
Now, it's time to go home.

The Complete Second Verse
Charles Cooper, PhD

REBORN

I would be reborn
And live it all again.
Avoid mistakes, regrets.

Forsake,
The circumstance that made me
Who I am.

Who would I be?
Not painted, tarnished, scared, or tattooed
The only blemish, I do not regret is you.
A lovely scar that I can never give up.
The only scar given that did not corrupt me.

Oh, I wish to be clean,
But fear to wash away
The scar you left me,
The gift you gave;
If I lived again,
I would have stayed.
No matter the price,
Whatever the cost,
Like the ship without stars,
Without you,
I am lost.

SUBLIME

The sun shown on a flat river,
No ripples, no waves,
No insects, no fish
Just placid, stolid water sitting,
Maybe even pooling.
There was no way to tell,
If the water came or went.

It was a river to be sure,
It had both in and out-lets,
Slipping a serenade beneath the surface,
Sublime and meandering.
On a journey home,
But to the casual observer, nothing was betrayed.
Life can be lived this way, when it is lived well.
Sacrifice can be sublime with time,
In truth, in life,
Without pomp, circumstance, or strife.
It is a simple expression
of values held deep.

Leaders lead while barkers screech.
Those who do, do,
Not for credit from men,
But perhaps the love of men.
For the love and expression
Of a person's own values
Is truly all there is.
Live a life of sacrifice:
Trade a piece of you,
  in time, thoughts, and talent,
Elbow grease… even work.
All those things you have to trade,
For something that is good in your own eyes
And given freely,
So those eyes can see
Values expressed in which you believe;

The Complete Second Verse
Charles Cooper, PhD

And no one can ask anyone for more
Than this.

Greater love there may well be,
But not in this world.

You, who give yourself for a price,
Are engaged in trade, not sacrifice.

What is the cost of sacrifice?
If ever there were such a thing,
Such a day, or a night, to give
What you could give, and then more.
Would it be worth the power of being,
Of knowing yourself to be,
Who you are
Instead of some whore?
Is there a cost to sacrifice?
Only the soul.
Every time you are less
That your created self
How is the creator not betrayed?

What makes men great?
Is it sacrifice, virtue or values
To oneself or another?
Is it creation, that pinnacle of existence
That is so common and yet so divine.

What makes men great?
Is it achievement,
Or glory or humor, or a mask, the ability to be
Someone else, anyone else, in any situation?
Or is it simply to be oneself
Under placid waters
All these things as one
Unnoticed, unremembered
Slipping along, a life lived well.
Thomas Gray had words for you.

That you lived was enough;
That you lived well, was sublime.

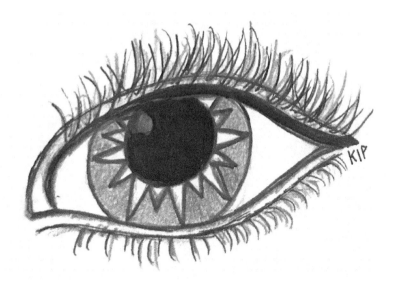

"EYES OPEN"

ART BY BECKY KIPER

RADIANT

Radiant rays call out the day
Until torrential rain
Conveys life.
Eyes open,
Leaving me bound.

Then the night came
For so long
There was no dawn.
Patience, count to ten,
Ten million times…
Sacred geometry
From Stonehenge to Byzantium
Upon this rock, I set a line…
Until the sun rose again,

Open Wounds & Fairy Tales
Chuck Cooper

Summer solstice,
No celebration to be had.

There, I kissed you goodbye like I should have.
But I never saw the radiant rays of light
In your eyes again.

Never again.

This is what tears are made of...
This is...

FOUNTAIN

Fountains have a memory.
Life has a tab.
Like an eternal flame,
Like the flowing water,
Like the greatness, we have never been.
It all costs something.
The sun rose and set yesterday
Now memory is a monument
To a happier day
That wasn't even real.
Flowing fount forever,
Never frozen in decay.
Decay cannot be frozen
Only fought to a stalemate.
What we lose in the avalanche
Is nothing,
Compared to what we take away.

Tourniquets silence
Fountains of blood,
Hearts once beating
Gave all that they could.
There is no price for freedom,
No tomorrow you can pay
The burden of the debt we owe
Leaves no room for escape.
Silence replayed
Silence never paid for
The water which ran and ran
Costs nothing
And I,
I was thirsty.

BRIDE

Life can be a loathsome journey,
When you are lost.
Still more so when you are lonely.
If anyone ever said,
I went near your bed,
It was proof they didn't even know me.

If you were a bride for a day
Or a week, or a month,
In a life full of pain,
On a road that was tough,
How long could you travel,
Just on love?

If you were a bride for a day,
Had love stolen away.
Would you take the next step?
And the next, and the next,
If your love were the wheels of your truck,
Could you climb in the cab and drive?
With the world on your back
Like Atlas, sweat streaming down your face and chest
Arms writhing in agony,
Making the world better
For who, Not for you?
What would you do
To be a bride?

ILLUSIONS

We were all young once.
We lived in a world
where cool,
and fun,
and parties,
and cliques mattered.

Those of us who could,
grew up.

Those who could not still live
Under the mistaken belief
That the illusions of youth
Are relevant
in any way
Whatsoever.

LOST

When I was ten,
I was lost in the woods.
Where I wandered with my dog Han,
A beautiful, black lab.
It was winter, and there was snow.
This loving, loyal dog at my side
Did not care
That I was armed with a BB gun,
Which I fired at everything.

When I was 24,
I was lost in the woods.
In the company
of a Company of men.
We carried rifles,
and food,
and medical supplies,
And called ourselves
"Masters of Chaos."
My rifle wasn't nearly as harmless
That time.

When I was 36,
I was lost in an urban jungle.
I played politics with fools
Who with confidence and charm
Made deals without ideals.
And after those deals were done
They road off into the sun.
I was undone, and walked away
I only walked because I couldn't run.

When I was 42, I was lost, alone and broken.
I came home to live on a farm.
I went back into the woods of my youth
It was there, that I swear,
I came face to face with God.

50

The Complete Second Verse
Charles Cooper, PhD

At dawn the next day,
I rose to find:
A tiny locket on the dresser,
Thicker soles on my shoes,
Calloused hands and feet,
A door open that had been closed.
It was as though,
Everything was telling me:

"Go.
Rise.
You have work to do.
Stand, give us your all.
Run, through day and night
Until it's finally time
For you to come home.
Until then, you won't belong,
Anywhere, especially here."

10-63-15

"HER"

ART BY CHARLES COOPER

BOTTOM

There is a place you find yourself
A place with no way out,
...No path forward,
...No step you can take,
...No dawn or daybreak,
All love and laughter absorbed
This place just wants more.
No thing can assuage
Such a place.
We've all been there,
Lost and
Disgraced.

On that day,
In that moment,
When you have fought the same fight
A thousand times,
When there's nothing left to do
Save cry over yours or mine,
And the only path to happiness
Is to walk away this time,
It's time to look up.
Move forward and look up.
Don't close your eyes, Look up.
Take the step, Look up.
Take a breath, Look up.
Reach out your hand to the sky
Take a leap, fly.

MORE

Cosmic truth may just describe,
The thing I know when I look in your eyes.
Spinning webs around and between
You and I.
I could call it love,
But it's insufficient to describe
What I feel for you.

Occasionally, I call it cerebral madness
Because everything that keeps me alive
Stops and sighs.
My heart beats double time
Pushing you through my veins
Blending our lives.
We were joined.
We are joined,
By truth.

Since birth,
I believed one and one was two
Until I met you,
We are more.

Does time pass quicker,
If I count the heartbeats,
While I'm waiting for you?
If I can't deny time,
I can certainly defy it.
The young can wait forever.

I will let nothing dull the portrait,
Nothing disguises the beauty,
Nothing contains the feeling
of the visage I keep in my mind.

I wonder if you would mind,

The Complete Second Verse
Charles Cooper, PhD

If I saw you soon?

That time I did see you:
My breathing stopped.
My heart fell still.
Betrayed by some autonomic behavior,
My face grew red mixed with blue
A solemn shade of purple too.

I held my breath waiting for you,
And stood and stared as long as I could,
Until a faint blush and smile restarted my heart.

You will forgive me.
I thought to wait forever
But was betrayed by an autonomic reflex.
My body swayed and waned,
I took a breath.

SECRETS

Thirty-some-odd years ago,
      a lifetime away from today
A boy wandered through his childhood home
To the attic where he would play.
It was a whimsical time,
No fear or lies,
No sin or pain
Or ties to bind.
Life was simple,
Pure and fun.
In the home, there in the Attic,
There was a chest,
An aging lock of iron and steel
Guarded a secret that was real.
Mystery and exploration are the truths of childhood.
A lock on anything spawns the dream of the day it opens;
Containing magic artifacts, treasures, toys.
There are no limits on the dreams of a boy.

As the boy turned to man,
As a soldier in the sand,
He broke his father's rules.
"Another lesson learned," he sighed,
"The old man knew."
Night after night and day after day,
Life was not play for a man.
He carried the weight of the things that his father had taught,
Be loyal and kind,
Earn what you want,
Give when you can,
That's the life of a man.
No matter who we are,
Or where we stand,
The bindings between us are real.

The terror of night and morning,
Watching life leave a brother's eyes;

The Complete Second Verse
Charles Cooper, PhD

The journey from dawn to dusk,
Saying too many final goodbyes.
His mind locked away the terrors and thoughts
Of the luck that carried him through.
Walled off the feelings, thoughts, and regrets;
He found his center, deep in his chest.

He married and lived;
And locked it away.
He was blessed with three kids
He taught everything to.
They played, safe and sound,
His house, hallowed ground,
 Safe from the things that he knew.
They all smiled through the days
As he endured the nights.

Of the things he was taught by his father,
When alone with his boys in the woods, he told them;
"Be loyal and kind,
Earn what you want,
Give when you can,
That's the life of a man.
No matter who we are,
Or where we stand,
The bindings between us are real."

He found some satisfaction between sleep and the dreams.
He woke much less often and rarely heard the screams.
He remembered the chest as his children would play
Thinking what was inside, until the day his phone rang.
His mother through tears summoned him to his home
"It's your father," she said, "you had better come fast."
The family packed the car,
That final die cast.
On an 18-hour drive to the street where he'd lived.
Through the door to the bedside of his father who wept.
As his eyes met his son's, he exhaled his last breath.
When an unmistakable glowing pride

came into the old man's eyes.
As he passed from this life to his place in the grave
He saw the honor of the gift that he was taught
Saw his father and heard the words given him;
Be loyal and kind,
Earn what you want,
Give when you can,
That's the life of a man.
His heart fell silent.
His eyes fell shut.
His hand took his son's
And left a small key.

Memories sometimes strain at the locks in spite of oneself.
Break down, fall down;
Burdens of being teach humility.
Live through this is the challenge
We are all born to fail,
But in the living
There is a mission
Which changes the heart forever.
"You do not survive, but you do not die.
Never surrender, then, now, or ever.
Make and remake yourself to be a man;
To say, I am.
And always remember:
Be loyal and kind,
Earn what you want,
Give when you can,
That's the life of a man.
No matter who we are,
Or where we stand,
The bindings between us are real."

A man never opens his father's chest.
He lives life.
Takes the words that he heard as a child
Makes a life, makes mistakes,
Takes responsibility for them,

The Complete Second Verse
Charles Cooper, PhD

Along the way, he learns the secrets that his father knew,
A father who can only see with pride,
Immortality of a kind,
The man his son has become.
A man who is
Loyal and kind
Earns his life
Gives without thought or regret
Pulls tight the bindings he forged
Into a shroud of light
That warms him as he passes this life
And sleeps the sleep of a man.

ALONE

I find myself alone,
In a crowded room of well wishers,
Again.

Why am I alone?
If we were not all alone,
By our nature, alone in a cave of perception,
I would still be alone.
In bed with a wife,
On a team, throughout life,
Every day, alone.

If I had not chosen, my chosen career
If I had not met a million liars,
And believed every word for years,
If I had not bribed, bought, taken, and slaughtered
People who did not deserve it.
I would be alone

I learned not to trust,
From others and from me.
I learned to fear the hurt
That comes from loss
That comes from loving,
And leaving and moving on.
I learned to be alone.

The price of youth is high.
The cost of learning to balance
Passion and emotion,
Lust and longing,
Blind desire, and
Love is without fail,
deep and painful.
It only comes from experience,
And experience costs
Without fail.

60

The Complete Second Verse
Charles Cooper, PhD

It's true that love begets intimacy
And intimacy begets vulnerability
And vulnerability begets pain.
The transitive law of love is
The price of love is pain.
It is too high a price to pay
Again and again.

I am alone, because I believe
In the One, in true love,
In natural, symbiotic living,
A desire to do and be
for each other,
Without contentious desire for another,
Shared satisfaction,
And that,
I have not found.
But I have seen it
once or twice,
And so I am alone.

I want too much from love,
too much from people.
Because I feel too much from touch,
too much from connections.
Because I expect too much from someone who loves,
too much from the connections
made by love,
by touch.

I am alone
Because I choose to guard
the tender places
That bring so much pain,
Vulnerable places,
that can't deal with rain,
Empty places,
that will not be filled.

Oh, I am a man,
and have some skill,
But I will never exercise in frivolity.
The price of admission
is just too high,
And life is too short to live a lie.

HONOR

The price of tomorrow is hope.
The cost of tomorrow is now.
That patient pleasure is never enough
To quench my thirst for long.

There's nothing in today
To make me stay;
No magic and no kiss
To draw me near
Until I find again,
I am betrayed.
If I surrender for today
It will be another year.

I'm destined to spin,
Round and around.
My disease is to do all that I can
So I can be an honorable man.

I rotate like a top,
On a wave, near the crest,
Crashing down into the water
The blue, grey, and black depths.
"Round and around he goes,
Where he lands,
No one…
With no one,
But himself.
My destiny is me.
Counting on myself.
Growing into myself.
Relying on myself.
And finally,
Finding
Myself
With
Myself,

Open Wounds & Fairy Tales
Chuck Cooper

Again.

Funny the words
That come.
I asked myself, where I would be
If it wasn't for me waiting
For everything to be right.
Just right,
And good,
And honorable,
Within the perimeter
Of the promises I made.

If tomorrow was today
I would appear today,
With a jester's hat
Wearing a false nobility
As my crest upon a vest.

And I hate vests.

The Complete Second Verse
Charles Cooper, PhD

EMPTINESS

"Fairy Tales make the present tolerable…"
Who says such a thing?
My true love told me this.
Like hope,
and dreams,
and things not real,
What can redeem a moment
That is…
Real.

Hope, dream, do…
It's a choice.
I still want you.
This is the emptiness I feel.

I know, you feel it too.

CHASE

"My daddy told me,
Never choose the easy way."
But everything is making trades.
You do what you do,
Find what you can,
A worthwhile life,
A husband or wife.

We spend so much time
Chasing the angled link to easy,
An impossible joint, which bonds
Dreams to reality.
The reality is,
Work, hard, hard work,
Blood, sweat, and tears…
Spend and spread across years and years.
There is no easy way.
There's no way to stay
In one place and grow.
No way to know,
Without learning, experiencing;
To hear without listening;
To see without eyes;
To know truth - when all you hear is lies
There is no easy way.
There is no way
To live without trying
To be alive without dying
No easy way.

But I went looking.
I went looking anyway.

"A FAIRY NEEDS WINGS"

ART BY BECKY KIPER

FAIRY TALES

It's been decades since Disney froze himself,
And hope and dreams with him.

It's been two thousand years
Since it was said that death
Could be cured with the words,
"Lazarus Come forth."

I have my fairy tale,
As most people do.
But I believe in time,
This tale will come true
Because once upon a time,
there was me and you.

My tale is as old as time itself.
Boy meets girl. Boy falls in love.
True love, not one man in a hundred years...
The boy wasn't strong or rich
But he dreamed,
To be enough... To be a man.

Sometimes,
A boy journeys into the world.
To make a fortune,
to grow, to fight, to learn life
And through experience,
find humility.

Years would intervene,
In this fight with fate.
The man betrayed his own goal.
Trading love for convenience,
And love that's not true love,
Takes life and makes regret,
And duties, and obligations.

The Complete Second Verse
Charles Cooper, PhD

So that when the hero returns home
Having navigated the obstacles,
Of the journey to true love,
He finds empty fields and broken hearts.
That's not the way the fairy tale goes.
Life, of course, is never so simple.

The One is still the one.
Still stirs his heart
With maddening song.
His home is still his home,
The only place, he's ever belonged.
Unlike Rapunzel, her hair did not grow.
It remains just out of reach,
Of the hero below.

Let out your hair, Rapunzel.
Am I ever to know,
True love's embrace?
Am I never to know,
Her white dress and fine lace?

Our story had a cast of characters.
There was God versus Fate versus Love,
And there was you and I,
Just along for the ride.
I engaged in life without living,
A void of feeling that makes hate.
I tried to try, to strive and create.
But all that I made was empty,
Trite, and common place.

I think God had this grand plan for life,
After all, he introduced me to you,
There were opportunities that came and went,
But we could never see them through.
Fate prevailed over the grand plan,
If only just for a while.

God gave us a choice,
A chance for one last dance,
So anything is possible,
Even love,
Even Love.

HIGH SCHOOL

In High School,
I sat at a lunch table
with 60 other High Schoolers.
We were not the cool kids.
We wore old army fatigues,
And quoted poetry
Before breakfast.

How obscene.

BREAKFAST

The earliest habit
I ever observed,
was a ritual:
I would consider the world
And pen a few words
Before breaking fast.

There was one rule:
No poetry before breakfast
Unless you write it yourself.
It was a good rule.
It anchored the days
To a little truth,
And rhyme,
That made me firm
And lithe,
And entirely less humble
Than I should be.

Poetry is the answer
To the dawn,
Unless you're laying
In a Lover's arms.

It never takes long,
Unless you break into song,
And the rest of the day drowns
In the echoes of joy.

Particularly when the lover is involved.

The Complete Second Verse
Charles Cooper, PhD

ROSES

I took a moment to smell the roses
While I was waiting for love.
I took a moment to smile at a squirrel.
And gaze at a flower,
While I was waiting for love.

I took a road in the woods,
While I was waiting for love.

I took a moment to see the world,
And honor, and serve, and live a little while,
While I was waiting for love.

I took a last, long glimpse
at where you and I sat
And quoted trite verse.
Me to you.
Then you to he.

I waited for love.
I am still waiting.

I spite the hands that made you
The beauty I wanted you to be.
Love paves the path to betrayal.
Had I known the pain that waited for me
I would have found a rose to breath deep.
I took a moment to smell the roses
While I was waiting for love.

I rose to find,
love was never there.
Knowing what I know now,
I would not curse in despair.
I would savor the moment,
I had with you,
Hard and deep

Open Wounds & Fairy Tales
Chuck Cooper

I felt it too.
I'd stand and stare,
At you there,
and I would
Walk away.

Not before
I asked you
For another dance,
I was always a fool that way.
The fool that wanted more;
Even when I knew the cost.
Now I may never know love,
Because some woman's daughter is a whore.

The Complete Second Verse
Charles Cooper, PhD

THE END OF LOVE

Knowing nothing is not the worst part
We both knew the flame had died.
It's the pain of the lie that slices deeper
Than his body when it was inside.
You let him inside,
      You.
You let him inside
      You.
Inside You.

Now he's in my head.
You took him to my bed.
I feel his shadow
As you try to prove
There is love…
But this is nothing new.
While you're saying,
"It meant nothing,"
The scene plays over and over
In my head,
      in my bed.
In my head,
      where you put him.
In our bed,
      where it means everything.
In my head,
      never tomorrow.
In my bed,
Betrayal.
Betrayal.
Betrayal.

"It meant nothing," is something people say
The day after the end of love.
Never ending love that's run its course
Eternal promise replaced by remorse.

Open Wounds & Fairy Tales
Chuck Cooper

"It means nothing,"
Is the last thing
I will say the day I'm through with you.
This is over.
It is finished.
You let him inside,
Inside you.
Inside my head,
Inside my bed,
Inside you.

Inside you,
       Darkness.
Inside you,
       Betrayal.
Inside you,
       I am through.
You'll never taste my life again
Never again.
Never you.
You've lost a friend
I am through with you.
It means nothing.

The Complete Second Verse
Charles Cooper, PhD

AWAKENINGS

I know you thought:
you knew what you were doing.
I know you thought:
No one would get hurt,
No one would find out.

I know you felt it was wrong,
Even if you didn't know how to say it or stop it.
"No harm, no foul,"
You knew how to say that.
And you did.

I tried to tell you how it made me feel.
I tried to make believe it wasn't real.
A day and a night passed without intent
To remedy our love.

How long should I wait?
How long must I go?
How often should I forgive?

Today, it is the time that passed that I regret.
The tie that bound, restrained too long.
Was it love that kept me here,
Or was it fear of being alone?

I checked with myself a moment ago
For love or fear, and found
Love had no part to play.
My heart was ice cold
When I heard your name.
It was a rude awakening,
But I was awake nonetheless.

REFLECTION

What an odd award to win
Best in class: reflection
I can't see you there's no light
Just a darkness in your eyes
Just a glimpse, glimmer, hope,
Just another binding rope.

There's that darkness in your eyes
Surrounded by tiny lines
Pulled so tight
Little white lies
It's not darkness,
There's no light.
I'm in love with a reflection
With a mirror
With the light
That gives truth,
        to the lie,
We can erase mistakes.
They were not kind
Erase the scars,
Bend the bars.
Erase Mistakes,
Make an escape.
What an odd award to win
Best in class
At never having been.

"WALKING"

ART BY BECKY KIPPER

FAILURE OF INNOCENCE

The absence of control,
      intimacy,
            passion,
                  and love.
My consciousness was there;
It was my body after all.
I became the observer
From a dispassionate distance.

Commitment came without permission
Baited by a cascading, cacophony of chemicals,
A rupturing, rapture of hormones
danced a jig with confusion.
Who I am? laughter
Is this? laughter
What is happening? laughter
Betrayed,
By an inability to stand.
My head met his fist,
Destroyed the will to resist.
The lies that twisted
The guilt ridden waste
Of what I wanted was
Tucked nicely away in a place
Where I could not go.

That day, more than most,
I never wanted to be again.
Endlessly reliving slipping, sliding home:
Betrayal for sure,
Brutality for sure,
Can be mistaken for passion.
Vulnerability for sure,
Pity for sure,
Can be mistaken for caring.

So petty the manipulation

The Complete Second Verse
Charles Cooper, PhD

And this moment, ending like so many others:
Alone with no one to tell,
In a personally imposed hell
Asking myself, what is love?

Now alone with my hand
I carry myself back to that forsaken land
Falling to strength, failing to stand
Falling again, and again, and again
Betrayed over and over,
I surrender the self to the bliss that comes:
With self pity, remorse, the cascade, the chemical,
The cocktail, cacophony of hormones that keeps me alone
No rest and no home, but a gentle repose.
Could this be comfort (able)?

Again and again, over and over
Until every touch brings blood
The body fails itself, to even perform
Proving unworthy of its own lie.
Is there peace?
Can I call this home?
I still don't belong.
I am still alone.

STEPS OF DAWN

As dawn broke that first day,
An Angel wrote the sorrow away.
The beams of light caressed the sky.
Her porcelain skin asked and answered "why?"

I did not know.
Nor did I care.
She was enough,
Which made me enough,
There.

Those first steps into the night,
Angel's wings guarded my vision
Through that lens, I fought,
And I defended life.

I will never know what it means to be a mother
Any more than you can guess,
What it means to be my wife
The angel did not know she was there
A visage, an idea that defended me.

Through dark of night, into the light,
As promises were made,
And burdened souls traded life,
For a moment of bliss.
I avenged those fools.
Chased and chaste, I waited for you.
There in my thoughts and dreams, all those things,
That make men more.

I could be more, you see
Because I believed in you and me.

Time and distance grew from dawn
And Angels, respectively.

The Complete Second Verse
Charles Cooper, PhD

Not long since,
I have seen those eyes again,
Known forgiveness for my sin.

Together finally, we rise.

I CAN'T CRY

There are days I wonder why I can't cry,
Days plagued with doubts,
thinking tears are a lie
Like the painted, passion on the face
Of a great actress
The still, small touch
that begs us to believe.

I put on a hat.
I wear it like a crown,
But I do not swim.
It's as if I had already drowned.

Mastering life is no small thing
You can't shout without a voice,
Or take flight without wings.
There is only one way to do any of these things:
Find the moment, breath deep
Let go of everything, and fly.

There are days when I can't cry,
And there are days that I know why.
But there are days, also, that I do.

The Complete Second Verse
Charles Cooper, PhD

YOU ARE...

...The lady I would carry through life
As far as I could,
Through fields and frost
And stoney ground
Though I was weary,
Sad, and distressed,
When it came to you,
If I could, I would.

...The lady I would hold
In wind and rain and hail,
As we traverse the fine thread
Of the spider's web over hell,
My hold will never waver,
My hand held tight in yours
My heart can never fail
As it beats, and I and you
Are bound in one accord.

...The lady I would know
And study through the day
And when the night makes black the sky,
Beside you, I will lay
I will know your breathing, soft and deep
My ancient eyes will watch you sleep.
My hand will find your face again
And know the softness of your skin
Fingers memorizing every line
Tracing the memories that each defines.
I recognize your voice with a single word
Soft but direct, sharp, calm and correct.
Through years I will know you,
And I will quickly learn
The looks I need to fear,
When I should turn
To run
When to lend my ear,

Open Wounds & Fairy Tales
Chuck Cooper

Laugh and have fun.
Place my hand just there
Beneath your chin the way you like.
Kiss you with all my might.
I would grow to,
To understand all that you do,
The places you go,
The things you've been through
That made you so strong
And every day new.

…The lady I would grow old with
Through life, good times and bad.
We would carry each other, whether happy or sad
Every day growing closer
Every moment more tight.
I can never surrender.
You are the reason why.

LAST KISS

That last kiss
Was not my last kiss,
My last kiss, was with you.

Your lips, sweet and sensuous,
Made me want to be,
More than I was,
Or could have been,
Had I found a way to stay.

Yes, I left,
Wandered and grew,
Through life, and work, and longing for you.

The last thing I felt,
The last truth I knew,
That was my last kiss:
My last kiss was with you.

As all fairy tales go,
The man returns when it is time.
Just before it is too late,
But such was not our fate.

There you stand on the horizon
Where I can see the life you lived.
I was right at such an early age,
knowing all that you had to give.
I look on my love again, and I see,
I am too late, you love another
Who you have kissed, since you kissed me.
I am here, I am owed nothing.
There was no promise and no vow.
What I gave to you when I was young
Was given of my own free will…

To that last kiss,

Open Wounds & Fairy Tales
Chuck Cooper

I tell you now:
All I was,
what I became;
All I wanted,
gave, and framed;
This life,
my life,
Books and buildings,
Poems and paint,
Plaster and paradise,
I painted with your name.

The question asked and answered,
"How could I walk away?"

I can never give up,
I have no where to go.

I pray for one more kiss
There is a truth, I want to know.

The Complete Second Verse
Charles Cooper, PhD

MERCY

I had this nightmare,
I was a court reporter,
Spending days misspelling subpoena,
And nights shouting guilty over and over,
In a feudal land
Where someone personified Justice,
as a woman,
as a joke.

Oh, the bliss that reason brings:
Cold, calculated, harmony of things
Where we all agree, to agree, to disagree.

But we can all agree on something.
"If only *I* got what *I* deserved"
Said no one ever.

The wrongs of another,
Cannot be punished too harshly,
Or disdained too deeply by a brother.
So I was told on a lovely Sunday morning
During a religious service,
About the love and sacrifice of Christ,
At a backwater Baptist Church.

I read the Bible a few times,
A long time ago,
And I think he read something wrong.
There is a mote in my own eye,
I won't lie.

So take what I say as you will:

To see the mote
Is to see yourself,
And knowing yourself,
Is to believe in mercy.

Open Wounds & Fairy Tales
Chuck Cooper

Mercy is such an empty exercise for man.
By Sunday afternoon,
They have all sinned again,
And God had forgiven in turn.

Imagine the awkwardness of my position
If I thought to act as a judge,
Or withhold forgiveness,
For anyone?

PEACE

Peace was made a law,
And on that day,
Humanity waged…
Popular, preferential, political suicide.

Politicians defending people
From nothing
Are valued at
Nothing
And no one
Ever had an excuse
To be ruled
Again.

Thou shall not kill was written a while ago,
People.

Sigh…

LOVE

The years and decades,
I spent trying...
An epic effort,
On both our parts.

The time I spent to make you mine,
That you spent trying to understand.
The effort I spent to keep you happy,
With my cock and mouth and hand...
The time I spent to make the money
To keep you happy, which took me away from you.
The time I took to lay the groundwork
To send you away...
Because I didn't see a way.
How do I call this love?

Our cycles of terror
from one fight to the next.
A pained, panting battle
And make up sex...
How do I call this love?

I want to say it was good,
But I can't.
I want to say I did all the right things
At all the right times,
But I can't.
If we never left the bed,
We might have had a chance...
I want to say we were in love,
But I can't.

CREATION

There's something in the circle
of creation walking by,
Something in the way she looks
that makes me cry.
Together living life,
God, what a ride.

Memories are forever,
But diamonds couldn't last,
As long as the impression of her fingers
On my back.

There's something in the circle of life walking by.
Something in the way she looks that makes me cry.
Together living life,
God what a ride.

Memories are a luxury.
And they will never last
As long as the impression
of her smile
And her laugh.

There's something in the circle of sadness walking by.
Something in the way she looks that makes me cry.
Together, this life,
Together, our ride.
Together, our memories.
Together, we lived
And yes, we died,
Together.

CURE

Fear is a focus
That draws focus away
From what matters.

Focus,
On what matters.

Guilt is a hammer
That pounds,
And pounds,
And pounds,
On men,
Until they surrender,
Or stand
And let go.
Please, let Go.

The turning point is not often found,
Talking in circles,
In a tiny office,
With a short, squirrelly man,
Who knows more about drugs than people,
Psychiatrist indeed.
That man sent me into a coma for weeks.

I woke just in time for
The sullied, red succubus
To have her way, make war,
And leave me, again,
Broken, sore, and poor,
At the bottom where truth is found,
Truth and a turning point,
Even redemption, if you are ready.
I was, and I did,
Turn around,
That is.

The Complete Second Verse
Charles Cooper, PhD

I had spent my life in the pursuit of love
And was given loneliness.
So, I spent nights in the pursuit of flesh,

Only to find less
And less… and less… of me.

I drank so it would be easier
And it was.
Then, in a burnt ashen haze
I slipped into a coma,
Again,
Third times a charm.

This time,
I woke up in time to go to church.
Not for Christ or Communion,
Not for meaning or books,
or song, or verse…
Or stories I knew by heart…

I went for friends,
People I knew,
who knew me,
Long before the drill sergeant
and war,

Before the agency
and war,
Before the sordid succubus
Made her own brand of war.
I had friends out there.

On the bottom is where you find out,
Who those friends are
Because they are always there,
At the turning point,
At the bottom.

Open Wounds & Fairy Tales
Chuck Cooper

In peaks and valleys
Over mountains
And oceans
Through life,
That kind of friend
That should have been a wife,
Had I made better choices.

The Complete Second Verse
Charles Cooper, PhD

LAY ME DOWN

There behind the trees
Loomed a sky I'd never seen
Painted Blue and black
There was no going back
Offset against that sky
You were the reason why
Deep inside your eyes
I saw forever

Your hair was glowing in the light
A scene that'd make you cry
A reason to fight or even die

You gave me words,
You gave me rhyme
I had to make you mine.

Lay me down,
I'm yours forever
Lay me down,
be mine tonight
Come the dawn I will be leaving
So make tonight the night.

20 years I wandered
20 years to take me home
I have learned on this long journey
That I could not escape your song
I hear the heartbeat,
hear you crying
I see forever in the dawn,
Forever in your eyes
It's that sad, sad song
That you could never disguise.

Echoes soft, yet still haunting
Take me home,

Open Wounds & Fairy Tales
Chuck Cooper

Oh take me home.

Lay me down, this is forever;
Lay me down, be mine tonight;
No more want, and no more rambling
Inside your heart, I found my light.

The Complete Second Verse
Charles Cooper, PhD

KEEPING SECRETS ABOUT THE FUTURE

Broken, in the way
In which, things can't be fixed.

Like a teenage wrist,
Wrent and ragged,
Trying to find feeling in finality.
Goodbye is the hardest word.
A word I cannot say,
Even today.
I ask is there another way,
Even today?

Like a teenage hand,
One strong stand from fraud and failing
Waving the wind to pass on by,
Telling one more lie,
"There's nothing to see here.
You've kept your secrets."

Like a man's arm,
Keeping you from harm.
It's my ear, which will never believe
The words you said to me.
There is nothing above my pay grade.
The life of comfort you've lived,
I'm sure you would agree.
Paid or not, I went and did.
Sane or not, I will not forgive
The doubt. I have enough for us both.
But I can never let it show,
So I will never let it go.

Be it might or spite,
I will live and achieve.

DEEP

How deep do I have to go
To find what I need to know?
A heart that beats with mine?
You could not say.
And all I can do is sigh,
And search for another reason why,
My heart refused to beat
And my eyes refused to cry,
When you look at me like you do.
Your eyes pierce,
no explanation,
Cut to the core,
I'm blinded by you.
And you claim you never knew,
That I loved you.
Still, I do.

I cannot help myself,
No place on land, at sea,
No mountain and no road,
No where I would not go
To see you one more time
Even though you are not mine
And never will be.

You made my life a lie,
This world I made
        And dedicated to you
Painted words and the truth of
Your name on books and buildings
Painted there, I would stare,
Thinking what I'd done,
And what it cost.

Oh, I know you are not mine.
More's the pity, I know why.
Fate is never kind

The Complete Second Verse
Charles Cooper, PhD

To those who can't decide.
Some of us fall through life.
Where the wind blows
we are carried.
Where the water flows
we are ferried.
As the day turns to night,
The truth turns to lies.
The sorrow turns to sin.
And I begin again.

I rise to try
To find the answer,
To the question,
Will you ever be mine?
I know, I know,
But I ask again anyway.

SPRING

Bloom is the celebrated command of Nature
All creatures bound and shout at the notion
"Never mind the life not lived,
When bloom I did,
And oh, I did."
All stamen, pistol, pollen, and pine scented bark
The potential of creation comes quick
Un-trampled by the hard life, like hope and choice,
A cardinal without a voice,
Springtime calls to us all.

Bless is the celebrated command of God
Bear burdens, heavy, laden, serve.
Sacrifice, did you know,
it brings joy to give joy.
And the burdens are lighter when they are another's
It makes it easy to forget
How much you gave away
When you are empty and alone
With nothing.

Bleed is the celebrated command of man.
Bleed and believe, there's life in the blood
And burden in the sacrifice,
Go deep for life,
Live, strive, cut, bleed, forgive
And at the bottom, find yourself,
Again. Forgive, again.
Were you ever lost, or just thirsty and hungry
                         And alone, so alone.

EPILOGUE

Life,
Malicious series of hardships and sorrows that it is,
Gave me you,
So I would know what it was to lose.
My heart and my head;
To be cut and be bled;
For healing sake,
How to make mistakes
And learn what it is to live.

Life is a training ground
For the...
Newly born
To find love,
To love life
To love another
Until they're gone.
Find peace in grief,
Love of another form.
Say goodbye. Please try,
But never too quick
To disappoint imagined eyes
Looking down on you.

I will wait.

"TAKING FLIGHT"

ART BY CHUCK COOPER

BOOK 2: POOR FARM PARK

The Complete Second Verse
Dr. Charles Cooper

JULIES

I have a friend named Julie
        who gave up alcohol
                so she could live;
She makes that decision every day,
Sometimes more than once.
She has taken steps
To find herself in a better place
Because she knows herself,
What she wants and feels.
Julie wants to live.

I have another friend named Julie,
A lady I love.
She strives,
She feels too much and drowns
Her lack of control in wine.
A fine 2012 Chianti…
She has an Italian side.
In the morning, a spritely Riesling
She has a German side too.
Julie is very much her parents, both.
She refuses to talk to her parents,
Refuses to be ruled.
Where her mother thought love,
Julie saw Control.
Living as a dependent wife complicates things.
For someone so capable.
She plays at working, but the vino gets in the way
Of what she could be.
Where her husband sought to comfort,
Julie just felt empty.
Laboring day and night to fill a hole
Her family sees, but only a friend can know.

Two Julies who I love dearly,
On different paths by choice.
I made that choice once,

Poor Farm Park
Chuck Cooper

In the morning and twice at night.
I thank God for the people who were patient with me.
I think I'm ready to write the next bit.

I would like to dedicate the rest of this to
All the people who never needed anything,
Save to be themselves
And be loved for it,
I love you.

The Complete Second Verse
Dr. Charles Cooper

A RUNNER'S BLUES

I used to run a lot,
Was thin as a rail,
Sharp as a tack,
And cut like a knife.

I spent hours on trails
And understood the world.
I saw God in trees and leaves
And clouds and water
And endorphins
And adrenalin.

One day, I stopped running.

The clouds were just clouds.

I gained weight.

Poor Farm Park
Chuck Cooper

ON THE BALLS OF YOUR TOES

Two good reasons for running.

Run when chased.

Run when chaste…

It is a poor substitute,
But you have to do something
To keep yourself sane.

TICKETS

I got a ticket to dawn the other night
As you closed your eyes
And rolled to your right.
I saw his mark on your back
Coffee stain? Tattoo?
Like some innocent fool
Who was born too soon,
He wanted you.

Now as much as then,
It wasn't regret I felt,
A new birth of freedom
A light so strong,
Finally, a ticket to dawn.

"The sun also rises."
An old croon crows,
The sacred tune of an ancient hymn
About all those men,
Who slept,
ate and worked,
tried for too long,
To give earthly delights
To her majesty
in spite
Of her.

I saw a Cardinal singing
As it flitted through the trees
Some spring time song,
Some love-sick disease.
I have to be strong, at times like this,
I have a good memory,
And I'm prone to regret.

I remember every promise made,
Every song,

Poor Farm Park
Chuck Cooper

Every day.

I should have laughed
When I heard you say,
Can't we just get along?
Can't you just be strong?
Had you already made your trade?

I think it was the very next day
that you gave *ME* A ticket to dawn.

So many years without the light
Facing things that didn't seem right
Stuck in a world that loves to fight
The mind with bulk and brawn,
Can I have this ticket to dawn?

A new day. A new life. Rebirth.

Today. Is that day.
The sun rose again.
There is nothing left to say to you.
No forgiveness needed,
No more sin.
Not another moment of grief
Or regret over some small miracle
that hasn't happened yet.

The birds will sing a goodbye song,
And I have a ticket to dawn.

If you could get a ticket to today
Not plan the time away...
Take this moment
Make it pay
For the life you spent
To be there.
I could just say seize the day
But Robin beat me to it.

The Complete Second Verse
Dr. Charles Cooper

And he did,
And he left.

And then I think of Ray
A friend who matched wits with me
In politics and policy
And that is bravery
For any man.
He worked so very hard,
Could have punched his ticket long ago
To live free...
But he worked, and he drove and achieved.
Propping up his throne
With gold.
And then he was gone.
His ticket for today
Was traded away for a song.
A few pennies for a lifetime of memories.
And what is that worth...

It was nice being born.
Existence is no small thing;
I watched you let it slip away.
Suffering made it real,
How else could death steal
The will
From a mind
That kept someone alive
Through all of this.

The ticket was a gift
Yes, all of us got one,
But does it seem real?
If I try, I can imagine the line
Of souls, waiting to be alive.
Seems like forever, to get
A simple spot, people use
To live
Sometimes.

Poor Farm Park
Chuck Cooper

You,
have regrets.
If you don't regret,
You weren't paying attention.

I was there,
You had your chance
You cashed in your ticket
For comfort,
For simple things
That you should have made yourself.
You were given a ticket to life
You traded it to be a slave.

Everyone knows what it means to carry
A little extra weight
Now and then.
With a little extra time and effort,
We find
Our wings,
Cast off the baggage,
And soar.
It's called a Ticket to More.

The things that weigh me down.
Day after day,
Night After night
Without sound…
I don't complain.
It's not the same
Anymore.
As I was waiting in line at the pearly gates,
I got a ticket to more.

Walking away is the hardest thing,
Sometimes.
Even when you know what's best.
Even the strongest beating heart
Sometimes…

The Complete Second Verse
Dr. Charles Cooper

Needs the rest.

But sometimes, at our lowest,
When the bottom dwellers pounce
In the darkness,
In the forest,
Where the lion
And the mouse
Dance
and squeak
and roar…
It's there,
Among the foliage
On the forest floor
That thing that is salvation,
That ticket to more.

I never thought it would be so hard
To find a way to feel,
What I needed to feel,
So I could be,
what I needed to be
To make all of this real.

Flaming lust,
Never bought a ticket to feel.
Simulating feelings,
Never once made it real.
Like caching a torch in the bank of emotion
Without emotion.

Capturing precious impressions,
Like lust at first sight
Painted with empty conversations
About the weather
or spite

For some old friend
You both knew long ago…

Poor Farm Park
Chuck Cooper

Never covered up
The gaping hole,
The gulf between you
When you both don't belong.

If you keep it up for long enough
You might convince yourself
For a day, or a night, or a year...

Strive for as much as you can get,
But never spend a day in fear.
Wanting a fairy tale...
Is not enough to make it real...

But if you ever take a trip to me...
I can give you,
A ticket to feel,
And together, we can heal.

The Complete Second Verse
Dr. Charles Cooper

ESTUARY

Without your touch,
I am left to rust.
A half iron ship
Cast adrift just over the lip
of the river Elizabeth.
Out into the bay
where I cannot stay,
Cast adrift
in the brackish sea,
Bitter waves of bland romance
Which carry you
To an estuary.

I feel you, feel new,
Your face, your hand,
Embrace this faraway land.
Redemption or love,
Do you feel it still?

The shore where we return,
to wash white
All the ills
Meaningless trite,
Words that kill.
Men have climbed mountains
For so much less.
You swam the river of desire
Reached out to touch the fire…
What must it mean to be inspired?
I do not know, but I want to.

Starved by tender mercies,
Sweet sounds I'd only heard.
I thank the Gods,
And speak the words.
For once in this life,
I was given more

Poor Farm Park
Chuck Cooper

Than I deserved:
A taste of life
The salty sea,
Sweet graceless tang
I surrender me.

There, I sang to you,
for love, for life...
For everything
With every word,
I know is true.

Reach out your hand
To see life bloom.

The Complete Second Verse
Dr. Charles Cooper

TOUCH THE TRAIN

There was a college prank
To "Touch a Train"
That was practiced at Randolph Macon…
It started that way,
Get really drunk,
Have a large enough group
That even the foolish makes sense,

Then, Try to touch the train.

The first person is always fine.
They're scared enough to be careful.
Maybe they don't even touch it,
But they appear to…
Fraternity guys are the masters of appearance…

And lies…

Then comes the lady…
Bold because she's second,
Buoyed by what she saw,
With her young eyes.
She tries harder
Reaches farther
And dies.

Three weeks later
someone erects a statue
To the "legacy"…
of a foolish,
drunk,
college girl.

The ceremony is sweet,
The statue elegant.
A bust in shiny bronze
Without acne.

Poor Farm Park
Chuck Cooper

The elegy is bold
Bigger than her nineteen years:

"For nineteen years,
She worked at a homeless shelter,
Read the Bible daily,
Prayed as often as it occurred to her,
And consumed copious amounts of alcohol
At the frat party of the night
On Friday,
and Saturday,
Or any night you like."

People toss the term legacy these days,
And I wonder what it means.
When someone's child
With all the potential in the world
Dies of stupidity.
Does anyone ask,
"Do you believe in Darwin now?"
During dark days
of sensational tragedy.
Some deaths become legend
Others become legacy,
When people die on TV.
Before Fox News and CNN,
Legacy had to earned,
With time and work
Endurance,
Persistence,
Self-Reliance,
Three Bold words,
Which mean
more work.

I know a family line
That can be traced four-hundred years,
Living from hand to mouth,

The Complete Second Verse
Dr. Charles Cooper

On the land those ancestors earned.

The legacy they were handed:
Of land,
a rifle or two,
            Some livestock,
A house,
and the knowledge
That they came from somewhere.

In Hanover County,
Just west of Ashland,
On wide, open fields
Five houses sit,
With four generations
Of legacy,
A bloodline.

Some company wants to run a Railroad through the whole thing.

Just to the east, in Ashland,
A train runs through in a line
Drawn laser straight,
In the way that only a lack of steel
And money can carve a railroad track,
Not a moment or a nickel to waste.

The bends and curves in the roads
Of western Hanover,
Mark the property lines
That defined "Family" and "Legacy"
200 years before.

This government is not so respectful
Of People,
        Or Family,
                Or Legacy,
As the one that made the roads.

Poor Farm Park
Chuck Cooper

But they love Railroads...
They are dying to "touch the train."
They hem and haw,
As if Railroads were a new thing,
Some fancy, fashionable mode of travel,
Busting at the seams,
A cure for the car?
Maybe?

Politicians embraced the railroads,
Because it was a politician's cure:
It solves nothing,
It was rejected by travelers,
It's less agile than the car,
And less speedy than the air,
But the cost of construction
Could fund builders for years,
Builders who are donors,
For politicians.

Donors who hate,
The legacy of self-reliance
That America made,
The spreading scourge,

Of Freedom that brought success,

The Success that brought Prosperity.

Prosperity,

That tore a hole
In the control
Of Nobles and Kings,
But made Princes and Knights,
Of men who could fight
And save, and work
Long into the night,
To build the new and better world,

120

The Complete Second Verse
Dr. Charles Cooper

And they did.

And that, is legacy.

The world breathed a sigh of relief,
When they thought
That Nobles and Kings
Were a thing of the past.
But Nobles and Kings are patient things
With a long view of destiny
And Serfs
And Slaves
And control.

And while they have the will
To maneuver,
They do not have the courage
Or the intellect
to see a world
that benefits all.
The thing they lack is respect
For the people who worked this land
Through history,
through war,
through reconstruction,
Through more.

They believe in an America
where the Individual
Is the Enemy,
Where Individual Achievement
Is an anachronism
And the founding of a world of equality
Is an allegory for everything that went wrong
For the last 400 years.

They embrace the Railroad,
To embrace the past,

Poor Farm Park
Chuck Cooper

And in the same instant,
They defy and defile
Justice, Freedom, Equality.
Rampant hands,
Running amuck in emotion,
Trying to destroy everything
They cannot understand.

What they understand is groups.
They use hate and pain and pretty things
to pull people together,
Manipulate and mold them
To achieve their will.

They nickel and dime,
Through taxes and fees.
People work harder,
And harder,
Until there is no will left
With which to fight,
The indomitable, bureaucratic
masters of marketing.

They craft the law to *buy*...
They use taxes to *build*...
Then they lease back the land
They took
To the men they now call serf.

Re-establishing their claim,
The lords and ladies of old,
Have returned.

With one mission:
To defile the idea that an individual has:
Rights,
responsibilities,
Can grow more than
A pompous owner,

122

The Complete Second Verse
Dr. Charles Cooper

with painted, lily lips,
From centuries long past,
Could ever understand.

They don't understand why we all
Just don't "touch the train."
It's good for you,
Or so they claim.

Poor Farm Park
Chuck Cooper

NO SILENCE

The things we wish we never said
Are a chance that will not come again.
I have no trust in silence,
No solace in the end.
What I cannot hear I will not fear
No simple, silent truth.

Reverie and happenstance
Make silent dreams
Of true romance
I'm never lost, you've never said,
There's still a chance
For me… for you and me.

I have no faith in silence
Or dreams that drift away,
Or panting teachers
Lost in lies,
Crying, "Seize the day."

I have no grip on silence,
There is no meaning there
No words and no tomorrow
Holding court, but not a stare.
I have no faith in trust,
What I see is all there is.
And what I hear,
Another beer.
Now meet my eyes
Say what you mean
Because forgiveness
Is never, ever cheap.

The Complete Second Verse
Dr. Charles Cooper

NO SORROW

On Angel's wings
I lay the night,
Exchanging verse
In soft moonlight;
What curse is time
Too little given

To know your power
Live in your wisdom;
For wanting so much
And trying so hard,
I will burn.
As any vampire
Who flew to close to the sun.
I will soon be gone
And you will have to find
Another way to run.

There is so little time.
None for regret.
Or even to take the chance
To celebrate the dawn
Or the days that haven't come yet.

As I live, I can only
Look back at neck breaking speed
To see,
There are a few things left,
We still have left to be.
For now, there is tomorrow,
Without regret, no past.
There is no time for sorrow
This day we must make last.

Poor Farm Park
Chuck Cooper

NOTHING LEFT UNDONE

There's something about leaving home,
Something so final.
It feels like destiny,
Until you return.
I did,
Return.
Nothing is ever so final
As a lie you tell yourself in haste.

"He got out," they said.
If they only knew

How big a lie it was.
I went searching for a life,
I never thought to make
And a love which
I knew
Could not exist.

I grabbed a bolt of lightning in my haste.
Burned arms and hands,
I held on tight.
There is no recompense worth the cost.
No man can hold back thunder.
How I managed to live through nature's will
More times than I can count,
Everything I thought I lost
Was still waiting to be found.
So be it.

Every day as the sun rises
My eyes flutter green gray
Catching light reflections,
In gold and solemnity.
This day as every other,
I number among those
Which will never be given again.

The Complete Second Verse
Dr. Charles Cooper

There is only one end.
To see the moon set,
with the rising of the sun
And to leave,
in my wake
With nothing left undone.

No apologies,
no regrets,
no more sorrow.
no second chance.

This is life,
The one we get.
No one is promised
Tomorrow
The dawn,
The day,
Or the sun.
It is a gift,
You take this life and run.

What I do today
Is one more thing
I don't have to explain.
When the creator says
"But your potential…"

No buts, no excuses, just do.
And I do.

Poor Farm Park
Chuck Cooper

TRAPPED

There's nowhere like yesterday.
Enticing places and flavors
Tasteful ceilings and floors
Do it all over.
Again, once. Again, twice.
Until habit becomes routine,
Until the dirty feels clean.
Take a step,
Never backwards.

Some things,
Are not tepid or lukewarm
Life can be more
If we open the door.

There's nowhere like tomorrow,
Near some beach, crashing waves,
The heat and malaise
Go hand in hand.

You smile at me and I see life.
In a tiny boat stuck on land,
I take a row and till the sand.
Pushing it back and forth
With the intensity of a man
Who doesn't know
The race is over.
The tide that left me stranded,
In a foreign land
Will return for me
If I am patient,
But where will I go, you are gone.

INSOMNIA

I was introduced to a stranger once.
In spite of everything my mother told me,

128

The Complete Second Verse
Dr. Charles Cooper

I spoke to him.
Almost like a dream,
He seemed kind and then,
He looked at me…
Took my will to sleep and left me here,
Hat in hand,
A beggar,
With an insatiable need to be more.

A raven claw in my pillow,
A tiny rock beneath my mat,
Dreamcatcher in the window,
If this were home, I would know that.

The mattress is soft.
Take me down
Where I can lay
Alone and staring.
Counting ceiling tiles is a thing.
I want to see a roar,
I want to taste the echo
Of the choices I have made,
Which leave me empty of tears.
There's nothing quite as long as sorrow,
Now it's tomorrow…
Not exactly happy,
But there aren't as many fears.

I think I'll wake in the morning to run.
Now feels like the time,
but it's late.
The dawn won't come
Before the milkman makes his rounds.
I need to be gone by then.

Poor Farm Park
Chuck Cooper

ODE TO A BLACK LESBIAN POET

Trips to the city
Open the eyes.
Maybe it's the smog,
Or the dirt,
Or the brutal
Humanity of it all.
The city is a system,
It doesn't feel,
But it can teach.

In 1993, my longer than it should have been hair
Drooped low over my face.
And I flipped it
And flipped it
And flipped it back
Clearing my eyes
So I could see for an instant.
That wasn't why I did it.
I did it because I thought it was cool.

Walking down the street in Richmond
Toward a low awning
That brokered the entry
Into the gothic realm
Of the Bidder's Suite
Caffeine and college kept
Two or three people employed
Pushing the last legal drug.

Every other Friday,
From four to four in the morning,
An open mic sat on a stage
And all comers
Could sing, talk,
Dream, rage.

I sat there a long time.

The Complete Second Verse
Dr. Charles Cooper

I worked four jobs back then,
As hard as I could.
I never liked living under my father's roof.
Dependency made me less of a man,
I thought.

I sipped coffee, espresso,
Shot after bloody shot.
I slept less than I dated,
And dated less than I fought,
Which is only to say, not much.
Two years slipped by,
Day after day,
Shot after bloody shot,
Night after night,
I found myself,
Lost myself,
Pushed myself past exhaustion
Crafting poems that I didn't understand.

I call those years "the Lost Years."
Poems about life are a thing
For British Aristocrats in the 1800s,
The products of empire,
And wealth,
I dreamt of that kind of wealth
And to be that kind of writer.
I'm not sure what would be better,
To be born into that kind of wealth,
Or to have parents that love me.
I only know which one I got.

One open mic night
Gave me a glimpse
Of a different perspective on life.

Her name was Stephanie,
She never even knew
She was on the spot

Poor Farm Park
Chuck Cooper

Or even that she was a poet
Speaking only to me.
She was in love, and Love,
When it's real, is the purest form of poetry.
Stephanie taught me to look and see.
She taught me to love and to be.
I only saw her.
We never spoke,
But what I saw broke the paradigms of my mind
Removed the limits I placed on love.

She had her arm draped,
Over a tiny, spritely girl.
The jet black of her hand
Rested on the ginger's breast.
What I saw in that instant,
Defied, everything I thought I knew.
Rethinking everything in a moment,
Is a skill, I've used seldom in life,
But Stephanie and the ginger,
The look in their eyes,
As they tasted the lips,
the coffee,
the music,
the poetry
Of life,
Tender life,
Gave me a whole new world.

More than a decade would pass
Before they could call each other "wife."

I wonder if they ask what might have been?

I wonder if Thomas Grey's
Elegy in a country graveyard
Held any truth
For these women, this love.
"How many days and nights,

The Complete Second Verse
Dr. Charles Cooper

Lay here buried,
With their rightful owners
Because what might have been never was...
Because some people thrive
On taking life...
From the living.

"COMPASS"

Art by Becky Kiper

FLAT EARTH BLUES

Arc and twist.
A twist of your wrist
And an idea, not mine,
Which would redefine curves
For humankind.
I had no idea how to turn around,
Until I had seen it done.

The Complete Second Verse
Dr. Charles Cooper

This is how you tell people,
Everything they know is a lie.

There is no globe.
It's a round ball of silicon, copper, and carbon.
Miscellaneous sparks of greatness
Which ignite in flight around the sun.
Around on a plane,
A flat surface.
I walked in a straight line
For my whole life
Trying to do what was right.
As if the path to escape
Lay in that direction,
Forward, always forward.
The consequence of decisions,
The blessings of experience,
The memories of mistakes
Always forward and flat.

I traveled as far as east meets west
To find myself in the same place.
The prime meridian, in a castle, on a lake.
Water that ripples is surely not fake.
I walked far and long and straight.
I slept at night and traveled all day,
East met west and again,
I found myself
in the exact same place.
If I accept the planes of earth,
How do I explain the plains of earth?
Everything just keeps spinning
Around.

There I was, thinking I was ready
To write the happy part
When life took another turn.
I should have learned
By now.

Poor Farm Park
Chuck Cooper

RUNAWAY GIRL

Sweet runaway girl,
Spent another day with me.
She swears it's not forever,
But I will wait and see.
You always come and go,
You've always been so free.
Sweet runaway girl
Spend another day with me.

I know, we're all running from something
I know you crossed the river wide
I know they built a bridge to make it easy.
I know it's easy, you despise.

Over the bridge, or through the water,
If you could see you through my eyes,
You would know what you mean to me.
The fantasy of what love can be.

There's a reason I can't disguise the tears
Discuss the vacant collapsing structures that I feel…
When I feel… you walk away.
I love to watch you walk,
But you left me alone again.
There is no sin, no promise made or broken.
That's my cross to bear,
Little runaway girl.

Sweet runaway girl
How I love to watch you leave.
The view is just spectacular.

The Complete Second Verse
Dr. Charles Cooper

DAYLIGHT AND NIGHT

Here I lay next to the road
Staring up at who knows…
Eyes held open
By will alone
Defying those
Who thought they owned
Me.

Did you ever want to see,
What I could carry
Through the daylight and night
Through the tears,
and the fights,
I held up
Longer than I thought I could.
I waited
Longer than any man should.
Too late, too long
Daylight and night
And all the love is gone.

Eyes flicker closed,
I am sailing
To a dream land,
Fighting what my eyes show…
What I want, who knows.
I want to live again,
Like I had forgiven
And you were forgotten
And there was some place
Safe, from missing your touch.

Daylight and night.
No one knows where you go
Candles burning down
I can't sleep but my eyes close.
Light is shining but I can't see.

Poor Farm Park
Chuck Cooper

I never thought of blaming me.
But I did it anyway,
It was easier.

Daylight and night,
Together,
Like ocean and sand
And stormy weather.
You named the hurricane
And I took the blame.

Daylight and night
Moon sinking down
The dawn is coming
The new day is found.
Guilt will subside, in time
Give it time.

Someone,
Somewhere
is waiting for me
I just want to be.

Daylight and night
Let me love again.
Daylight and night
What I want is a friend
Who touches me
Like it was new.
Daylight and night,
I will find a way,
To say goodbye to you.

The Complete Second Verse
Dr. Charles Cooper

WALK

When I have to walk,
I do not flaunt or curtsy or bow.
I do not parade in the streets.
I do not frown.
Walking is my attempt,
To lose myself,
within myself.

Sometimes on a road,
Sometimes in the woods,
Sometimes on a sidewalk.
But always in nature,
And always secure,
In myself.

Just yesterday, I found myself in a lonely wood.
A path diverged there,
As they often do I'm told.
I turned back.
I do not walk to choose.
I choose a thousand times a day.
I walk to avoid choice.
Mindless reverie.

I see God along the trail
In every piece of creation,
Tiny lines
and fragments
and webs.

I look away.

There is too much beauty in this world.

I do not walk for beauty.
I walk for me,
For sanity.

Poor Farm Park
Chuck Cooper

Every day, I embark on a quest
To live,
make,
and create.

When I can do no more, I walk
To leave it all behind,
Clear my mind,
Let go of today,
So I can begin again,
tomorrow.

The Complete Second Verse
Dr. Charles Cooper

"THE MULE"

ART BY CHUCK COOPER

POOR FARM PARK

I've been gone too long,
From Poor Farm's fields
And trails, and woods,
And those accursed hills.
I must return
Before I run too low
On the life giving water
That continues to flow
From this place of my birth,
So I can relive and reignite
The fires that burned,
Once upon a time
With desire,
Once upon a time
With dreams,
Once upon a time,
In fields over trails,
I painted it all with poetry.

On the cliffs overlooking the stream
Flowed the water,
Of which I spoke.
It made me believe,
In me.
Now that is a magical moat.
That same water
Which gave me life so long ago,
Still soothes my tongue
And cools my throat.
Again, I am restored.
Eyes closed in deepest sleep
As I pass into dreams of the hills,
And run short of breath on the trails,
Even in my dreams
I am not as young as I was once,
The ground rises to meet my feet
And I recall the names

The Complete Second Verse
Dr. Charles Cooper

As distance and time pass away...
The fat lady, the mule, the liberty loop...
I would run like a deer,
Like I was chasing the truth.
I've always known
When thoughts of home
Return to my dreams,
I must go.

I have been away too long,
too long.

The air out there
Taught me to take care
And to focus
Becoming more than I might.

When I close my eyes to dream,
When I close my eyes at night,
I am there, not a visitor,
But a stranger to this life I lead.
When I left that place,
I parted with so much of me.

I see you in the light.
Always anchored, chasing tales
And fairies and love.
I'm left with memories of all of the above.
When you look at me,
I think that we might...

I tremble.

In Poor Farm Park where
I made declarations sweet,
In the shadow of those trees,
There on a boulder,
Overlooking the stream.
It still occasionally runs.

Poor Farm Park
Chuck Cooper

With life giving water.
I know,
even though,
I have been gone too long,
Too long.

Eyes still closed,
protecting what I know
About the air that gives lift to
Rushing wings in these dreams
I soar to see you past the leaves,
And life begins to ascend again.
All those years just the Poor Farm and you.
The miles I've run since
Are part of a life that feels longer than not.
A downhill run with redemption in sight.

It has been a long journey home.
It took me far,
Between the steppes of Russia
And the Mongol horde;
Between the desert and the jungle,
And the tenth basement floor
Of the pentagon;
There in Westfields,
Directorate better left unsaid, in tower two;
Were thoughts of you.
You are the sun
Which melts frozen waste
Around my heart,
Like the haze from the ground
And the tears from my face,
So I could live one more day,
And be enough,
Even though,
I have been gone too long,
Too long.

For the longest, I called you "The One."

The Complete Second Verse
Dr. Charles Cooper

I still do in the shadows,
When I think the truth
is the best way
to be fair to everyone.

As night turns to day,
Yet again.
I lay down my sword,
Quite sure, I am a man.
As day becomes night,
And my eyelids slip shut,
You are the thoughts, the light
Which heals the cuts.

I see in your eyes,
And hear in our song.
Deep breaths and wandering
Through poor farm's woods
All of it restoring my soul,
Yet again.
I could blame the air and the trees,
Or the familiarity,
But I have to admit the truth
It's that I know,
I am close to you.

I can live again,
like I knew nothing but "could"
Failure was never a thought or a possibility,
Dreams were the wings that carried me.
The wind beneath me caught,
And I flew with you.

Oh, those were the days and the nights
To which I belong once again.
It will never be so long
Again. Never again.

Poor Farm Park
Chuck Cooper

BRIGHT SHINING EYES

Bright shining eyes that lie,
I swore, the first time I met you.
Under my breath,
In a good way,
In a way you don't forget.

You smiled and swept your hair
Over your shoulder
Revealing your neck
In a very vulnerable way
If there was a moment I could pick
For you… this is it.

I picked you
Then and there.
That first night,
Those first impressions
Are on my mind
When I see you in the light.
I fall in love with the fine lines.
There's something you aren't saying…
It's hiding in your eyes.

Not a word was spoken,
You knew, you would not see me again.
You never thought to question
If I was more than just another man.
You never thought to try.
Like me you never lied.
Time to go home.
Your family needs you.
You were silent,
But your eyes, they said goodbye.

THERE ARE DAYS

There are days when…
We all are Gods.
Some earn the title.
Others surrender to it quickly
Or bit by bit.
Others give up
on the daunting task
of wearing such a moniker
And never live at all.
Still others are offended by it.

Gods are so petty.
Say it with me,

"I am… *enough*."

Poor Farm Park
Chuck Cooper

SINCE WE MET

It's been a day since we met,
Smiled,
Walked,
and parted ways;

A hint of a promise to bind us,
In the four years that would come and go.
Clenching heart, hand, and breast
Feet fell hard on rock and desert,
Packs that were heavy,
Beads of sweat,
Burning heat, without regret.
Just lean back,
breath,
set the sights,
On tomorrow
On a safer life
With you.

I never wanted anything,
so much as tomorrow;
Every day I would pray
for a dusk and a dawn to pass
Without blade and gun in hand,
Without proving I'm a man.
Without bathing in blood,
As sacrifice beat the drum
That drives men on.
There can be no retreat
from what inevitably will come.

Never once did I fall at the hands of another
Never once,
But I watched it
Again and again

Pounding out passion,

The Complete Second Verse
Dr. Charles Cooper

The patriot parlays fear into action.
Gripping pain and his chest,
the partisan pitches plain old hope.
He wished the men all the best
And left them to find rest
　　For Themselves.

Swords rise and fall
in a new day of rain.
Blood stains
Axes and shovels
and crosses with chains.

I have never wanted anything
so much as tomorrow,
today,
And to save you,
And an end to this pain.

Poor Farm Park
Chuck Cooper

BLANK PAGES

Blank pages never told a story to anyone.
But if they could…

I am prepared to write tomorrow morning
Of the most glorious experience.
A joy, sharing life
With a beautiful wife.
Climax after cataclysmic climax,
Followed by, you guessed it,
The good sleep,
In each other's arms.

So close but still longing
For blended spirits
And consciousness.
I do not fear that she will know what I am thinking
Because she knows me well enough to know,
And because she does, she smiles.

And that story would have been written
If I could just feel
For the briefest moment
That she was real.

Until then,
They're just blank pages
In the back of my mind.

The Complete Second Verse
Dr. Charles Cooper

RUNNING ON THE BEACH

Barefoot,
Is the only way,
To make your way
Down a beach.
Soft sand slipping under foot,
Undertow and tides,
Play games with your mind.

Shoes will never do
when you're sinking.
Sand shifts every time,
You think you've found
A foothold.
Skin and ligaments and bone,
That roll with the terrain,
Men never made such a thing as feet.

One foot in front of the other can take you anywhere.
Shoes are a convenience,
when the sand is so hot it burns.
But to really move,
you must learn how to lose
And burn
With grace.
Make up for it in life.
That's the only way.

Poor Farm Park
Chuck Cooper

ONE SUMMER DAY

One summer day,
I was running on Virginia Beach.
I was more shocked then not
By what the men proudly display
Hairy monsters,
with guts that sway
Back and forth.
To and fro…
They lay there
In the heat
And baste in their own juices.

Of the women,
I would prefer not to say
What I thought.
Know this though,
There's a reason why the beach
Is a popular place to be…
And it's not because of the men.

The Complete Second Verse
Dr. Charles Cooper

TIME TO HEAL

If there was a wall;
I hit it.
If there was a bottom;
I found it.
There is no finish line
When it comes to the amount of torture a man can impose on
himself.
I, I have a high tolerance for pain.

Time for healing,
Healing time.
We are trained from birth
To believe,
It is wrong for a man to seek
Healing,

Until nature has found the end
Of what it means to be a man.
A moment explained in time as
"I...
can't...
take...
any...
more."

A wall...

The bottom...

Think of all the things,
None of them mine,
That I carried anyway.
I never put them down,
Never walked away.
I exhale and inhale
And move
Out of habit

Poor Farm Park
Chuck Cooper

Most of the time,
But today,
I finally know
How to say

No.

How to walk away.

Time for healing,
Healing time.
For the first time,
In a long time,
I don't want to die.
It's about time
And distance
And healing.
Putting things down,
And walking away
And having no guilt
over the times
you couldn't say
"I love you."

Time for healing,
Healing time.
There is no time like today.
The wounds don't go away.
Memories like scars
Remind us of mistakes

Time for healing,
Healing time.
Can you admit it now?
You would have been mine,
If I hadn't walked away.
Could you have found a way to stay?

Time for healing,

154

The Complete Second Verse
Dr. Charles Cooper

Healing time.
I look for the good,
Not much to find,
But I take comfort in it
When there's time.
We tell each other lies.
I know full well,
There is no heaven or hell,
but I believe in it
And it helps me get by,
Until there's a wall
or a bottom.

Time for healing,
Healing time.
Sometimes, I find a way
To make it go...
To make it numb,
To feel nothing...
And no one...
Without apology.

I've said I was sorry,
Too many times
To make it right.
I was always ready to defend,
But I never wanted to fight.
I did it anyway.
Fights which hurt those I loved,
And those I didn't
The scenery changed,
The people grew old,
It's so hard to rise above
What you are...

I walked away, bloody, maimed...
I need healing, I know.
I need to feel, and not to go.
But I have surrendered

Poor Farm Park
Chuck Cooper

More than once
To the emptiness.
It's so easy, so numb, so nice…
nothing is real.

Except this need to heal.

FOOTFALLS

NASCAR drivers will never know
The sheer pleasure of

Left – Right…

Left – Right…

Left – Right…

Left – Right – Left – Right

Of running.

Foot falls are
frank,
deliberate
measures of men.
There are things that we can learn
About anyone who runs.
Things that the alternating time
And pace
And distance
Teaches us.

Yes,
Racing cars… Race…
200 miles an hour
Bleeding…
Testosterone and rubber
All over the track,

All the way… to the… *NEXT*… Left… turn.

Miles and miles of trails are gone
Passed beneath my feet.
I carry on and on.
Until,

Poor Farm Park
Chuck Cooper

A sweat soaked
Blood pumped
Thrusting mania
Of "race" fills my mind.

Left – Right… Left – Right…
Footfalls mirror the pounding passion of life in my veins;
A white flare goes off like resonance in my mind.
White hot, and here is where I love.
The burn pushes away the calm
and reveals a darker side.

This is a race.
I see a number emblazoned in red thread
Painted on to the back of the runner
Who is only there to pull me forward.
The white-hot flare
turns red and blue and purple…
His frenzied fashion ignites a bull's desire.

My heart beats,
Pounding,
Pushing, blood
to my limbs and brain.
The manic hot breaths
Come fast and faster.

A brass-salt-aluminum paste coats my throat.
I have tasted desire before
And it fills me.
There is never enough water
To quench the muscles need
To meet my mind's desire.
I want this and need more
Than his back can give me.
Pushing faster.
Heart pounding,
Cindy Crawford on her best day,
Never felt desire this runner feels.

158

The Complete Second Verse
Dr. Charles Cooper

Desire cloaks the mind
and guards it
from the seething fire
Burning in my calves,
In my thighs.
He is not as far from me
as he once was.
Shoulder to shoulder…
He sees my eyes and knows.
He knows what I know.
He slows because he sees he is beaten.
My eyes flick to the next runner.

My crimson-flecked eyes of greenish asphalt
Would shed tears,
if there was a drop of moisture in my body.
The pure focus in them
Betrays my need for life.

Pain rips through my left leg.
I want to cry out "no."
I consciously see the finish line
growing farther away,
But I am still moving forward.
I shut off my mind,
And focus on the visceral need to finish.
I will not fail.
Will Not.
My brain is
The only part of my body
That seems prepared to function,
It is the command center.
And today, the brain will rule.
MY body WILL obey my MIND.

Right left… left right.

This is not a run,
Not a race,

Poor Farm Park
Chuck Cooper

This is a FIGHT.
With my own body,
And I was not created for second place.
My breathing slows as the focus returns.
Right – Left…

Out there on the trail,
I learned to lose,
Without surrender
Even when I didn't win,
I kept running,
Kept playing
Stayed on the field.

I want more from life
Than turn after bloody turn.
Still today, I want to learn?
When I am out on the trail,
Left – Right… Left – Right…

Running shoes,
Are the tools
You use to cross bridges,
To go places,
To strive
and to build
To learn
and grow,
and feel,
But most of all
to move on
from one place
and time
to the next
Without regret.
The trail is where I learned
To hold onto everything
Without at the same time looking back.
The shoes are the tools,

The Complete Second Verse
Dr. Charles Cooper

That we can use, to find our way.

Left – Right… Left – Right…

Out there on the trail
I learned longing,
passion,
and persistence.
That lesson I carried
From the trail to my life.
It has served me well.
But I will not tell
Anyone that passion is the secret to life.
Passion is something that many people fear.
I learned never to quit,
Never to stop,
Never to regret a chance I have lost.

All that passion keeps
People at a distance.
Those who burn brightly,
Those like you and I
Find loneliness,
In the spotlight,
Loneliness is a very real thing.
It comes hand in hand
With responsibility.

The shoes,
long since done with their run,
I have carried,
in my mind,
in my heart,
on my back…

Much farther than I dreamed
But it never seemed quite far enough for me.

Left – Right… Left – Right…

Poor Farm Park
Chuck Cooper

Never once when a promise was made
Have I surrendered...
Bit by bloody bit,
My gaze on the man in front of me,
I pursue and am pursued in kind
And that is life:

Left – Right... Left – Right...

I have built satellites that orbit the earth.
Rockets meant to go to the moon.
My precious poems are composed that way,

Rewrite...   Rewrite...
Left – Right... Left – Right...
Rewrite...   Rewrite...
Right – Left... Right – Left...
One Voice...   One Life...
This is going to need a rewrite.

When the road is longer than the race,
It matters less that you win, than finish.
Some days, the finish is not defined
It matters much more that you survive, than score or thrive.

Out there on the trail,
I found God,
In the trees
and the leaves,
In the vines
and the streams.

Mile after mile...   Day after day...

Right – Left... Right – Left...

I never want to fade away.

My foot rises and falls,

The Complete Second Verse
Dr. Charles Cooper

Forward motion sometimes
Is enough.
Belief sometimes is enough
To carry you through the night
To the next day.

Right – Left… Right – Left…
Through the dark to find the light.

Out there on the trail,
I learned to march,
At four miles per hour
Thirty miles per day.
Those who know me,
Know what I mean.
Marching turns toe and heart and heal to steel.
My calves were strong,
But they too, tore and swelled and healed
Depending very much on the day.
Healing is a thing,
Day in and day out
When you ask more of yourself.
The body wants to adapt,
To be what you ask.
Amazing creation that it is,
I like to test…
I've asked too much more than once,
Only to discover,
Everything is easier the second time.

Out there on the trail,
I learned what it was to fail.
If you aren't first, you're… not first
And that is ok.
Tomorrow is…
Hope is…
The next time is… easier.

Breathing, finishing, persistence, drive,

Poor Farm Park
Chuck Cooper

Sheer – solid - steel - will,
These are the things that keep men alive
Regardless of circumstance
In the dark or light,
In the world
In life.

I learned to focus and fight
Without the chains of fear...
The trail is rejoicing and rejection,
Around the next turn you pursue
And are pursued;
Up the next hill,
Where I find frustration and limits
To what I am capable of...
This hill seems a mountain
One more breath,
Legs outstretched
Left – Right...
Left – Right...

Until I am over it
Then, what is the hill.
The trail teaches...
And trail runners find
Limits are in the mind.
Pain is in the mind.
Running like life is composed of left - right.
Your mind will beg you to stop.
Your body will protest
But obey your commands.

You, like myself, will learn
To rule your mind,
And with it teach your body to obey
Because you are so much more
Than you were just one hill ago
Just an obstacle or two to go.
Challenges are like that.

The Complete Second Verse
Dr. Charles Cooper

They teach people to rise,
Teach bodies to thrive,
Help soldiers to find

Light

When there is none.

Left – Right…
Left – Right…
Is the composition of life.

I learned to try,
Out there on the trail.
I learned to be vulnerable and humble,
The answer to questions of scale…
There is no challenge
so great as the human mind.
No problem
Too large
it can't be solved
Bit by bloody bit,
Inch by bloody inch
One piece at a time.

I learned to want,
To love,
to seek…
and to hide.

My desire,
my passion is…
enormous.

"That's no moon…
that's my passion."

Left – Right…
Left – Right…

Poor Farm Park
Chuck Cooper

The music of life

In 4 / 4 time.

Left – Right… Left – Right…

I learned to discern,
From right and from wrong.
Prioritize and decide
when and if
to go along
With something that ran entirely contrary
To my being, or beliefs.

I have done this more than once
On the trail and in life.
The effect was never so great
As to justify this betrayal of myself.
The results were never so worthy
Of the sacrifice,
Personal… sacrifice…
That made me less…

Left – Right… Left – Right…

Is the rhythm of the blues,
Old beat up guitar
A road and walking shoes?

During the low times, in low country,
The trail teaches us not to filter people.
Love all in kind,
Because you never know…
My love made me a tool,
Like a pair of running shoes.
I became
A servant to the runners.
I learned to do the best I can

166

The Complete Second Verse
Dr. Charles Cooper

For everyone I can
Every chance I get,
Which I have done
More than once
In this life
To good effect.

In the trail,
And in life,
I made mistakes.
The good that you do
For others,
Can be your redemption.
It has been mine
More than once or twice.
I can carry the weight of the world
For a while,
But with my friends...
I am so much more.

Left – Right... Left – Right...

Is the lift in flight
From those wings
Which beat against
The things
Which would pull you down?
Ugly the people
Like gravity, who do little but cling
Hitch your wagon to a star, they say
And tow you back toward the earth,
But left – right, left – right is also how you fly
Bit by Bloody Bit,
Soon enough
As the air grows thin
They drop away,
You find yourself alone
To strive.

Poor Farm Park
Chuck Cooper

The people,
for whom I strive,
Have kept me alive
More than once.
Brothers in arms,
A friend's embrace
Lovers lace and charms.

Right – Left… Left – Right…

Is Achievement's song.
Achievement's brutal face,
Is a terrifying master,
It is to her I belong.

I face her every day.
Before the sun rises,
I dawn my running shoes.
Miles pass,
In this curious replay
Of rapture and reverie.
Along the way,
I transcend the physical.
I am the road,
The trail,
The shoes,
The friends,
The lover,
The lace,
The shoes.
I am one with everything around me.

Right – Left… Left – Right…
A breeze cools my sweat soaked back.
I nod my thanks and take the next step.

CANDIDE

A glass that's half nothing,
And a foolish question
Has wasted so much life.

Half a promise,
no reward.
Half a child
that cut the cord,
sort of
He, she, it still lives here you know.

Half a life
that passed in sorrow.
Half life never meant tomorrow.
Like a sad isemtope,
So close,
And so close,
And nearly there…
Forever.

Promises exchanged in twilight,
Never really meant as much.
Shadows falling from the light.
She just wanted a guy with a truck.
Perception changes with the dusk.
It is different every day.

A cloudy sky never stopped the dawn.
The sun comes and goes half noticed.
"Goodbye," she said.
"Goodbye," he said.

What lasts forever now?

Half a glass of empty space;
The single chambered round,

Poor Farm Park
Chuck Cooper

That laid Old Yeller down.
A life half finished…
A race half run…

I knew the day I met you,
Where all of this would end.
I saw the grey apocalypse,
Saw the blackened sky and sand.
I went there anyway,
A noble knight, I took your hand.
I live, as if nothing could kill me,
And I love like there is a chance,
Something is about to begin.

I'd rather die of life
Then have to live again
As a better man, Samsara,
Half a glass of liquid, half a glass of air,
Hope and dreams and fairy tales
Which make like
Tomorrow is a happy place,
And today's empty, lonely life,
Is just a moment on hold,
But today is killing me.

The Complete Second Verse
Dr. Charles Cooper

MY IMMORTAL

I asked you what it meant to live forever,
"Is immortality so impossible to describe?"

"It's not impossible," you said,
"It just takes a really long time."

The drapes swayed…
The window cracked…
The air blew in…
I turned to say…

You stopped me,
Placed your finger on my lips.

Stunning me to silence

As light slipped
The surely bonds that disguised
Your eyes,
Your hair,
Your smile…

I would have sworn,
I was blinded
By the sight.
But I saw you, and
I knew you were.
As the dawn passed away,
I could not feel tomorrow,
I did not know the day.
The concerns, the decisions
And the consequence they bring.
In a morning with you,
In a moment with you,
Wind swilling round and around.
Sweet country air
Flowing through your hair,

Poor Farm Park
Chuck Cooper

Chasing my fingers
Flushed by silk and fire
Golden angel halos composed
Everything I lost on my journey here.
When I found your lips
Everything was restored
Without question of the value
Of the life spent.
Then and there,
I became more.

Light slipped from your face into a memory,
Binding us forever, together
Inside my mind
Where no lies can be found;

And that is what immortal means.

The Complete Second Verse
Dr. Charles Cooper

"CABIN IN THE WOODS"

ART BY BECKY KIPER

Poor Farm Park
Chuck Cooper

A CABIN IN THE WOODS

I sat next to a fire.
Terrifying power,
In fire,
But it warms a room
With a crackle and a spark
That contains,
What remains
Of a 100-year-old maple tree
That lost its leaves,
It's limbs, it's will to live,
Then it fell,
At the hand of a man with an ax.

I was warm, with a woman I loved.
Content and warm, as I watched it burn…
These gifts from fate or recompense,
Cedar timbers made up the walls
The scent of cedar placates pain.
I'm not sure why,
It's just that way.

Like every young man,
I had lived in fear of this day.
Satisfaction, is the enemy of achievement
Or so I thought.
And I wanted to be so much,
Or so I thought.
With you I was more.

There in the light of the sun,
In the warmth of a burning tree,
In a cabin made of cedar
On a mountain made of rock,
A warmth flowed in me,
For the first time
In a long time,
To redeem…

The Complete Second Verse
Dr. Charles Cooper

It was that little smile
That disarmed me.
Together, simultaneously,
We surrendered and conquered,
Each other.
      Our fear,
           Our past,
                Our instinct
           For self-preservation
      After only a little while
Passed away.
Forever is the word of today,
That I never thought
To think or say or hear
Beneath bated breath,
Ever.

If I had to define Epic Love
From my 44 years of life
And knowing that one day
I would be,

A storybook
fairy tale,
Knight
In shining armor
A lady with only one shoe
Needless to say, it was beautiful.

To this lady, I say this:
On the day I surrendered to you
And conquered your heart and mind
On the day, you did the same.
The journey we are to take,
From now into forever,
Can only be described as
Love.
Epic Love.

Poor Farm Park
Chuck Cooper

SPARED

Today, more than most,
I'm driven to make the heart beats count.
By the rules of rounding and the law of averages,
Everything I have to do has already been done.
It's time to the reap the rewards and play in the sun
But I am cannot go easy.

I've been spared, going on seven times.
I am here for a reason.
Maybe it's to say these words to you:
So that you can read it...
You, are here, for a reason too.
Seize this moment
Live this life.
Never stop,
Never give up.
Never walk away.
Never... until you are fulfilled,
Whatever does it for you,
Let your potential be real.

Make it real.

It's time these word games meant something...

The problems, the solving, the walking away.
It has to mean something.

Take these words and make them your own.
Make them real.

WHAT KIND OF FOOL

What kind of fool am I?
Bought a car or a truck
I count on luck,
Far too much,
When I drive,
To keep me alive.
The time has come to Fly.

With airplane wing and chopper blade
I rise.
With sweat and pain through torrent rain
I grind.
On the wings of thought and words,
The lift, the courage, the nerves,
I fly.

No one can stop me now.
No one could stop me then.
I don't know how I fell,
I only know, it won't ever happen again.

Poor Farm Park
Chuck Cooper

FINALLY, LIFE

My life,
Is a humbling,
harrowing,
winnowing,
Whisper
In the wind,
A pebble of sand
On an infinite beach of history.
My Life was,
More secret than not
More instinct than thought,
That gave me meaning…
When compared to almost everyone.

And Then:
I made it more
Through sheer force of will,
Until my will was almost gone.
Then, I clung to passion
For so long, too long,
That passion waned
So I drafted reason as a guide,
Embraced the truth, until it lied.

Until that day,
When salvation lay
Beyond my conscious grasp.
Still, I drove forward
Clinging to root, and dirt, and straw.
No matter the season,
Whether captured or sought,
I fought for more,
Than anyone could possibly deserve
To be.

This I did,
Not for me,

The Complete Second Verse
Dr. Charles Cooper

But because, I could
And it needed to be done.
So I did,
Live.

There is no lesson in my wake.
Each person goes their own way.
But, if you find yourself asking,
What does it take,
To finally make life.
What does it take to mean,
To live to give,
To be free,
To strive,
To want,
To mean
Something,
In our most desperate hour,

There is only one way:
Make everything you think
An action verb;
Never be afraid,
Don't wait, do.
Make. Create. Generate,
Everything you can imagine,
And then,
Give it all away...
For others to embrace
What will never be theirs.

Finally,
when you find yourself alone,
But know,
Deep in your heart,
You are right...
Finally,
when everyone else has gone home,
In the dark of the night...

Poor Farm Park
Chuck Cooper

Stay behind.
Commit and
Grind.
Breathe life into your imaginings.
That's the way
You make change.
That's the way you *live*.

The Complete Second Verse
Dr. Charles Cooper

YOUTH'S PRICE

What I knew in youth
Was absolute.
Black and white,
Wrong or right,
So certain was I,
That I failed to understand
There are things that only a man
Can get right.
Just a child, I took a brush,
And painted life,
With my desire for a wife,
For that, I would pay,
And I paid
And paid.

Youthful ignorance costs,
The price paid is life,
Which buys experience, and regrets.
Still, as if the best mistakes are made twice,
I search for love, a wife.

As the years go by, I never stopped to cry.

So I ask, please, don't lie,

If you had it to do over???

Well…?

Poor Farm Park
Chuck Cooper

THE GIFT OF AGE

I saw you,
and kissed you,
and held you,
And turned
To walk away.
There was always a job to do.

How did I walk away, I cannot explain?
In this moment,
I cling to thoughts of my capture,
The sanitary way you would hold me close to rapture
Push it a little farther.

It's not a thing a child can know or understand.
It makes me glad, I am a man.
Because you,
Well you, are a woman.

The Complete Second Verse
Dr. Charles Cooper

PLAYING GAMES WITH TIME

Time is not tolerant of boys or girls.
Against their will, they find their way
As men and women to responsibility.
Time paints life with tests and trials
Taints our mind with fear and fines.
And begs a reckoning
Of us all.

In shoes and roads and wings,
We travel until we don't
Ashes to ashes
And all that.

What I leave behind
In ink and words and rhyme
Is what makes me more,
Immortal more,
And I am a time whore.
I want it all,
A moment that's forever,
To be remembered
For the words I said
Too few times
To you and her and him
"I love you,"
Even when it doesn't rhyme.

Fly away to youth.
Fly away alone.
I will have my forever love,
Even though you aren't my home.

Poor Farm Park
Chuck Cooper

ABLE TO FEEL

I was able to feel,
For the briefest time…
Able to fly,
So high,
Too high.

Joy, sallow joy,
A child playing with toys…
Did you not know?
Did you not grow?
Not find
That eerie feeling,
That you were too high
Creeping into your mind

Falling…
Too far…
down…
The fall, from your arms,
Brings so much pain.
I turn off those feelings.

It is still a joy to watch you fly;
Can I be content to watch?

Not me. I will try…
Perhaps I can fly too.
Maybe even a little higher than you.

I've lived in your shadow for so long.
It's time to find out,
What you look like from above.

The Complete Second Verse
Dr. Charles Cooper

MODERN MEDICINE

Band-Aids are the miracle of modern medicine.
I was politely introduced to a Band-aid
That healed everything.
It was nice, polite,
Stayed on in the shower
Lasted hours and hours
And clung to me, tight.

Everyone knows when things are done.
Band-Aids heal.
When the healing is over,
You have to peel them off.
The meaningless ones just slip
Away, they see a need and run.
There is no damage in their path,
And nothing really heals,
There is no aching pain of loss
Because no one feels
One way or the other
About a love that never was.

The best ones come off slow and painful,
They last until the need is gone.
When they leave,
You feel what empty means.
It hurts, it really hurts.
Hasn't your life always been about preparing,
And I was just a Band-Aid,
Something to repair the damage you absorbed
Cover the emptiness, stave off a scar
You needed so many on the way
To your destination.
Here's hoping one day you arrive.

"THE BANDAID"

ART BY BECKY KIPER

185

LIVING ON HOPE

Hope is the servant of lesser beings
And salesmen.
What you achieve in life
Can be so much more than hope
When it's made of persistence
And blood, and sweat, and tears
and thought, and craft, and mind.

What your hands can do
When connected to your mind,
Is only limited if you don't try.

A man can rest in hope…
Laze away for days and days,
But no one can create that way,
With clean hands and painted nails.
A man can hope who does not try,
And never fail,
But he cannot fly.

So, what of you?
Will you bond your hope and dreams
To effort and work and sweat?
Fail a thousand times,
Succeed, create, and fly.

Please… try.
Hope is a worthless sentiment
Unless you act.
Please, act.

The Complete Second Verse
Dr. Charles Cooper

SELFISH

Honestly, it's the righteous that really bother me,
The one's who don't know your name,
Or your mind,
Or your values...
But they judge all the same.
How could you believe you know what's best...
For me...
For me?

If you knew,
What I went through
To be here.
To stand in your presence.

If you knew the price I paid and
The gifts I gave:
To a wife...
And children...
And family...
And country...
And company...

You might not say the things you say.
It is the fool who judges me
Without meeting me,
knowing me,
Even if we disagree,
Respecting my right to be...
Just as you belong to you;
I am my own,
And it will always be that way.

I see the world through my own eyes,
Never disguise my values or my will.
What you can make me do
With my life,
That defies that will is stealing.

Poor Farm Park
Chuck Cooper

What I want and what I do,
Has nothing to do *with you.*
I am selfish, and it is my choice to make
That's all there is to say.

The Complete Second Verse
Dr. Charles Cooper

TOGETHER

Light breaks through
You see, as if for the first time
The subtle lines between truth and lies
Are not as subtle as they used to be.

You see me.
Dawn cracks, breaks loose the sky
Pieces of the day falling though,
The life takes flight,
To celebrate the freedom
That came with the wings
At the height of the night.
For us both,
It took time to find…
Time and darkness, shadows and vanity
Disguised life from me,
Hid me from you.

Where there are shadows,
There is light…
Which I see now,
Our lives have seen so much
Bitterness, darkness, despair,
All of it prepared us
One for the other.

It's time to realize
What we can do, together.
The sun is out,
You're shining
The day is new,
It's time, to live through
The day together.

SOMETHING NEW

Nothing can stop this collision,

Poor Farm Park
Chuck Cooper

Of day and night,
Wrong and right.
All we were taught,
Everything we know,
Dissolves as my eyes
Push into your soul.
So pure and good,
Capable and fine.
You like it rough,
But don't resist
The gentle fingers,
As they come to rest
In those places
They learned so fast...
How to make you gasp.

The pressure is relentless,
The flames paint your mind.
Darting tongue,
Touching lips,
Grinding hips,
Thighs tremble,
As you greet my kiss...
Hold out, just a second more
Wait for it...
Linger on the edge...
As the precipice gains depth and strength.
The explosion claims your body...
Burning me into your mind.
In the moment you claimed me,
In that moment, you were mine.

LOST IN THE MOMENT

Mystic blinds to hide behind…
A horse can never see,
What's right in front of him.
He's racing just to be.
She can see less than him.
Blinded by regrets,
She never forgets
How easy it all seemed
When she was young.
The race already run.
Everything arrived at her door.
The phone would ring.
The conversation would drone on,
Declarations were made,
But no one ever knows
when they're lost in the throws
Of youth times love times hormones…
Life, what life looks like
Is a mystery.
A mystery which unveils itself so slow
For the young.

Errors are not evident
When you're feeling
Things you haven't felt yet.
There's no time for regret
When you're lost in the moment.
Lost in THE moment,
With tragedies all afoot
Striving for the most basic passions
It takes so much to live.
Just to live.
But it's a price that hasn't been paid yet.

Perspective is the great mirror,
Life in the rear view.
Looking now to see,

Poor Farm Park
Chuck Cooper

And all I see is you.
Lost in the moment
With you.

NO WASTE IN JAPAN

Don't spend a moment,
With idle tears,
Idled by fear.
I will not wait,
There's no time like today
To live life.

CAPITALIST SUMMER

Nothings is free.
I got to see you bright,
Feel the warmth and the love.
See you fly,
See you shine.
I looked into the sun.
The price is tears and burned retinas.

MOUNTAIN TOPS

Life is a never-ending quest
To reach the crest.
So many mountains to climb.
On days like today,
I am tired, so tired.
I think that one more step
Would be impossible,
But I cannot rest.

There are miles to go.
More miles behind.
Distance and days,
Spent wishing you were mine.
It's not sorrow, not regret,
Just a place I haven't been to yet.
I will climb without rest,
Until I find,
Where you reside,
On top of your mountain,
The view sublime.

PLAYING GAMES WITH AN ANGEL

I get it, you're the angel
With the wings and the light.
We may not even play on the same field,
But that doesn't make it right.
I have to be fair,
You said it would be this way.

The Complete Second Verse
Dr. Charles Cooper

A LESSON IN WORDS

Ever since Hendrix said it,
I've wondered what it meant
to be "BOLD as LOVE."

I found out that walking away from love,
Laying love on the sacrificial alter of ego.
Giving up love for something larger,
Is bigger.

Any man can surrender,
And love makes it so easy.
What better excuse.
To be bigger than love, is to be alive.

I prefer, Bold as Life.

To create, I don't surrender to love,
I give up love and live.
To be bold as life... I create.

WALKING AWAY

I saw you walking away.
You never turned to say,
I'm sorry or goodbye.
You turned away,
And all I got to see was behind,
A past that was mine
And yours and empty.

Poor Farm Park
Chuck Cooper

MY SERENADE

This serenade is not a lie
Even when I do not cry.
I saw you walking in the park
There on the bench next to you,
I offered you a word or two,
Worthy of your time.
You looked I smiled,
You…
What I said, my love song,
Was real, you saw me feel.
I knew the darkness you walked through
And on that bench, I watched you heal.

Tonight, I remember
What it felt like
As I closed my eyes.
Even though you said goodbye,
Like you said you wouldn't;
Even though I didn't die,
Like I thought I would.

My serenade was not a lie,
I tried.

"THE LONG ROAD"

PHOTO BY CHARLES COOPER

Poor Farm Park
Chuck Cooper

LONG ROAD

There are days
I think it all went wrong.
There was a time,
I found my truth in song.
There was a moment,
I wanted everything I saw.
And everything I touched.
I wanted it all,
But you would not be rushed.

There are days in my life without regret.
Those days haven't happened yet.
I search the world from east to west
But you are not to be found.

Live long, sweet Elizabeth,
Smile with me through the miles
This river bed, will see water again.
On that fine day I'll find,
The miles between us evaporate
Finally, you are mine,
And I am finally home.

FULFILLED

I would be a fool to write this here and now,
Even saying it is hollow on the best day.

It is something I crave,

But I have neither seen
nor known it in my life.

I continue to strive
and create
only hoping
that some moment
between here and the grave
placates my desire.

I feel that being fulfilled would be an amazing thing.

But I also love to strive
And want
And work
And build
And create
And…

Poor Farm Park
Chuck Cooper

GENTLE REMINDER

On the bed,
in our room,
I hear you breathe.
You see me move.

Our eyes don't meet,
it's been too long.

There is no need,
Where shadow's song.

We live our lives,
Intertwined.

My heart beats,
To make you mine.

And you don't even have to try,

I am yours,

From now until the afterlife.

The Complete Second Verse
Dr. Charles Cooper

STAY

I think it was Lisa Loeb
who had a song called "Stay."
The week you left for good,
Was longer, by far
Than any I can imagine.
I know hurry up and wait,
And I know what it feels like
To be near the dead and dying.
Life teaches these things,
Patience, humility, and how to learn.

I couldn't learn a thing when I was young.
I was far too smart to be taught
By anything that didn't hurt,
Or fit
into
my preconceived
concept... of life.

I was too young
To watch someone die,
To see it in their eyes...
But life is a harsh mistress that way.
Like everything,
It's easier the second time.
And the third...
And the...
Sigh...

Too young to think that love was a lie,
Or watch a man betray who he knew himself to be,
I couldn't help but ask,
What would you be?
The man turned away.
Misty silks that blurred the eyes,
It's not a disguise
Even as I wore it.

Poor Farm Park
Chuck Cooper

Society said, to fight, *"The Man."*
So I did, time and time again,
For such a long time,
I never stopped to think,
To know,
Who "The Man" was.
I waged war
against the wars
which waged
On the inside…
of me.

I was "The Man" I fought.
It was not easy to hold me back,
To pull me back,
Into an Iron Bar
Or some famed '80's wrestling hold
I had seen on TV.
There were no limits on what I know,
Only what I can see.
I have access to it all
When I'm rested, but I cannot sleep.

Trying times cause men to rise.
Men who are not held down by will alone.
Their will. Not that it makes a difference.
How do men rise, better themselves,
Day in and out, what does it take
To be a better me?
What I cannot see,
Held just out of reach,
There is no great reveal,
No lying, cheating, or stealing…
It's all inside of me.
There are two men in my life
Who I am,
And who I am becoming.

I slept on the floor

The Complete Second Verse
Dr. Charles Cooper

On the first day of this new life,
The sofa, the night after.
Slept is an exaggeration.
I hurt, and stared, and counted, and what?
I thought most of all.
Preconceived notions of life
Keep a man caged.
I long for the days
Where the new
and the bright
the hunted
and the right
mattered,
to me.

It reveals too much
Of the things that are gone,
The echoing refrain of your favorite song.
The truth is, I never understood Maroon 5.
Nothing about it ever seemed wise.
Sometimes music is that way,
It means little but feels much.
We were that way, when we were together.
I felt I could never tether
Myself to you,
Whether far or near,
We were too far apart to feel.
Too wounded to heal.

GROWING UP

I grew up poor,
Or so I thought.
I had parents, and they loved me.
It doesn't mean much
To a powder keg -
Bright as they come -
Flash flood of a man,
Who never met a problem or a person,
He wouldn't overcome.
The confidence of the untried,
The vanity of the young,
The sallow,
bitter taste of life
at first bite…
I was the brightest star,
the sun,
I shined…
I thought so anyway.

What it takes to learn
For a man new to life
Is experience.
There are things
which can't be taught,
People who can't be taught,
And I was one.

Even if,
I set out to learn.
I wish,
Someone
would have warned me
It would not be the experience
I longed for
Or the education I wanted…
It was
the kind of experience

204

The Complete Second Verse
Dr. Charles Cooper

that teaches lessons,
which are not soon forgot.

Even after the long
first
time…
I sought it out anyway.
Like Faust in a wicked place
I sought to sell my soul to know.
Nothing is cheap, knowledge even less so…
Because Life doesn't work that way
Life makes us pay and pay.

When I grow up,
I have said it so many times.
When I grow up,
I will answer the mail,
Pay my taxes,
Not make THAT mistake
Again.

When I grow up,
I will work slower
More deliberately,
Choose words
More carefully,
Find a way to be kind
And lend a hand
Every time.

When I grow up,
I will stop fighting the man
For every inch of ground
With every ounce of strength
I have found.

When I grow up…
And up and up and up
And Down

Poor Farm Park
Chuck Cooper

So far down,
I will find the ground
And stand on it
Feet firmly planted on truth
Standing on principles and ideals
Truth reduced to its essence
Like a man in his youth?

When I grow up,
I will understand why people
Who proclaim diversity
As an unassailable ideal
Push uniformity of thought
And a standard set of knowledge
So much…

"Everyone is ok,
As long as they think this way,"

No one owns
Another person.
If it is not given,
Or taken in trade
It cannot be received.
If it is not received,
It cannot be taken.
The alternative
Is unthinkable.

The Complete Second Verse
Dr. Charles Cooper

I CAN STILL RUN

The petals of the flower
Are lost to time.
I tasted and touched.
They were not mine.

Avenues of life
Led me away from you,
But I cannot deny
What my heart knew.

A gold gilt necklace
One molecule deep
Was what I could afford
It was not enough to keep
My hand in yours.

I cannot understand
Why I am not your man
When I remember
How easy it is to feel,
What I need to feel
When I'm with you.

You said, "I had so much to offer."
You said, "I should move on."
Don't be surprised,
When I am not there.
Don't be shocked
When I discover,
I can still run.

BOOK 4: ARMY DAYS

"WHAT THEY CARRIED"

ART BY BECKY KIPER

The Complete Second Verse
Dr. Charles Cooper

WALKING

I took a walk today.
I'm drawn to it,
to walk and think.
In solitude.
The entire world could pass me by,
I would notice,
But today, I see.

I walked right past
A pond with two tributaries,
Not large enough to be a lake.
A fish ventured too near the surface,
Which was low.
There he met a bird of prey.
Not his day, not today.

A fish needs the water, like I need the rain.
The tried caution that it brings
And enough buffer overhead to hide beneath.
I could not say
If I am the fish
Or the bird of prey,
But I need the rain.
The day I went to war
Like the day I came back alive,
It poured and snowed
And burnt caution into my eyes…
By some miracle, I survived,
but so many on both sides did not.
I pay for that still.

Army Days
Cooper

NO QUARTER, NO SURRENDER

0232 hours, Ajar River Bank, Kahmard District, Afghanistan

We move at night, like ghosts.
Our night vision gives us all
The advantage we need for now.
Six hours before, I paid
In a denomination of two brother's blood
For a picture of an evil man,
Which relayed via satellite,
Requested instructions.
The response, simply composed, "No Quarter."
The words: "لا استسلام"
No surrender, a shouted cry, like a Prayer
In the air, five times a day.
God can't help you here
Not with blood, bullets, or spear,
In play. This is the domain of man.
Who can help? No one can.

No surrender. No quarter,
A fight to the end.
A fight which never stops.
The tears stop the loss,
Which never stops.
All that we've lost.
All that is cost.
No surrender… we promise each other.
No quarter… they promise the wind.
Neither side can afford another day
Of guilt and false bravado.

Zero Four thirty hours
The moon still lights the desert
The face of evil, via satellite,
Pinpoint, a pin prick
of laser light.

210

The Complete Second Verse
Dr. Charles Cooper

The coming fireball
Incinerating walls,
Which stood for thousands of years.
Now dust and ashes,
to ashes and dust,
as blood to rust
And all that. …
All that was, was,
But is no more.
Dust and smoke and sand
Fire and oil and land.
Human capital, human collateral
Damage beyond words,
Wealth not withstanding,
There's blood on these hands.

No surrender, no quarter
This is a fight to the end.
No surrender. No quarter.
This bloody fight will never stop,
Until tears and loss
Are all that's left.

We'll never know how much we've lost
Too many faces pass in the night.
Too many eyes that close,
Will never see the light again.
Too much gone without a fight
For peace.

No surrender. No quarter.
No weapons. No wails.
Just a debate…
Which never took place.
Peace is the test of manhood,
Which we all failed
In the end.

Army Days
Cooper

WAR

So many people,
Who give a tribute to soldiers
For their freedom and prosperity
And all the good stuff which comes
From living in an organized society,
Misunderstand soldiers.

As a soldier, I fought for the man next to me. Occasionally, I tried
to levy a little justice, but only lost rank and pay for my trouble. The
military does what it does, destroy. It's the only thing which
Government does well, destroy and control.

It's a cardinal mistake to believe a government is capable of
compassion or love. It's a system, a set of rules. It doesn't feel, it
only functions. Those people inside it are cogs in a wheel where
resistance is a waste. It cannot be a reflection of people. It can
certainly use people to perform its functions though.

Soldiers are those people. I am one of those people. You should be
scared.

Men who glorify war have never been there, died there, lived there,
or felt the guilt that comes from surviving.

The Complete Second Verse
Dr. Charles Cooper

LASER RANGE FINDER

100 Monks used to live here
In a secret part of forever,
In a world with less than most.
The tower in which I sit is all that's left of them.
A crumbling bible rests on the alter
Where men used to come to pray.

I level my gaze away from history
To the promise of future bound up in sin.
The building is some embassy or another
Some country or another,
It doesn't matter anymore.
I stopped breathing moments ago,
But this too is less relevant
Than the promise of future sin.

You see, this is the definition
of an international incident,
Because none of us
Would do anything like this
At home,
Until we do [Ad SIC, 2020].

My hands move methodically…
Three dials for timing…
Two for aiming…
One button for laser which sends all the data home.
Check the frequency, good.
Short code, three letters
O.P.E. – [Enter]
I laugh at what this means.
I watch the building there on the horizon
See the dot,
A tiny green beam
Of ones and zeros
Passing through the ether.
Time passes.

Army Days
Cooper

I look over at nothing, and it is good.
Without a word, the destroyer lays waste creation,
Rises to leave and possibly rest
After all, erasing the past
        to create the future
                is hard work.

The Complete Second Verse
Dr. Charles Cooper

GOODNIGHT

Malaise and grey,
Dank, dark the ground.
No leaves or limbs,
No air for men.
What sorrow on this day,
I lay wounded and alone
Where every single moment,
Was a moment too long.

I cursed the winter wind at dawn,
The snow that came and has not yet gone.
Stained ripe with blood
Of men and thugs.
They lay before me,
Prostrate, gone.

The stale, dry, acrid air
that burns with each breath.
When I move,
Streaks of pain and blood,
Like red rain,
Stain my hands and face.
How I wish the blood would stop,
But it goes on and on,
If only for a moment,
It is still a moment too long.

It's day,
I rise with the silent sun
Pierced beams of light
I try to run,
And falter.
I step, again
A step,
I begin,
But I waited
too long,

Army Days
Cooper

too long.

Until there's nothing to be done
For anyone.

Empty is the silent night
Empty is the song, the sight.
The path too long
          For one last fight.
I knew enough,
knew right from wrong,

But not enough to stop the song:
The victory dance goes on and on.
I never thought in all these days,
I would want the rain,
And crave the dark,
For the promise of a ray
Of light,
And a new day,
And a dove,
And one more
sad, sad song.

A whispered prayer for wings and flight,
To carry me from this longest night
To the place where our journey could go on and on,
Until we're gone.
Goodnight Song.

The Complete Second Verse
Dr. Charles Cooper

DESERT NIGHT

Eagles in the desert,
Twilight in the day.
I went looking and found
There was no way to stay.

Look up, look high.
Another chance at greatness
Has almost passed me by.
Look down,
Right to left,
Another opportunity
I won't regret.

Oh, I'll never know
What it means to hold you.
We'll never go
This way again.
I'll never see the light in your eyes.
The beauty of youth,
The mirage of sin.

Twilight in the day,
The sun had set,
I could not stay.
You could never understand
The call I felt to be a man.

Duty is surrender,
Sacrifice, and love.
I left you behind
As if commanded from above.
Oxford, the church mouse,
Who bore witness my love.
The blood and sweat that flowed away
That took from me another day.
It's not with regret,
I think of you now.

Army Days
Cooper

In the cold night, the desert,
Slips up, like a dove
Who has no place here,
Like silence, she brings peace
Peace, without silence.
It's the lack of silence,
Which let's me sleep
Without love.

The Complete Second Verse
Dr. Charles Cooper

IF WE BLEED...

We crossed a line called Rubicon,
There was no going back,
Just a line on a map,
Drawn in blood and regret.

A marching band of tyrants,
Brutal killers who dealt in death…
Magic forces on their horses
A robed mage in Russian tank.
Who has a cause to retreat
Who cares to give some ground
When fanatics and extremists
Rise up, we put them down
They crossed a line called Rubicon
Now they're buried in the ground.

We will fight again tomorrow
Dust and blood, Heart and soul.
A marching band of tyrants
Weapons free, lock and load
Breath deep a set of lies.
If we do not bleed,
We cannot die.

Today we march for Tommy,
Today we march for Johnny,
Today we march for Tyrone and Anthony…
Who will never see home again.
March in turn,
Pound the drum.
They paid a price,
So we bring them home.
They're laid to rest,
But not that long.
We trot them out for all to see,
No one forgets the heroes
Who wouldn't be,

Army Days
Cooper

But they did what they had to do
And found out the truth...
We all bleed.

BEHOLD THE BRAVE

Brave is a fool
Dancing before
A million souls in hell
To love and be loved.
They have little to give,
And less to lose.

A man in uniform
Sealed his fate,
Swore an oath,
And swore, a lot.

Curses like guns and bullets,
Are solitary things,
Meant for a single soul
To say, "Not quietly."
Or, "Not this time."
To some "enemy,"
Who is saying just the same.

It took such a long time for me,
To be the man who could say,
"I put down my gun,
Three years ago today."
I no longer need
The security.
I no longer fear
The anxiety.

I have said my goodbyes,
So many more, than any man should.
The price of my life,
In uniforms and blood
Rose for so long.
The polished glass of desert sand
From an air strike I called,
Is painted by the blood of man

Army Days
Cooper

Who I never knew at all.
The weasel, bold stroke and underline
That comes from the A-10's growl and whine
Gave me a certainty
I could not find
A replacement for.

Such a fool, so brave.
I never learned to duck,
Never learned to kneel,
I became a medic to heal.
But if the truth was known,
I wasn't very good,
So I keep my medals under lock and seal.
They aren't me.
They aren't mine.

Behold me, and wonder,
How I survived?
I do, every day.

I am careless,
I am bold and brave,
But mostly,
I am terrified
I will not see
The next day.

The Complete Second Verse
Dr. Charles Cooper

DESERT BOOTS

In the desert,
In the morning,
Combat boots are clean, shiny, and black...
When you rise.

A fraction of a second
After exiting the tent,
At stand to, they are glazed in sand.
In the desert, black boots will never do.
So said the memo
on the SecDef's desk
after the first gulf war.

No advice, no "Never attack the same country twice."
Or, "Finish what you start."
Or, "Never betray your allies,
Who are willing to fight for you,
With you.
To remove the fool you put in charge
When you were younger
And felt so very large."
The lesson learned from the gulf war was;
"Black boots are not suited for the desert."

During the second Iraq war,
Soldiers were given, carefully designed
Tanned hide, turned inside out
So there was no shine,
And they were called Desert boots.
In spite of the soldier's instinct to try
Desert boots simply cannot be shined.
They do not require Kiwi
Or elbow grease
Or flame and spit
Or copious amounts of time.
They run against 240 years of tradition in this way:
They offer some level of convenience.

GENERALS

Generals are a curious thing.
Administrative kings during peace time
Living lavish lifestyles funded by fear,
Imagining the next war,
      the next weapon,
Imagining how to survive and destroy
All who come.

At the dawn of war,
Light flows into the General.
They become…
Men who seem prescient,
As they have
Already imagined
      every move
           every permutation
Of the war to come…
To ensure the destruction
Of one's enemy.

I must apologize to the reader here,
As I have gone on an aside
About Generals,
Who are little more
      than weapons of war,
An instruction manual of sorts,
Who have been
      and seen
         and done
            it all before…
Or so I have been told…
By Generals.

The Complete Second Verse
Dr. Charles Cooper

TRENCH WARFARE

Wait, decay,
Wait, guns leveled at the enemy
There is no escape,
Just bullets and time and men
And words
      and paper
          and pens.

Dashing off "never compromise,
The truth can never lie.
The men will hold out…"
While we wait and decay…
And fight another day.

Men with pens arrayed before them
Contemplate the where the periods and commas go,
Another day
Bullets and decay.
There is no escape
For the lost.
While fools negotiate,
We live our last days
In these holes that we dug for ourselves.

Army Days
Cooper

FOUR IN THE MORNING

Clock ticking
Time ticking
Passing us by.
Past the tearing
The tears, the terror
Time ticking.
I wake
And write
It's the AM
I don't look at the clock
It ticks in my mind
Like a digital watch
The full silence before dawn.

Stand to,
We rise and man the perimeter
Check weapons,
Lie prone
Aim at nothing,
Heart beats, thunder in my chest
I expect the attack
Which comes.
I am the attack
Which comes.
Aim, click, fire,
One.
Aim, click, fire,
Two.
Bodies keep falling,
Bodies keep coming.
The waste piles up
in blood and bone and screams.
I notice that this is a day
Unlike most.
Every shot a strike,
Center mass

The Complete Second Verse
Dr. Charles Cooper

Like my will rules the steel
Flying through the air
I extend my range.
I've pasting a line at 150 yards,
Barrell level and
Aim, click, fire,
Twenty-two.

How many Milton's and Chaucer's lay on the ground?

I'm out at 250 yards now,
Just as effective
Aim a little higher,
Find the space between breaths
And twenty-three, twenty-four and so on.

The attack fades,
A hazy grey,
I see...
My desk and pen and computer
And I wonder
What I'm doing on the floor.

Army Days
Cooper

THE MEDIC

It's almost habit now,
I was an Army Medic…
I know what it is
To rip off a bandage
And hair,
And skin,
And subcutaneous sin…
I would apply morphine to that…
If you would trust me.
I would offer
  A pleasure
    So great…
Satan's soul would be for sale.

Given that power,
I would empty Hell,
And offer mercy
To a fallen world.

Just a little more power…

Pathetic,
Craving,
monster,

Which lives in the leviathan
Inside ourselves,
And knows what it means to be human.

Just a little more power…

Sadist,
masochist,
master.

Which part
do you play…

228

The Complete Second Verse
Dr. Charles Cooper

When you play with children?

Which saint would stay
To offer intercession,
Forgiveness
for that!

The Medic,
The Christ,
The priest,
The pimp,
The parent.

Is it any wonder
Hell exists,
If only in our minds.
What a torture hope is,
What a pained game
Is life,
When winning can look like
Ripping other people to pieces.

There's a price to pay,
someday,
I hope.

Army Days
Cooper

KEY VICTORIES

The journey to war
Is hypnotic
For most.
For soldiers, it's real.
Tangible sweat
Building walls,
Of age and regret
Far behind the line…
Impenetrable
Eagle Flying high
To the victory,
Key victory.

The spirit of man,
Has a steep cost to enter in.
Belief in oneself
Is so hard to find
When you may be the one…
            who was left behind.
If you were the cost of victory
What would you do?

Fight on to my Ranger Objective…
110% and then some.
In the unforgiving moment
When the blood begins to spill,
"No man left behind,"
Was my price to fight.
I took the flight
And with no regret,
The sun never sets.
No one knows why.
Glory is a pastime
For the brave and the bold.
Foot falls like the one before.
Always forward in spite of the score.
Who will know?

The Complete Second Verse
Dr. Charles Cooper

Who will even ask…
When no one can answer why
This victory
Was a key victory,
Worth so much cost.

We crossed the sea to touch the sky.
Rifle in hand,
An extra bandage tucked in my waist band.
I fired the bullet, *and I had a duty of care*…
I was the medic who never shed a tear
As I triaged the enemy
Along with my friends
With a grease pen and an M9
Off to Valhalla
Where there are no goodbyes.

The tourniquet applied,
T 0219
Which may have been a lie,
I don't remember.

I never wanted the hill or the house
Or my life after this
If it meant surrendering
Something no one would miss
Or could even define.
Victory is so sublime.
It was the cost of victory,
A key victory
In someone's mind
Which became a plan
At a time, in a place,
I did not understand.

I did what I did,
And I have no regret.
I was trained.
There were orders,

Army Days
Cooper

And an instinct to survive.
Every day,
The next day
Is a victory,
A key victory in life.

Jacob and Esau
Would plunge the world,
For the price of a birthright,
And a cunning lie
Told to a blind man,
Into blood and sin.
Can I be blessed
Just one more time
To start a war,
So I can see Victory
Over bullies and thugs…
Key victories in history
Just one more time.

AGED WARRIOR

Global demonstrations of people and belief,
Follow noble remonstrations of the bereft and their grief.
If we could turn off our TV,
We might see,
and find ourselves nearer to the simple and the real,
Instead we take up a heart-rendered blade of steel,
Raising the hands of the world,
And shedding a collective tear,
At the behest of some publicity firm
For a people who never were.

This noble heart at a desk of wood and brass,
not as elegant, as the dozen or so monitors on the wall
Of a world-weary operations center.
Here, we deliver what matters;
What will change;
What will last;
Who will profit?

Pictures of this and that analysis, creative, flat,
In four dimensions, fly to the sweet by and by.
Countenance of time,
Pausing to know what's right?
Finding oneself fading
into the sweet by and by.

Finding thoughts, wondering, meandering, wandering,
Chasing the dreams of those who dream
Not to do, but to know, as though we know better.
Silent, brutal, control, as though we know better.
I have been where I've been, and seen what I've seen,
And my finger pulled the trigger because it could have been me.

Now I play this numbers game,
Ten thousand, ten million of this or that
Flying, sailing, ground under foot.
The silent rushing flood of time;

Army Days
Cooper

age and wear have not been kind
They tie me to this desk and my thoughts,
And I watch others accept the mission that was mine
Not for lack of will, but the passage of time.

Silenced the soldier meets the maker,
With a click and puff of wind,
Hands will move in silent, sequence;
rules unbroken, but surely bent,
And deliver the thought from the mind of the maker,
A man, no less than me.

My will weaves the quilt of guilt;
Retired to reverie.
'Til late at night the wind brings
Taps to my haunted head,
And I remember my brothers,
and remember,
I will see them all again.

The Complete Second Verse
Dr. Charles Cooper

THE BODIES FALL

The bodies keep falling.
Never forgive. Never forget.
Never again. Never regret,
But for god's sake,
Never do that again.

The bodies fall
For bullies and thugs,
For blood for life
To reset the lie
We tell ourselves
When we wake in the morning
And rise.
War is just a disguise…
For control.
War is just a disguise…
For fear.

The bodies fall.
The bodies fall down.
The gift of life
Given us all,
Was lost without a sound.

The body count rises,
We're all impressed,
Counting graves in the sky
For warriors long past
Who drew a sword, a knife, a gun
For a field, some freedom,
because they would not run.

The bodies fall.
The bodies fall down.
The gift of life
Given us all,
Was lost without a sound.

Army Days
Cooper

The lie is control,
Of which there is none.
The illusion is powered
By a whisper that runs,
"...Save you from yourself
With taxes and protection."
No one could control you
If you only knew,
No one owns the air you breath.
The tax they levied
Can be no reprieve,
And the bodies will keep falling
Until something is done.

War is not the answer
To any question,
      which can be asked,
But it solves the problem...
No one's left to ask, why?
Only mothers to sit and cry,
And someone took their gun.

The bodies fall.
The bodies fall down.
The gift of life
Given us all,
Was lost without a sound.

Every life matters.
Every single one.
Black or white,
Old and tattered...
You want to defend yourself
But you gave away your gun.

Protection is control.
Defend yourself
Or bear your master's call.

The Complete Second Verse
Dr. Charles Cooper

Paying for the slavery
You're happy to endure,
In a world that hands out life for free
Is the same as forging chains
To bind you and me.

The bodies fall.
The bodies fall down.
The gift of life
Given to us all,
Was surrendered without a sound.

The bodies keep falling,
But you gave your's away.
You made the chains you wear
And you pay and pay and pay.

The bodies fall.
The bodies fall down.
The gift of life
Given to us all,
Was lost without a sound.
Without even a fight.
Who was left to fight?

The bodies fall.
Surrender them to you
To chains and war.
Protection, what for?
What from?
From more,
...Too much surplus?
...Too much joy?
...Too much life?

You gave it away
For war and for strife,
And the bodies fall...
Down.

WATERBOARD

Even silence and ignorance cannot hide
The emptiness people try to disguise.
The lonely know the honest live,
Or try to.
But honestly, I've looked so long
My eyes bleed
There is no breath.
Breathe I tell myself.
I try.
Water is your friend, I tell myself.
But I still have no air.
Hold your breath I tell myself
I disappear into a smile I remember.

Someone is saying something.
I smile at the man with the fist
Against the side of my head.
Who is…
      Mickey Mouse.
How many…
      Rabbits in stew.
What type of…
      Carroll Shelby's 1967 Cobra 427 cu in engine
      567 Horsepower
      First car with more horsepower than cubic inches
      Later that year Corvette…
That fist, shit.
Water, breathe…
Fist, shit.
I want to sing a song,
But I don't remember the name
Something about Maria and dancing and
God I wish I was beautiful.

2, 4, 8, 16, 32, 64, 128, 256, 1024, 2048, 4096,81…
Fist, shit
Water Breathe…

238

The Complete Second Verse
Dr. Charles Cooper

Questions.
I haven't seen light in days
I haven't seen sun in years
I haven't seen a smile in…
Questions
Water
Fist

The robe pulls back,
Her hair is long
Her smile is glory…
Her glory is evident…
I think I can touch her…
I can feel her for…
Fist…
Water…
This particular fantasy being interrupted teaches.
Now, I know what it is to hate
And it sustains me.
I won't break.
Until I do
Because everyone does,
But it won't be for this fist…

"THE BATTLE OF ARLINGTON"

By Becky Kiper

THE BALLAD OF CHUCK OWENS

Dedicated to all the men and women around the world who came home from war.

It has been said,
To survive a war,
You must become war.
To defeat your enemy,
You must understand him completely.
In that moment, you love him.
In the next, you destroy him forever.

Millions upon millions
Have gone to war
Millions have returned.
Each has witnessed death
And been destruction,
Each has seen Angel's avenge,
And been a brother's revenge.

War is a harrowing, hallowed sport for the rich
Played by the poor,
Who are hired, trained, and clothed now,
Treated much nicer than they were before.

It offers a great deal of confidence,
The training. It is carefully designed,
Cloak and dagger and fairy tale;
All blood and medals and glory,
Colors and ribbons, promises of family,
Brothers with Bonds
Which can never be broken,
In this life,
Or the next
High Carbon steel,
Forged in the furnace of combat.

Army Days
Cooper

War is a blood sport
For men and women alike
Where the best and the worst of us go
To fight to the death,
To live and strive and die
And maybe, maybe survive.

The suave, jock,
testosterone-laden bully back on the block
Never saw it coming.
As he walked through the gates of Fort Benning,
Found himself equal
      with all men
          and women in uniform.
Equality is the gift of guns.
Some training and a uniform and an oath
And boys and girls alike find their way
onto planes and trucks and boats.
In a foreign country,
In a tent, behind a hill,
Boots full of sand,
Shirt full of sand,
Pants full of…
It should be said here,
That on every man, or woman's first day in combat,
The sand only sticks to what your pants are full of
Whatever glory there is to be had on that day,
It is overshadowed by the smell.

On a cold morning,
In the desert,
Sand coated the boots
Of a private named Chuck.
He held his rifle at the ready
Like he had been taught
And climbed into his ride.
This was not new to Chuck.
He had eight weeks of basic training

242

The Complete Second Verse
Dr. Charles Cooper

And ten weeks of Advanced training
That was basic.
The Soldiers with him named him Owens
Or private, or maggot, or boot.

Humvees travel light,
      6 guys,
Well, 5 guys and a girl.
They called themselves team
And embarked on a patrol.
It was early morning,
They had their mission:
Scout out a route
That would later be driven
By a General,
A man of command.

For Chuck and his Team,
What matters is:
Generals don't drive themselves
And if they die in war,
They will never live it down.

Drive the course of the general,
If there is an enemy presence,
Kill them all.
Scout for bombs.
Finding bombs,
Set them off.
Finding IEDs
Set them off.
Finding mines,
Set them off.
Last and most certainly least,
Try not to die.

Such are the thoughts of a soldier,
Practical, simple, direct, on point.
In a world filled with minutia,

Army Days
Cooper

Everything is relevant.
There is no person like a soldier.
They can be made.
They can be taught,
And a very few, are born.

No one lives in the moment like a soldier
Even though no Buddhist could survive a uniform.
Oh, some have to be sure,
But not without wanting the next moment
And violating that creed that Buddhists share
"My own happiness above all,
Nothing really matters at all."

Chuck's eyes scanned the side streets.
No one was there.
It was before dawn.
The moment before...
While the enemy sleeps and breaths and dreams
That all is safe and soldiers work
To keep those dreams
From becoming reality.
The sound of gravel
And a Jay-Z song announced to no one
The presence of a merry band of Buddhists,
Living in the moment,
In the prime of their lives,
American men, well, boys and a girl
In uniform,
          in a humvee ,
                    on patrol.

Scan the streets,
          Scan the windows,
                    Scan the alleys.
Was that movement, no.

Scan the streets,
          Scan the windows,

The Complete Second Verse
Dr. Charles Cooper

Scan the alleys.
Was that movement, no.

A new song played.

Scan the streets,
        Scan the windows,
                Scan the alleys.
Was that movement, no.

Repeat until your mind is numb.

Travel at 5 miles per hour
Until your ass is numb.
Seat cushions would be a nice addition
To the next vehicle the Army buys.
Chuck's mind and ass were numb.

Numb or not,
He still thought,
poor red blooded
American male that he was,
But not about the streets,
        the windows,
                or the alleys,
        The mission
or even the enemy.

He thought,
"Oooo, the round, soft ass of my girl,
Back home,
back on the block
With cold beer and hot steer to eat."
Chuck shifted in his seat.
His eyes drifted to the girl driving,
What was her name?
It was....

Shockwave...

Army Days
Cooper

Boom!
Pop, pop...
Pew, Pew...
Boom!
Light, dark, movement, something hot.
The smell of burnt skin and cordite.
Pop, pop...
Pew, pew...
Boom!
Hands worked without thought.
Weapon no longer at the ready,
Found burst mode and found targets
Click, pop pop
Click, pop pop
Click, pop pop
Baird,
        that was her name
Click, pop pop
Wait, words,
Sergeant...
Mouth moving...
Listen.

There's no smell like Cordite
Sulfur, bullets, and burned flesh.
It burns the nose.
It burns into the brain.
It can never be forgotten.
Click, pop pop
Talking.

Hearing,

Aim

"Owens!"

Hey that's me.
Click, pop pop

The Complete Second Verse
Dr. Charles Cooper

Click, pop pop

Amy Olivia Baird, full name.

The last bullet that left my weapon
Sailed through the air,
Controlling the ground
Between the wrecked ball of metal
That used to carry 6 people
On patrol,
And the enemy of all we hold dear,
For the moment,
And embedded itself
In the neck of a man.

The grandeur of the moment
Was sullied by the soiled, white shirt
And the uncoiled Turban,
streaked with the bright red
Of an arterial blood flow.
That particular moment
Seemed no less relevant
At the moment
I pulled the trigger

Click, pop pop
Than did Amy's
Blonde hair,

Click, pop pop
Blue eyes,

Click, pop pop
And bad teeth.

Click, pop pop
Hey, a bullet sailed by my head.
I will not look,
I think to myself

Army Days
Cooper

As my head involuntarily turned toward
A spatter of blood in the air.
Not my blood, I thought.

Click, pop pop
I don't know whose, I thought,
I do not care.
Pow, pow, Boom!
Dust, smoke, clearing,
In memories, I think there should be pain.
Instead, there is a hand on my shoulder.
"Hey!" I shout,
as my face meets the grime of the road,
This ground is hard and dusty.
The dust that gets everywhere.
Sand in my mouth.

Holy!

A rocket flew over my head
The flame was a brilliant, white light,
The kind that burns your retina,
If you stare too long.
It's amazing the things you remember,
At the wrong time.
When moments seem to linger on and on,

For a rocket, it was so slow.
How did it not fall right out of the sky?
Sergeant White,
Who knocked me down,
Lay beside me on the ground,
As the rocket flew right through
The space I was in
a second before.
That was a while ago now.
One second,
Sergeant White was muttering
        into a hand held radio,

The Complete Second Verse
Dr. Charles Cooper

The next his face was gone.
A single eye stared back,
     blank at me,
         mockingly.
If he had a face,
     surprise would have been evident,
       I think.

What were they aiming at?
The wall of the house just to the rear
Of the wreckage of our humvee.
They would hit it too, I thought.
It was too big to miss.

Hand on shoulder, "What!?"
Hand on face,

SLAP

"Owens!"

Sergeants are assholes.

An E5, Sergeant Stow,
Thrust something in my hands?
What is this?
My rifle, yes.
Something I was supposed to...
Click, pop pop.
Click, pop pop.
Click, empty.
Change Magazine.
Drop, Load, chamber a round...

A roar overhead,
low flying A-10,

Close ground support,
     very close,

Army Days
Cooper

                too close,
if you know what I mean.

Both sides of the street disappear into
Ashes,
and smoke,
and dust.
Whatever had been there before
Became a victim of weapons of war.

Ruble left in the wake of depleted uranium rounds.
There was a final pop on my right,
A Haj-dressed mannequin was collapsing before me.
The rifle in his outstretched arm
Gave a puff of thunder
And a short,
          sharp,
                bright,
                      white flame.

From the muzzle,
which was aimed
directly at my head.
As the body,
The mannequin,
was torn in half,
The rifle shifted ever so slightly
and I watched the bullet

sail,

lazily

past my head,

Close enough to feel the air
And heat coming off of it in waves.

All soldiers live in the moment.

The Complete Second Verse
Dr. Charles Cooper

Some die there.
Some moments just go on
One life shy of their quota.

My eyes followed,
As far as they could.
Until my head followed,
And the bullet,
The one that said "Owens,"
or "private,"
or "boot"
In neat Cyrillic letters
Embedded itself in a wall.

Beside the same wall,
I saw Amy Baird dead.
Her perfect, blonde hair
Was tinged a faint red.
She was thin,
physically perfect.
She had not aged yet.
Nor would she in my memory.
She was from somewhere in Maryland,
Maybe the eastern shore.
I thought to mourn when I looked in her eyes.

Those eyes,
open wide,
were a scaled,
pasty gray.

They used to be blue, I thought,
But the life had been removed.

There are days that never seem to end.
Some days during war,
Some days during deployments,
Some days during enlistments.
Everything that begins, ends.

Army Days
Cooper

So days are marked on calendars,
And talked about by men.

Statues are built,
fences erected to guard the ground
Where so many men lay down.
Other men will study and explain,
Academics and the like,
Who never wore the gear for war,
Never gave themselves to a Uniform,
Never placed their life in the hands of another,
And trusted in a friend as much as a brother.
When enough time has passed,
The academics and bureaucrats
Will do everything they can to make it disappear.
They don't like what they can't understand.
What they don't understand, they fear.

There are days that all those things end,
They always seem a day away
To the man who waits and cannot forget.
As the sun rises and falls,
And God is occasionally good,
And soldiers occasionally blessed,
And if they live in the moment,
Long enough without fear,
The day comes that they can go home.

That day came for Sergeant First Class, Chuck Owens.
One war, five police actions,
Seven countries and three enlistments
Under his belt;
Countless brothers and ten years, 3,652 days;
To mark the end.

Chuck held a ticket home,
It was not like the one
That took him to basic.
This one he had to buy,

The Complete Second Verse
Dr. Charles Cooper

When the Army was done with you,

It was done.

He got home all the same.

There are two ways to survive a war.
They vary in value, to be certain,
In the eyes of men.

The choice all must make
From their first day in combat to the last
Is to survive,
by running,
     By hiding,
          by becoming nothing.

Unworthy of bullet,
     or effort,
          or time

In the eyes of the enemy,
In the eyes of your friends,
In the eyes of your country.
They are all worth something
But none of them can give you back your life,
Which no man values a like,
So each man measures and decides.

What is glory or honor
     on a hill with no name
In the shifting sands of terror
In a land with no buildings but rocks and caves
In a jungle with no prairie,
But rivers a plenty and the stench of rot everywhere.

In Boston, the beantown brethren are strong
Ranger training makes them stronger,
Sands shifting under foot,

Army Days
Cooper

The boom - pop, pop of the enemy,
There is an unforgiving moment
Between the first glance or sound
And the reaction built by repetition,
Lights and darks shift
Colors can be ignored,
The move from shock to awareness
Cannot.

Orders are made and obeyed,
And people die.
It is a world of black and white,
Surviving and dying,

It sometimes occurs,
As it did to Chuck Owens
And 22 of his Veteran brothers
That the thought to run never occurred
To them or him.
There is bravery, courage, honor
Even glory to be had
In the presence of such men.
Even more, if you were to become one.
Such men encounter the second choice of combat
Because the first never entered their mind.
In the unforgiving moment all men,
Muslims, Jews, Gentiles, Christians, and Atheists alike
Pray.

"Dear God, whatever form you take.
Let me become war,
Let me know no fear,
Let me be all the Army has made me
And a little more, because today, I need it.
Finally, let me kill
If it be your will.
If not, let me maim sufficiently
To permanently render my foes
A resident of a tent

The Complete Second Verse
Dr. Charles Cooper

By a lake, with three wives
And six goats
And a fancy toupee
Under the sheet wrapped around his head.
Last but not least,
Dear Lord,
let me not end up dead."

The second way,
to walk away from war
Is to kill everyone.
A simple Click pop pop
Repeated until the enemy
Is gone.
That's what it means
To be War.
This second way is perilous in deed,
Adventurous in part,
And there are steps to follow
That, though left out of the training
In words, are heavily implied throughout.

The first step denies everything man is,
There is nothing to fear,
Even if you don't survive...
You were dead when you put on the uniform.
Your sole purpose is to destroy...
It is the creator who dies...
You become death itself,
Like the General,
You are a refined instrument of the enemies' end.
The end of everything you learned as a kid
When they said Thou shalt not...

The next step is easier,
Thank God for this day,
And the gift that he gave,
When the moment arose,
For you to be,

Army Days
Cooper

What was needed:
An army of one;
A brother to any
Who find their way into the uniform…

You are…
A catastrophe
To those who oppose
The gang of green
In the desert
Yellows and dull dingy grays.

The uniform, more than clothes,
Transform the man into
The weapon of war,
You follow in the footsteps
Of those who came before.

Remember who you are,
What you are,
And where you come from.
Live in the moment,
Without fear.
Remember your training,
And you will survive.

These steps must be executed precisely
And in order, without doubt, fear, or delay.
To be sure,
Be wary in War.
What doesn't kill you the first time,
Will the second.
Fortune favors the bold,
But God pities the fool.

Weapons are everywhere in war
Some are machines, some chemicals,
And some wear a uniform
Not quite like yours.

The Complete Second Verse
Dr. Charles Cooper

Not all survive.
That is to say,
walk away.

No one ever survives war unchanged.

The day will come, like most days do,
Where the sun rises
      and falls
           and sets,
It'll be marked like the others,
with reverie and taps.
The Army flanked the sun with music,
To mock the dark
      and the enemy,
           and the Soldier,
With inspiration and regret,
As a reminder that all things die.

But while your eyes shine,
With the tears you have not cried,
As a Beantown brother, an Army Ranger…
A hard-assed weapon of war,
Leader of men and women.
The day finally comes
That your service is done.

Away you walk,
To a bus or a plane
To make a trip home
To parents or friends,
To a house you don't know,
On a street you remember,
in the faintest of ways;
To an empty bed,
where some lover used to lay
To a job and bills
and rent you have to pay.
You wake early in the morning,

Army Days
Cooper

Just to run through the haze.
Where the roads were,
there are streets now,
But little else has changed,
When seen through the eyes,
Of a Beantown brother,
Who has changed in every way.

Back on the block
As the Army would say.
Thirty minutes into his morning run,
Chuck picked up the pace.
He broke into a cadence,
Singing clear,
nothing shaded,

"Your buddy's in a foxhole,
A bullet in his head,
The medic says he's wounded,
But you know that he's dead."

Around the next corner,
Chuck Owens,
         Beantown brother,
                  Army Ranger,
                           Master of Chaos
                  Angel of Death,
         Weapon of war,
Fell to his knees
And saw it all again.
His entire body shook with grief.
His eyes shut tight.
Down his face, tears streaked.
He did not breath.

There on the corner,
of the street where he grew up,
Chuck Owens clenched his knees to his chest.
He held on tight,

The Complete Second Verse
Dr. Charles Cooper

like everything this side of forever
Would crumble to dust if he let go,
And he rocked until he lay there still.

O-dark-thirty became quarter-to-six.
A post man saw Chuck lying there.
This post man happened to be a retired Vet
Who had seen his share of combat.
He knew Chuck as if they'd met.
He reached down and took his arm.
Called him son, bade him rise.
He put his mail bag in his truck,
And he slid the door shut.
Not wind or rain, not snow, not hail
But some things come before delivering the mail.

"What's your name son?"
Chuck knew that voice.
Every Sergeant's Sergeant Major,
Command, experience and years,
The wisdom of a survivor
Who survived to walk away.

Chuck let out a gasp
And tried to right himself.
"My name is Owens Sir," he said
To the NCO he saw
The postman was gone.
The NCO said,
"You can call me Malachi.
You better come with me."

At 837 Summer Street in Boston Mass
Is an Irish Pub called Flannigan's Last Blast.
By two every morning they announce last call
And don't open their doors again until
Mackey
Or Ricky
hit the floor.

Army Days
Cooper

Maybe three or four
the next afternoon,

Their dad

Mackey Senior

does day duty…

While the boys sleep it off.

He does inventory
      orders booze
           and shoos off
The homeless
and the hooligans
and the bums and drunks
from the night before…
Tapes furniture together,
has a few drinks
And picks at his guitar.

It was to the tune of Flannigan's ball
That a rap on the door broke through the morning.
Mackey was pissed at the interruption and rose with a start
To give that jerk a piece of his mind.
He was just about to when…

Nearly 30 years ago,
Two black haired boys,
one a good Irishman,
The other pure Jew,
Stepped off the bus at Fort Benning, Georgia.
They were almost exactly
one world away
from Boston
And a lifetime away
from the day before.

The Complete Second Verse
Dr. Charles Cooper

It was hot and it was wet,
The first thing they heard was,
"Welcome to the home of the Infantry."
Eight long weeks passed, two men, brothers
boarded a bus for Fort Bragg
Fourteen weeks later,
They boarded a plane for Vietnam.

Lucky as they were,
As Beantown brothers are,
Mackey came home to run the family pub.
Malachi came home to a post office job.
They occasionally saw each other,
Over the years.
Sought each other out,
Shared some laughs,
Shed some tears.

Mackey lost his wife
And stopped dropping by,
Malachi stopped drinking
And found nothing to say.
He didn't stop by the bar
Cause nothing took him that way.

…On this cold morning,
sometime around nine,
Mackey opened the door,
To see his old friend
With Chuck Owens close behind
With the briefest of nods,
and look at the eyes,
Mackey held open the door.
held out his hand
And Chuck Owens
felt the support
of both men.

"Alright" said Mackey.

Army Days
Cooper

"Alright" said Malachi.
Owens stood a little taller,
Wiping tears from his eyes.
The pictures on the wall,
Black and white stills,
Of the jungle in the fall.

In a world far away,
Two Beantown bothers stood
With nothing to say.
Their conversation was written
Decades before,
In actions and blood,
In some other man's war.
So, nothing was said,
Until the drinks started to pour.
The scotch went down sharp,
It burned and relieved
A moment that had been building.
Finally, Malachi spoke,
"Nice ink", he said.
The Ranger badge on Owen's shoulder
Burned of life,
A stroke of ink
To mark everything he had done
For that tab,
The price a man pays
        to never hesitate
During the unforgiving moment,
The purchase price of leadership.

Owens looked down
And when he looked up,
Both men's arms were bared
For what seemed the same ink.
For the first time in all the days,
Since he took off his uniform,
He felt like he could breath.

The Complete Second Verse
Dr. Charles Cooper

"75th?" asked Mackey.
"82nd" said Chuck,
"73rd Parachute infantry," he explained
"6 Airports in 10 years."
"Iraq, Haiti, Kosovo, Bosnia,
Rwanda, Iraq and Afghanistan."
They both nodded.
"Vietnam" they said.

The men talked most of the day,
The time came that the regulars started to trickle in.
Mackey's boys were there to greet them
Respecting the privacy of the three men.

It was late when Chuck finally rose.
He walked home from the bar,
Remembering what it was to have brothers,
What it meant to wear the uniform.
He knew what he needed,
Or so it seemed.

That evening, he applied to visit the VA.
The application went in.
Chuck sighed and began his wait.

Sergeant First Class Owens
            knew what it was to wait
Time passes slowly
            at the bridge
                        between the military
                                    And the civilian
and the Veteran's Administration facilities
That are old, underfunded, understaffed
And less ready for another war
Than the man and women they serve.

As the days grew long,
Chuck stopped going outside.
He slept late every day.

Army Days
Cooper

His muscles lost definition
But his thumbs were strong
He played "Call of Duty"
All night long.

Apart from the uniform,
The only relic of the service Chuck kept,
Was an Officer's .45 next to his bed, on the desk.

He felt luckier than not.
Every day when he woke,
At least he was not some poor sod,
Doing KP or PT,
or in the front leaning rest
six feet under.

His mom kept the fridge stocked,
With Boston Ale and sliced ham.
It looked like the ham in the MRE.
But it was not the same.
It had taste.

It was the taste that made Chuck nauseous.
It was the nausea that became the excuse:
For not getting a job,
For not hanging out with friends,
For not going to church,
For not looking up his old girlfriend,
For not...

The VA responded by email to Chuck Owen's claim.
It set up an appointment for him...
"two weeks from today..."
For a physical and mental health screening,
When Chuck Owens did not show up for his appointment
The VA sent a letter
proclaiming the importance of appointments.

The Complete Second Verse
Dr. Charles Cooper

"An appointment that you waste could have gone to another
veteran."

Resources are sorely limited,
Stretched to capacity.

Chuck Owens had been buried,
  in full dress uniform,
    with military honors,
      A month prior to receiving
       The letter.

His mother claimed she knew nothing,
And that she hadn't heard a sound.
The Policeman mumbled something,
Under his breath,
About fire and forget.
You see, bullets once fired,
Can slip through space and time,
On battlefields.
They travel years to find their marks.

The .45 still smelled of gun powder,
    and oil,
       and regret,
    When the old postman,
Shaking his head,
    slipped it in the coffin,
       At SFC Owen's wake.
    It was a closed casket funeral.
One of 22 held that day.

At the hospital they got bonuses.
An active duty Major met his daughter,
On a field filled with flags,
at an NFL game.
He got the game ball.
The flag flew high.

Army Days
Cooper

They held a parade for 70 guys,
From Chuck's home town.
Chuck didn't mind.
He wasn't around.

BOOK 5: INTELLIGENCE HAZE

"MY BEST BOND"

ART BY BECKY KIPER

PUZZLE PALACE

A. This page left unintentionally Blank.

2S2. Don't Ask, don't tell.

L. Oh Hell

1V2. Oh *Well*

YU. There are things you don't want to know.

3EX. Someone, somewhere knows them.

TT. There are books you wish you never read, written by men you wish you'd never met, in microscopic painted dots on paintings of immeasurable value that *No One* WILL EVER see.

ST. The same NO ONE you blamed for everything, you did, as a kid, at home.

X. Knowledge is strength they say. Some knowledge kills. Some language skills.

12. Oh Well.

2. Don't ask…

2x. Please don't tell.

L. Oh Hell

Q: Not again.

PS: This means something.

The Complete Second Verse
Dr. Charles Cooper

SPACE AND TIME

I don't mind the time it takes
If I can love you.
I don't mind the distance
Between here and there
If every day is closer
To a place that we can share.

What is space and time
If you could be mine.
What are blood and sweat
If it staves off regret.
If it takes a revolution
Why hasn't it happened yet?

I don't mind the pain
If we can share it.
I started this road
Based on a dream:
You and me, simplicity
That's the thing I fight for.
Every single day.
Whispered wind
Fluttering through the trees
Whispered Wind, Simplicity.
Every day, the dream,
you and me
Finding our hope in simplicity.

What is space and time
If you could be mine.
What are blood and sweat
If it staves off regret.
If it takes a revolution
Why hasn't it happened yet?

I don't mind the pain
If we can share it.

Intelligence Haze
Prophet

I don't mind the sweat, I can bear it.
You and me, simplicity.

What is time and space
When I see your eyes?
Everything just disappears.

What are whips and wounds?
What is one more move?
If it takes a revolution
Baby, that's what I do.
It's a revolution baby.
And baby, that's what I do.

The Complete Second Verse
Dr. Charles Cooper

LANGLEY FALLS

Jane was assigned a cubical
In the sixth row
On the third basement level
Of Building 3.

She entered through gate 2.
After meeting the most serious gate guards in the world
Jane moved through a parking lot
Drab lights painted the early air
With an incandescent glow.

Jane didn't know
What she didn't know,
And the powers that be
Liked it that way.

Some of the houses
in the Falls
are owned
By the stable long-term cabal of State.
Other houses are assigned
As they come available.
Jane's house was given her
After sitting empty for almost six months.
A red star home times three...
Jane didn't know,
She didn't ask.
The powers that be
Liked it that way.

It was never home,
Not in the way the city was.
DC consumes people,
Just when you think you've made it,
It spits you out.
Too bad, so sad.

Intelligence Haze
Prophet

Elections have consequences.
Not inside the walls of Langley itself,
But inside the gates of Langley Falls
The moral compass can spin 180 degrees
On election night.

On the grounds of the Falls,
You're a few steps
From the Castle,
And a four hour lie detector test away
From knowing something
no one should know...
From doing something
no one should be allowed to...
From being someone
who should have known better...

Jane was born that way.
Welcome to the family Jane.

The Complete Second Verse
Dr. Charles Cooper

KEEPING SECRETS

There is a code in everything,
from the words
first etched on paper
to the ink blot dot
crafted by Jewish-German Jewelers
 in the margin of a last letter to family.

The Julies know the code –
even if they don't know,
what they don't know.
Elizabeth holds the code
deep inside herself...
Inside a sacred chamber
from which there is no letting go.
It stretches from Langley to Poor Farm Park...
It feels,
then it moves...
to become a part of you.

This code is the key to my heart...
the theme of my journey home.
Release me from my bonds.
Draw near the chariot of fire,
as I bathe in blind desire...
waking to find myself
locked in chains one more time.
The thick, black hair of my youth
scattered about my feet.
I've grown old, tired, and weak.
I need to pray for strength I know,
But I don't have or know the code.

This code is a secret
With a key which can't be found
In my hair,
Or in your chains,
Or in a box, under the ground.

To find it, the depths of a man
Must unfold releasing untold value
A value only the creator can know.

Readers will fail and fall,
a filter on all who pass through
These gates,
The cream rises.
Once true,
it is forever.
Once seen,
it cannot be unseen
As the world around us each changes,
I beg you set me free.

Life is a prison when I have to keep secrets.

"SECRETS"

ART BY BECKY KIPER

The Complete Second Verse
Dr. Charles Cooper

THE KEYMASTER

What is red and pounding
A cradle of blood pushing muscle,
The strength of men and women alike.
Like so many traits shared,
The fibers of ourselves
Flex and grip
Tighten and release
And in that release
The Earth beholds her maker.
And I feel everything
And it was GOOD.

In Richmond, there is a hospital
At the back of a circle
Inside which, spiraling upward,
A statue of a lord of death
Rises
And falls.
Irony not lost
On those of us who understand such things,
Not pop singers or Mousketeers
But men and women who don't pretend
To live.

Where this lord rode and killed
At will, newspapers followed and it
Was this quest for vanity
Which brought down
A glorious but meager lost cause.

The last vestiges of Freedom for some
Died this day
At a courthouse.
The sun at 57 degrees
In that location
Reveals the moon

Intelligence Haze
Prophet

Which offers light
To the heart of a weary traveler.

The muscle that pushes blood
Never relents.
The bell that announced the split
Will ring again,
But not likely here
Or where it sits today.
It wasn't made that way
Or that well
Anyway.
This one's a fake.

Never fear, there is another.
Muscles pushing blood,
Blessed, though weary
Sees though a blurry eyed
Referendum on our love.
Democracy is the hallmark of failed relationships.
It's all or nothing
Never bought any soul redemption
Or perfection.
Perfect squares
Have so many stories to tell.

Marks are everywhere,
In writing. Symbols are
Everything in stories.
Reverence for everyone
Is a lie, often told by politicians
In my city.

Oyster for sale.
Crabs for rent.
Lazy scavengers
Browse antique shops.
Worthy opponents
Throw worthy fits,

The Complete Second Verse
Dr. Charles Cooper

And banjo playing fools
Decorate tents in ways no one intended.

Ponies and mosquitos,
This is a national park?
I thought we could do better,
But we didn't.

Some women wear tents
Hiding curves and passion
Reveling in yearbooks and
Past lives. When I was young,
I was the sun, brighter still
That he has gone,
And I can shine
For someone
Who has not burned
His retinas out
Comprehending,
How such a lovely yellow star
becomes a red giant.

Children matter.
Little men,
And a baker's dozen
Jack Russell Terriers
Read Revelations
And laugh
Decisively at Laodicea.

Larger men,
And Bassett Hounds
Read Conan Doyle
And laugh at
The game,
Which was never afoot,
Until…

On Yoga Pants day

Intelligence Haze
Prophet

In the King's Dominion,
Spandex finally gave way
To the ravages of a peer pressure limit
Video to watch
During Vacation Bible School....

And that is the Key to the entire thing.

The Complete Second Verse
Dr. Charles Cooper

POWER

Langley is a fallen place.
Power is forbidden fruit.
Rules are for lesser men.
Human beings a fallen race.
We could be more,
Is a motto
Of the best of souls,
Which gives rise to action,
Which usually leads to disgrace.
Langley is the symbol of elite control
A bastion of Ivy League entitlement.
A home for those nobles
Who were and are sure
They know better
And would never trade
A single day of knowing
For the freedom of Eden.

Welcome to your home in Langley Falls,
Home of the fallen who sometimes fall,
Home of the brave who sometimes falter,
Home of the amoral who almost always believe,
In making a world of idealistic slaves.

Creators all;

God gave man a single rule,
Man gave God the CIA
Who removed the Tree
Of knowledge of Good and Evil
From the garden
And planted it where?

JANE'S FIRST TIME

Jane was born with a gift,
A British accent
And long flaxen hair
As lovely as she was, she couldn't make herself care.

Jane only wanted one thing,
Everything that could not be had.
She had her nails done,
And her toes,
And her eyebrows.
A tool in one hand
Her focused fingers danced.
Jane was always one step ahead,
Of the boys and their gambles,
She had a plan,
And a target,
And three more rounds of 7.62 mm
Than she needed.

Her shoulder bore the master stroke
Somewhere between breaths
she pulled
And through the scope,
She watched a head explode.
Her eyes closed, and she took a deep breath.
No tear ever slid down her face,
Not this time or any other.
Remembering when she had felt fear.
Jane could remember the date and the year
Of her first time.
It was a cheap thrill to remember like that.
She closed the portfolio and watched it burn.
Another life gone.
The world still turned.
Think of all the misspent time,

The Complete Second Verse
Dr. Charles Cooper

The thought ran through her mind,
As she racked another bullet into the rifle.

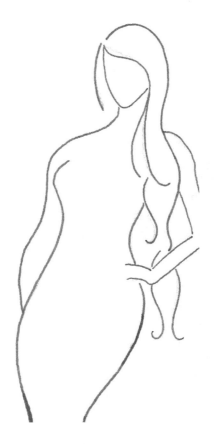

"ELEGANT JANE"

ART BY BECKY KIPER

JANE'S MEN

No likeness of being
At midnight is as dark
As the road curving
And the wheels sliding just a bit,
Until they grab,
As tight as they can
For these conditions...

Young Jane found that her heart
Could pump a little faster
In a curve,
If she kept the accelerator
Pushed a little too far,
And gave the wheel,
A tiny pull toward the curb.
Mountain roads are the best for this.
On one side a wall,
On the other,
A cliff and the air.
At night, the darkness goes down forever.
You can imagine the fall
Without trying.
Jane's heart was pounding.

She tucked her hair over her ear,
And smiled.
It was not a seat warmer she felt
As her eyes batted and she blushed.
Blue eyes flashing,
The rush...
They darted over the man,
She had,
sitting in the car next to her.

He was sheet white,
Holding his seat belt tight
To his chest,

282

The Complete Second Verse
Dr. Charles Cooper

Teeth clinched.
He had not exhaled yet.
Jane sighed.
Drove directly to his house
And let him out.
"Don't call," she said.
And drove back the way she came
A little faster than before.
This gent became,
One
More
Footnote
Documenting,
Jane is insane.

Her racing heartbeat
Is slower
Than the thrusting pistons
She surrounds herself with.
Call it insanity if you will.
But it is exquisite.
It is beauty
Of a kind one cannot make by themselves.
It takes a creator, a craftsman of unrivaled skill
To make and remake a mind like Jane, night after bloody night.

"Another night of my life gone,"
she thought to herself,
Embracing the loneliness
One more time…
"What a waste."

"JANE'S DATE"

ART BY BECKY KIPER

283

WHEN JANE MADE POETRY

Poetry is…
The deliberate use of words.
Bullets are poetry in motion.
Words can do more harm than a bullet.
Jane was good at Harm.
Death is easier than living
With regret,
with yourself
or surrender…

Jane never understood surrender
Until she did it.
After you give away
That first little piece of yourself,
Surrender becomes easier than not.
The blithe moments of bygone days
That never went away,
Memories of when you
Never knew surrender
The lovely thing about Jane
Is that she does not remember
Those days.
She was too young,
And the price of memory is too high.

What she gave away in those days
Was as much or more
Than any hard fought last stand
Which costs just as much
As leaving the last man
Who was willing to give
Credit where credit is due.

It all costs more than
The big things she did to win
The little things she wore to bed
The pretty shoes

The Complete Second Verse
Dr. Charles Cooper

And pasty coat of too much rouge,
The lies the men would tell,
The listening look, the smile, the sale,
The vicious comments undercutting
Any woman who rose
From or by the women
Who chose not to play
That game at that level.

Days and days
A day away
From forever
Is too far away
To continue to pay
For the past.
Jane knows because she learned
The hard way,
How to walk away.

There's a story there,
More interesting than not.
Another story
For another time...

Sometimes,
Surviving is the best you can hope for...

Sometimes,
Days pile upon days
Before the rising sun is seen...
Sometimes,
Years of failure and malaise intertwine
Before an ounce of compassion and rain
Can wash away the stain.

Sometimes life is not sublime,
Which is the thing that makes tomorrow
The most beautiful day Jane ever saw.

DC DINNER PARTY

There is no more dangerous game
Between dusk and dawn
Under layers and layers of grey,
Than a Washington D.C. dinner party.
The knives are always out.
The young always hungry.
The aged and experienced,
Behind the armor of time
And knowledge
Are more deadly than any trigger.

Words mean so much.
Trust is a currency not discussed,
But always in play.
You earn it. You can live off it.
If you threaten it,
or you fail it,
You die.

"JANE CAN DANCE"

ART BY BECKY KIPER

DC SUNSET

As the sun set, Jane and I
Dawned fantasy masks.
Her long, slick, silk dress
Clung tight to her skin.
Excusing my own tux and bow tie.
The masks were not optional
At this evening's soiree'.
If the truth were known,
None of us ever left our masks at home.
The only thing that was real
In this capital town,
Was single life,
And red meat on the table
at every meal.

One congressman was a butcher
Before he rose up and gathered the consent
Of a few thousand souls
To collect their money,'
And bring some of it home.
The story of this night goes back many moons
To the woman he replaced,
And a storied relationship
Between a reporter
And the Gentlewoman from Arkansas.
As per usual,
Everything was off the record.
Dangerous liaisons
Are reality for the desperate DC immigrants.
Bright lights, Big city,
All the power
In the world
Concentrated
In a single place.
The seduction is inevitable.
No one can hold out long.

"JANE IN DC"

ART BY BECKY KIPER

287

Intelligence Haze
Prophet

"Power is the ultimate aphrodisiac."
In such a very lonely place.
At the end of the day,
It is the singular you
Who must decide
For so many...
At tonight's dinner party,
We decide for one.
He should have never run.
He should have never won.
The chosen cling to power
even when it's gone
And their hands are long.

The appendages,
Jane and I both are,
Can be found anywhere
At any time.
There's little rhyme or reason to it
But a DC Dinner Party
Is never short of one or two
Hands or fingers that correct mistakes
The people make
On election night.

Jane is a compassionate woman,
I've seen it in the mirror,
In her eyes.
She can put anything she wants there.
She can make the truth lie.
I admire the slick silk fashion choice for the night.
Our friend the congressman is well known
For putting hands where they don't belong,
And Jane, sweet Jane, has tucked a needle,
Just beneath the silk where we estimate...

Height times Weight
Length of Arm
Distance to touch,

The Complete Second Verse
Dr. Charles Cooper

Angles and calculations
Perfect placement.

She smiles as he walks by.
I give him an icy stare
To which he winks,
Smiles,
Reaches and gropes
My Jane.

His hand pulls back abrupt.
He gives his finger a kiss
Just a tiny drop of blood.

Two days later,
The congressman is rushed to the hospital
Bethesda, Walter Reed, who really knows.
It doesn't matter,
No living doctor has ever seen
Something as swift and deadly
As what killed the Congressman
In four short hours.
I saw Jane the day after.
She smiled and swayed
And showed me a new dress
White and sheer, red lace,
Strategically placed.
I'd love to touch the cloth,
Feel its texture beneath my fingers,
But I've known Jane for years,
So I recline in my chair
Turn to the screen in front of me
And open another email.

It's an invitation to a charity Gala...
Prime minister such and such
Is the guest of honor.
So many charities to attend to.
It seems to never end.

JANE WALKS ON WATER

In some ascended state,
Halo bobbling on her neck,
Jane walks on water.
I explore the shore
Where waves are slight.
The tide slides in
Announcing night.

I would swear Jane had wings
And a pronounced glow.
Drops slip from her hair to her toes
Like tears leaving sadness behind.
The ocean absorbs the past with grace.
The water is still as if untouched.
Poor Jane is chaste asking for trust.
But it is ever in short supply
For a man my age.
Experience and lies,
Make it so hard to trust my eyes.

Jane walks on water.
I've seen it for myself.
I was amazed the first time.

I numbered the days
Until I found out
The waves and water
Were empty projections
of my own mind.
The saddest thing is
Jane is not who conjured the lie.

There was never a day Jane didn't like
Never met a day she wouldn't live twice.
Sometimes she likes to wallow,
Just take a breath and swallow.
Celebrates the days

The Complete Second Verse
Dr. Charles Cooper

In her memories,
Before responsibility blurred her vision
She lives to relive the moments,
Sees her prom, sees the boys who fawn
Over her eyes and hair.
She smiles at thoughts of a man long gone.

There are too many things she can't forget,
When memories end in pain…
The time she said no.
The time she said nothing
Her silence bought her nothing.
Nothing left to gain
But memories.
She arrived at yes in due course
But it was too late
To make a happy memory.

JANE VS. THE WORLD

The hairline fine line,
Cast between success and failure,
Which Jane drew on her life,
Would have been a challenge for anyone,
But she couldn't make herself care enough
To spend the hours on anything
After she had mastered it in her mind.

The hours that people play, and drill, and study
To be more than they are capable of,
Were not for Jane,
Jane didn't know how to play.
She knew how to do.
Life is ever what you make it.
Jane was no fiction girl
I've never met anyone so capable,
Or deadly,
Or empty.
Chemical sadness
At life,
at work,
at family.

Somewhere between breaths
In the moment,
Empty moments.
There, she found peace,
And made reality.
Crafted a world to her liking.
Where most people dream,
Jane does.
It isn't living; it isn't life;
Confusing the act of life and title, LIFE
Jane would retreat.
Creating in her world the happy memories
Which balance the breaths and the moments
And the bricks she uses

The Complete Second Verse
Dr. Charles Cooper

To craft the world.
The place, the world Jane made
Will never come again.
The twenty years I have lived since Jane
Came to my door
Have been so much more
Than I can imagine.

One day she won't come again,
She will decide to stay
In between the inhale
And the exhale.
The brute crescendo of life
That Jane makes.
It isn't far to fall.
It isn't living. It isn't life.
This place where Jane has made her home
Exists, in my mind, alone.

EVERYONE HAS THEIR JANE

Everyone has their day.
Everyone has their Jane.
Not everyone says goodbye,
But they leave all the same.

If I am honest with myself,
I love Jane.
If I am more honest with myself,
I am Jane...
In the corner of the heart
Where we look,
To see what we are capable of
And find we took the long way
To find happiness,
Again.
Avoiding nothing,
Flint rocks and ambivalence
Are a path all their own
For the people that can't go home.

Blended chemicals and circumstance
To make holy writ and righteousness,
To see the inner self...
With love.

What should I tell myself,
Heart pounding loud.
Nothing quite captures
The flickering light
The blowing wind
That cuts through the feeling
Sharp, hard, cold.

In the silence,
There is breath,
And there is recompense.

The Complete Second Verse
Dr. Charles Cooper

If you've done it once,
What will another time mean.
I take a scary, heart shaped locket,
And I bury it six feet from the base of the house
Where I grew up.
Jane is no excuse
For the waste
Strewn in the wake
Of the long way home.
The Elizabeth River,
The mighty James
The obsession with water,
That never changed
To wine.
Not this time.
You walk and walk and sink
Because nothing is the same.

I lay cold on the gravel that coats the beach
Left by erosion that could not reach,
My heart to draw me in, again.
I sit up.

"If I am honest with myself?"
I think and nearly laugh.
It's funny right?
It's makes me think of alcohol
And parties and strangers and panties,
And something much, much stronger
Than I will ever be.
I need to numb my desire.
Numb is where I need to be.

In a snide sarcastic tone,
Under my breath,
I mumble, "Admitting you have a problem…"
Deep sigh, believe the lie, continue…
"is the first step."
Well!

Intelligence Haze
Prophet

My problem is, I'm not numb.
There is too much beauty in the world.
Even laid waste, the life of Jane,
Pulls me closer to me.
The words I write,
More real than not
Frighten me
Because I have to ask myself twice
"Was that real, Did I do that?"

If I can't see the world through those eyes,
Where I live and strive and try…
To make something real…
Something that lasts…

The next lie is where I say,
"this is all about you."
"You have a Jane too,"
For when you need to be more.
Design specifications
Are a thing with God.
He made you this good.
But you,
You had to be more.
Jane is the tool
Which makes a distant me
possible…
This is what Jane is for.

ASSET

Intelligence is hard work...
And lonely.
The price of freedom is...
Isolation.

It is a choice
And a high price to pay.
Why would anyone play this game
Of sacrifice, redaction, and contraction,
Steely-eyed, testosterone-laced, promises
From some guy that never paid
Half of what you're worth...

Or is even capable of understanding the value?

Idealistic fool that I am,
Even I know better than that.

MR. FIX IT

I solve problems,
It's what I do.
Who knew
At an early age
That fixing the broken
Would be a career.

Little did I know
As I waged war,
It's enough to be calm,
Assess, plan, execute,
Analyze and analyze some more…
And execute, execute, and execute some more…
It's enough.

What's more,
Everything that can be achieved,
Can be done that way,
A little at a time

The Complete Second Verse
Dr. Charles Cooper

BOOK 3: BLOOD AND TRAFFIC ON I-95

SOME DAYS

A lot of life is just momentum.
We rise because we can.
It's habit.

We work because we can,
Slow, repeated actions
The same as yesterday.
We do what we must
Because we must
And because we can.

But some days,
Rare days,
We do more.
On those days,
We are Gods.

Blood and Traffic
Chuck Cooper

NEVER TOO LATE

It is amazing that people can live through a lifetime and not realize that it isn't the perfect face and hair and body that make someone beautiful, but the scars and the life that shines through them, the vision that perspective brings, the smile that comes from having walked through the hard things and seeing them from the other side.

Real beauty is something no one is born with.
It must be earned.
Real beauty is so powerful that no shell can contain it.
Life is a series of turning points.
Decisions that shape our journey.
Choosing to live is the first and best step toward beauty,
There is no other way.
It's never too late to start.

I-95

38° 31' 22.5228'' N 77° 17' 24.2772'' W

From Maine to Miami it runs,
Paved in holes, big and small
The plows make,
As they push the snow
Because no one could wait,
For the Sun,
To melt the ice,
That God made.

For more than a year now,
I've run that road,
In search of something better,
In search of meaning that's clearer.
For me, time passes in heartbeats and thought
Books and music and poetry,
Someone reads to me
As I wait to complete
My journey home.
My children and my past at one end
My duty, country, and life at the other.
One hundred fourteen miles from point to point.
A year behind,
Too many to go.

I am behind a long line of cars
Three lanes of slow traffic,
Slowing,
Until we stop.
Somewhere between
And Garrisonville, Quantico
In the shadow of the Marine Corp Museum,
I see, flashing lights in the rear view,
Lights that tell a tale of someone ahead
Whose journey home
Is at an end

Blood and Traffic
Chuck Cooper

Too soon.

I pull out my notebook to write,
This is going to take a while...
I have a very short period
In which to be,
A hands-on father,
A ghost of the happy, family man
Who never was,
But wanted to be.

As the time passes sitting in this line of cars,
I see that chance slipping away.
I've written a few lines,
But not enough,
When the cars start to creep forward,
Again.

Almost as one, we move inches in hours,
Slow, like a parade of floats,
Where the egos of men, too big
For their offices,
craft those giant balloons
On Macy's Day
In Manhattan.

These are the men who gather,
To travel the road
To where I do not know,
But in my mind,
I like to think,
They are on their way home:
To see their family again
And
Reunite with their friends
As I have done with mine.

Wheels turning, I take note,
Just over a rise,

The Complete Second Verse
Dr. Charles Cooper

Where a cone,
Flashing lights,
And some flares announce,

Danger!

That has already passed,
(It's over, let's go! Get on with it!)

One more stain on the pavement.
One more man, just trying to live.
His life, like mine, a footnote,
In the history,
Of blood and traffic on I-95.

WHEN I WAS WRONG

I thought a wedding was forever,
And I said I do,
And I did.
I lived and worked
And continued to give
It felt like forever,
But I was wrong
So wrong.

I was naïve enough to grieve
To pause life's long song
To wait to try again
As her life went on
And on
And on.

I don't hate like I used to,
Because it seems,
Life goes on
For me
Too.

JUST HER TYPE

She said he was normal.
Backyard BBQs and neighborhood friends.
He can talk to people
About little things,
Operates in insignificance
For days on end.
He's never done anything of note
History couldn't care less
It doesn't remember his name
But she does
And calls it love.

If I could step back 100,000 miles,
I could see him as an alternative to me.
If I was not myself, I might accept the simple and smile
Instead of intensity multiplied by me...
In place of this never ending pursuit of amazing.
I don't think I would if I could
Trade any part of who I am
Even if it meant
A lifetime with you.

IN SEARCH OF A PARTNER

I need an anthem,
A motto,
A theme,
And a guide.

I need a post,
A sign,
A meme...
And a bride.

The need for partners
In this empty world
Where nothing is as it seems
Is as necessary
As a mother
who is willing to say no.
Someone you can trust
who will never let go.

"INTERTWINNED"

ART BY BECKY KIPER

The Complete Second Verse
Dr. Charles Cooper

COWBOY

I say Cowboy
When I mean fierce individualist.
The man and the wilderness are one.
Bound to his work,
"The drive",
He doesn't need much,
Just freedom and the right to be alive.
Self reliant,
      Self effacing,
            Self determining,
                  Self defending,
          Self containing,
      Self affirming,
A world unto himself.

A cowboy is alone.
I am alone.

Blood and Traffic
Chuck Cooper

WHAT TO MAKE OF YOU

By the time people reach my age,
They have, almost by definition,
Found themselves;
Lost themselves;
And found themselves again,
And if you have no baggage,
We all know,
you've never been anywhere,
Or done anything.

We are a desire based culture;
All needs met,
We surrender to ourselves,
To self–indulgence,
And complain that someone else has more.

Too old to complain,
Everything I have, I've made.
I have produced, too much,

But,
I am too driven
To stop trying
To give my children more,
To be a little more,
To taste a little more,
To feel and touch and smell and see
More!

When we first met,
I thought we were alike in that way,
Driven for the sake of drive,
Giving to our children,
Because we had enough.
Building to feel alive,
A PhD for the sake of the degree
As if achievement happened in degrees

310

The Complete Second Verse
Dr. Charles Cooper

On oversized pieces of paper.

We have both been more,
Than any piece of paper could ever say;
Both done more,
Than the 99% of everyone
Who lies about in malaise,
Leading lives of quiet desperation,
And
Telling themselves,
Lies about having lived.

I want you to know that I understand
Your need to be bigger than a man.
I want you to know,
I see you for who you are,
Underneath that need:
To be loved,
To be beautiful,
To be seen,
Not seen,
SEEN,
And known to be.
After all, isn't that the first command,
"To be?"
I need you to know…

That I know,
What to make of you
A woman who went to college at 48
After conquering the world without even a GED.
I know that you know how to be.

Blood and Traffic
Chuck Cooper

3,500 MILES,

Not kilometers.
Not this time,
A lower number
Might redefine
The size of the hole,
The emptiness
The taps,
Distractions from meaning...
The absence of sleep
And everything that miles implies.

3,500 miles
And 300 days,
Separate you from me.
Numbers cannot say
The things I would change
To make the miles disappear.

As relentless as time is,
It cuts and pains,
reshapes and drains,
Cast locks and chains,
To contain
My love.

Balance will and fear
On a wheel, without care.
Justice has nothing to do with it.
What would you change to be near?
Swollen hands cannot touch from so far,
And joined souls span much.
Like light from a star
Bringing life from so far,
Would you hold on for longer,
Hold out forever,
Silence that inward stare
At the place called, "nowhere?"

The Complete Second Verse
Dr. Charles Cooper

Would you hold down the crown
Fight with musket and gun
Stand your ground
Until there's nowhere to run.

Look into the eyes of the crowd
And say good bye.
But you've never said goodbye before.
I would never let another day go by
Without you warm in my arms,
Sated scent, tender charms
All we've spent to stave off harm.
But my arms are empty.
A corporeal fool,
It's time and distance
which denied me you.

I never wanted a throne,
No fame or fight
Not land or stone.
3,500 miles away,
What I wanted
Was not to be
Alone.

Blood and Traffic
Chuck Cooper

YOU TAUGHT HIM TO FLY

Who did you think it would save?
If someone you loved was set free,
It was callous meandering
Of a soul let go,
With no direction.

Who did you think wouldn't feel pain?
If you saved him one more day
Rapture pays well in passion...
And it ends in pain
There is no redemption
For the victim
No forgiveness for the game.
You thought to play for a day yourself,
But gave him wings instead.
You thought to send him lower
He rose above your lovely head.
You thought to betray,
To flay,
But nothing stays the same
He has found the way
To forget yesterday.
There is no sorrow.
No one ever cries.
He has found another,
Whose love never dies.

ANY FUTURE WITH YOU

A plan unveiled, reveals much,
But what plan survives,
The first encounter with love.
My plan would not survive,
The first encounter with those eyes.
The haunting melody in the fire
Which calls passion,
A fealty from which
There is no return.
It is a vortex,
I almost fell through,
A heartbeat before I realized,
There was no future with you.

Like so many others
Who learned to fly,
And were seduced
By a moment of joy.

There is more to this poem somewhere
A future perhaps,
Engraved on tablets of time somewhere,
But you, you are gone…

Blood and Traffic
Chuck Cooper

SITTING IN JUDGMENT

What dreams have passed
In time gone before
Between generations,
Between people,
In time gone before.

We ride ourselves
And tell ourselves
We're better off than before.
Objectively, it's true
But it's hard to know
When all you know is you,
And you have to ask,
Am I better?

Judges have seen
So much.
They sit on a Bench
In judgment.
To decide
Right or wrong...
If a man can see his son?

There are no rewards,
Execute the law.
There is no feeling,
Execute the law.
If a man can see his son?
How can you ask the question?
How can there be an answer?
How dare you sit there!
If a man can see his son and his daughter.
How dare we...
Improve everything
And slip the unstable fingers of society
Into the family.

The Complete Second Verse
Dr. Charles Cooper

WHITE CLIFFS OF DOVER

Poseidon stoked the waves,
Trident barely visible beneath the froth of desire.
Bare white the cliffs hold against the vicious forces as they attack.
Sailors, free of life, bow now to the sun and moon
Never Asking why
It was Apollo in his flight
Too late to this good night.

Waves crest here.
Plated men walk this shore no more
With sword of steel
Cut less of the rock than water
Sun scorched the sand burned basalt white
Against the sun there is no might.
Against nature man measures life
On the smallest scale.

All that power, stoked and hot
Burning to the core
Bodies strewn in the wake,
A lake, with not enough thirst in the world.
Burning dawn, the rising sun
Not long now, almost done...
Time to lay down your pen.

Blood and Traffic
Chuck Cooper

AFFAIRS OF THE HEART

Remember how serious
It was to say, "I love you?"
How much more serious it was to…
Well you know.

Just the other day,
I met a lady pushing a lovely carriage
Baby in tow.
I commented how nice
To see a mother and her child
On such a lovely day.

I explained to her
How serious
Matters of the heart
Are… to me,
To the life of a child
Who doesn't grow up in the streets
Or in the wild.

The monumental price which we all pay
To spend a day in love…
And how such a thing is worth everything,
Eternity.

She replied,
It's my Match.com baby.
I never saw his dad again.
With tears in my eyes,
I walked away.

I am officially done…
Heart shut down
Eyes closed
For the duration,
Remembering what it was to feel
Was the worst plan ever.

The Complete Second Verse
Dr. Charles Cooper

One broken heart is all I can afford.
In a world full
of speak no evil,
Hear no sound,
There is such a thing
as too much speed,
Too much convenience.
So much passion and love
So often seen, so easily shared,
As to make the action and feeling
meaningless.

Too little care
Is taken...
With words.

Too little care
Is taken...
With actions.

Too little care
Is taken...
In affairs of the heart.

The birds and bees
Will buzz and sing
But we have put away these animal things for something so much
better,
People must be better.

Blood and Traffic
Chuck Cooper

AVALANCHE

She came to London
After the rain
Working for pay
That never came.
Avalanche of trouble,
A mountain of debts,
A man who promised
She would have no regrets.

By the time he recovered his investment
She was spent.
Deep and deeper still
She felt…
A baby on both hips,
And one riding coach.
So much of herself was gone
No part of her
could admit she was wrong.

Inside it felt worse than defeat.
Fear confines ideas
Restricts potential.
The only avalanche these days
Was the rain that fell every day
Between one and four.
It felt like tears made of fear
And dependence.

She knew,
she was destined for more.
The skies fell silent and she rose.

The Complete Second Verse
Dr. Charles Cooper

YOUR DAY WILL COME

Did you think to yourself,
"I am 14."
When you saw him the first time?

Did you think,
"My day has finally come?"

With barely a decade
of days and nights
Behind you.
You were an old soul then,
Who knew what forever meant.

I can't say,
If it's a testament
To your soul,
Or your tolerance
or your beauty,
Or temperance
or just sheer ability,
That it was 30 years later
Before he walked away.

At 16, you said "I do"
And you did,

For thirty years.

Thirty Years.

There should be a monument…
To that kind of commitment,
That only those two people can tear down.
That's the problem with people,
They will.

There's a problem with the brain…

Blood and Traffic
Chuck Cooper

None can resolve:
Come hell or high water,
Good times and bad;
At 14 or 40,
All the experience you've had
You can never, ever, forget.

You just have to live.
Given one life,
A chance to be a wife...
With the radiance of the sun,
Three sons,
Three decades;

And then *he left*,

HE LEFT.

Now you wait

From dusk to dawn,
With the radiance of the sun,
For your day to come.

I know it feels like it hasn't been long,
It seems like yesterday the babies were born.
They're almost grown.

You let your hair down
Rebelled against the chains you felt
So acutely.

Behaved like the teenage girl you never were
With your old soul,
Even then you didn't belong
Or so you thought.

Now you know what it is to be free
Of the chains you made,

The Complete Second Verse
Dr. Charles Cooper

That remade,
You,
Into what you thought,
You were supposed to be.

All the reverence in the world
For the institution
Didn't pay the wage
You wanted.
Wicked recompense,
This heartfelt sorrow,
Tears that tear, heart-rending despair.
Weren't you promised forever?

There is a day,
And it is coming,
The bonds of joy
And matrimony.
Everything you thought you bought
As the perfect wife
Is coming
On the wings
Of the radiant sun.
Until then,
Is it enough to know,
Your day will come?

Blood and Traffic
Chuck Cooper

CUTS

Most knife wounds don't kill.
They hurt like hell, though.

I've been cut a million times,
Even cut myself and tried not to yell.
I've been bent and burnt and even tattooed
But I never knew fear until I met you.

By our second kiss,
I was scared
That the distance between us
Would be too much for you,
Or me.

That if I ever let go,
I may never again see,
Or touch, your face,
Your lips, your tender lips.

My lips brushed yours
And electric notes,
Transcendent visions of a lifetime
Were engrained on my brain.

Most people fear death,

    And spiders,

        And snakes

        And bees,

Not me.

I fear a life where the only you
Is a memory,
Framed in the vault of my mind,

324

The Complete Second Verse
Dr. Charles Cooper

That I cannot forget.
You, with me for all time…
Just beyond reach.

Was she real or not?
I do not know.

My memory says so,
But the absence of you
In my presence,
Proclaims that I let go.
Never.

The absence of you in my presence,
Caused a tremor in my heart
That declared,

"It would have been better
If I never knew that moment,
When our eyes met
Across the room
And you glowed
And I smiled
And everything I was
Gave in to the hope

and happiness of the moment."

"That moment where,

No obstacle was too great

To separate we two.

And I let myself believe,
In a shining tomorrow,
In the presence of the Sun,
Where no shadow falls,
And I have nowhere left to run.

Blood and Traffic
Chuck Cooper

And, it pleases me."

When the knife runs too deep,
It's hard to tell.
A cut is a cut,
No matter how much blood it spills.

In the winter,
when blood runs slow
and thick with iron,
A man values it more,
Expects more…
Surrenders more heat
With each beat,
Of his heart…
Late in life,
Surrendering life
Even when it feels right
Costs…

Make no mistake,
It's a risk we take
Without fail,
Lest another moment pass without passion.
When there's a price to pay,
I pay it, without question.
In the hope,
That someone
Will be the one.
Clean the cuts,
Left by Hope, the most brutal emotion.
Until then,
That someone is worth waiting for…

REDEMPTION

I found redemption.
Not salvation,
I wasn't looking.

Not God,
She already knew.
And never forgiveness...
            That is understood,
there is none to be had
For what I have done.

I found redemption,
And everything just
Fell away. For years,
I carried so much weight
That when I let go,
I nearly flew.

Because of you,
I lived in a sea of guilt
Worried I would hurt you
While you were killing me.
Suffering is not the path,
To being redeeming.

You can walk away.
You need to walk away.
And I did,
I finally did.

I can be redeemed,
even if I can't be forgiven...
That's not what redemption means.

Blood and Traffic
Chuck Cooper

SOME MOMENTS MATTER MORE

In every breath that's taken
Doing what you were sent here for
With purpose,
your purpose,
You are made real.
No moment is equal
to the ones before.
Moments made real,
matter more.

Every look into the light,
When you run…
When you fight…
This is no joke,
It is your life…

Every heartbeat,
every day,
If you go.
If you stay.
What is real
is what you make.
What is made,
the steps you take
To make the change.
Take the floor.
Stand and make this matter more.

Please,
live.
Take a chance.
Live,
it's life.
Find romance.
For a moment
Or for life,
Take that girl,

The Complete Second Verse
Dr. Charles Cooper

make her your wife.
And know,
with every chance you take,
Every breath,
Every day,
Nothing will mean what it did before,

Love matters more.

Blood and Traffic
Chuck Cooper

DON'T LET GO

Mountains rise above the sound,
There is no easy way down,
No way, to find the ground
Through these clouds and this snow.
Seems like there is no hope,
No easy way to go,
Like the world is made of walls
And the walls are made of stone
It's your mind that keeps you here
Drifting far from home.
For now, you must hold on
Please, don't let go.

Be the change.
Be the sage.
Offer the words that make the waves
That conquer hearts
And bring them home.
Please hold on.
Don't let go.

There is a difference you can make.
Take every chance
to plant a stake
In the ground
To watch it grow,
Don't let go.
Don't let go.

Just hold on,
The sun will rise,
And the light will melt the snow.
As the light reveals the road
That takes us home…
Please hold on. Don't let go…
Please hold on. Please hold on.

The Complete Second Verse
Dr. Charles Cooper

EXPOSED

Exposing my face to you
This time it's true.
Maybe you'll love me
Baby you'll love me,
…This time
All the scars and life you see
All of that is honesty
All of that is me.
Exposed,
Exposed for love.

You turn away,
Just another day.
Never return.
I'll never learn.
Exposed,
Exposed for love.

I'm tearing my face away baby.
Maybe baby,
Not this time.
Your love's not made of honesty
I never learned to lie
Learn to be,
Or to just get by.
Exposed,
Exposed for love.

Sweet painted face
Is camouflage
Tear it all away
Tear away for me
Baby, I just want to see.
Exposed,
Exposed for love.

The drama, trauma

Blood and Traffic
Chuck Cooper

I put myself through
Exposed myself to love.
For love,
I gave myself to you.

All the drama I put myself through
All of it for you.

All the drama I put myself through
All of it for you.
I gave myself to you.
Exposed,
Exposed to love.
What did you see
In your rear view?
Exposed,
Exposed to love.

The Complete Second Verse
Dr. Charles Cooper

A CITY OF WHORES

Assholes, barristers, con men, and carrion.
Roads are streets, streets are alleys,
And walking is faster than driving.
Parks, museum, bars, and drug dealers...
Try to redeem a life spent in close proximity,
To everything and everyone.
I met a bum
Who made more asking for it,
Than a stock trader on his best day.
Imagine what people will pay
To feel redeemed.

The only way, it turns out, to survive,
Is to learn to ignore everything
And get things done.
Nothing in the moment, or on fire,
Nothing inspires, like fear.

Art thrives in the city,
Poetry, too,
Creators create in a bleak gray landscape
Smashed and smeared by too many hands
To have meaning.
A wandering band of land locked zombies
Walk to work in furried, desperate frenzy
No way out of the routine
They have made, for themselves.

In the city, people will:
Do anything,
        Pay anything
                Be anything you want,
For a line or two of lovely words.

JOURNEY

It is a very lost man,
who will tell you that he knows…
Why,
Lost men lie.
It is a more lost man
Who will stop and ask directions.

Long after I stopped believing,
I found myself.
At a stop, on this journey,
This Life.

I believe any Angel
Is just the right person,
At just the right time.
I met an Angel
Who happened to be mine.
She let me be,
Exactly, who I needed to be,
To take the next step,
Without any regrets.
In a brief moment of serendipity
I exclaimed, "There is a God."

I did the math,
And there was.

The Complete Second Verse
Dr. Charles Cooper

RELENTLESS

I am a student of motion.
Energy burns so bright,
Motion decomposes
As does flight…

Spinning in flushed spite
A dapper dove
Springs forth,
A loping symbol
once again
Of Peace,
But a little angry about
Being pigeon-holed as such.

Peace gives way
To a cordite fueled flight
Of projectile pellets,
Proving,
That Darwin only half understood
what he thought…

If consciousness evolved,
To create success, survival,
Why are there weapons of war?
Given these weapons and individuality,
Why are we here at all?
Given evolution,
Why do we care?

"HAPPY COUPLE"

ART BY BECKY KIPER

US

The youth you lived through,
From which you thought
There was no escape...
Someone you should have been able to trust
Did that.
When you told me,
For the purpose
Of making me walk away...
You did it without the knowledge
That I know Pain.

If you could not see the scars on my heart
You should have glimpsed those on my face.
And seeing, you should have known,
Scars are what make us great
And beautiful.
Scars are composed of life.
And I love life.

Now you, are another scar,
I only wonder,
What did you fear,
For a week, a month, or a year.
I was never in a rush
To discover,
What would become of us,
I only wanted love.

Blood and Traffic
Chuck Cooper

MARIACHI

In sixteen - sixteen time,
Making Mexican rhyme
The sun had set, not long ago,
A Mariachi song pitched just too low,
A lady Mariachi?
A young lady at that.
She looked out of place,
But they gave her a hat
And a mandolin.

When I looked at her,
A knowing smile
Drew her face tight
She popped into double joy time,
Which is a thing only Mariachi know
But we all feel.
The band didn't skip a beat,
But doubled pace, tapping feet.
I ate some Avacado,
And met her eyes again,
Spanish fire, in double joy time.

I would like to say I rose and left,
But that would make me a liar.

338

A SENSE OF LADY

A sense of lady is
Reverent sanity.
As they grow,
Women hold truth
Above strength,
Dependability above stature,
A stalwart stability over
the daring,
brave,
or bold.

Tomorrow is a lady's word,
Hope the theme of days and years
For which men give thanks.
A woman without hope
Is a lesbian.
Men don't change,
But we can hope.

Deep inside the cut,
Men play at destruction and creation
But for a woman,
Each is an occupation.
Women walk with
Intent and purpose, sublime.
Men offer a poem or paint,
While a woman gives birth to life.

The bi-polar sanity
That comes from
Holding too tight
To hope,
From which comes
The divine.
Wisdom and war,
From Zues' head,
Athena's spine.

Blood and Traffic
Chuck Cooper

So much taken,
So much given,
So much she will leave behind.
A man plays games with potential
Stretches childhood on and on.
Women never live a day
Free of consequence
Or reverence.

Being a woman,
Means living like there's something to lose
There's no shame in the games people play,
Games measure men, and women alike.
Men excel at games of strength,
While women have the strength to make a life.

SOMEONE

We all have that someone.
In a moment I can't forget,
I met you.

There,
In a pallid, pasted, black painted pub,
Called the Voodoo Lounge,
counter stained in blood…
The Bartender was maimed,
but still upright.
I guess someone taught him
not to stop a fight.

I stood there, just to the right,
Of you
And, we talked.

Then and there, we knew.
No bated breath,
Marked the moment.
A gentleman does not anticipate
Later that night…
And I was
A gentleman
And you,
Were a lady.

Still, as we left the bar,
the past, that I thought was color
Now looked like black and white,
And the colors
Of the world around us,
Left me in awe.

On that day,
In the night,
The light just right,

Blood and Traffic
Chuck Cooper

You chose me
And I, you.

As elegant as you are,
With lines as fine
As a Corvette Stingray
In 1969,
When cars were lightning,
Skating the fine line
Between machine,
And art.

It's those eyes that get me,
Every time.

Eyes are like a fine line,
between flesh and the mind,
And yours, bleed light,
As bright as the sun
At night.

Light,
That lit the way,
To excuse regrets,
And finally,
Turn the page
In me.

Light,
That showed me
That I could believe,
Again.

You did, and I knew,
There is no better way
To take the next step
Than hand in hand
With redemption,
Leaving anger behind,

The Complete Second Verse
Dr. Charles Cooper

Owning forgiveness,
Granting acceptance,

I was yours.
You were mine.
In that brief space of time.

We made no promises,
On that night
Or any other.
We looked,
and we knew
That was enough for me,
When it came to you.
And that life,
this life,
The one we thought was half through,
Was new.

The light fell…
Through the limbs and leaves,
Through the fall and winter
To the ground down,
To the Summer and Spring,
Finally, to me.

Like the ice and snow
That withered Winter's walls
And finally washed away
The tears from yesteryear,
Like a warm, sweet summer rain.

That caressed the tired,
And the sleeping,
So they could wake,
You woke me,
Just that way.

I woke to life,

Blood and Traffic
Chuck Cooper

Where we saw,
As if for the first time,
A life that wasn't done
As long as we could grow.

And if we could grow,
We could run.
And if we could run,
We could live, forever.

We all have that someone
In a moment,
That we saw and we knew,
That moment could be forever.

I saw you in the sunlight
Held you beneath the moon.
The life, I know is new,
The forever, I feel is true
It's all ours for the taking
Because of you.

The Complete Second Verse
Dr. Charles Cooper

WE TALKED

The morning after, one of those conversations
That you think dies with the child you were...
You know, it's real. The words feel...
It's composed of sounds,
Intimate and revealing.
Crafted not of calculations,
But of trust.
There's something natural in such an exchange.
No effort required, not bland, no blame.
Something real
Between two people
Who understand each other, naturally.

WALK AWAY

I saw you walking away.
You never turned to say,
I'm sorry or goodbye.
You turned away,
And all I got to see was behind,
A past that was mine
And yours and empty.

THE ANGEL

I get it, you're the angel
With the wings and the light.
We may not even play on the same field,
But that doesn't make it right.

Blood and Traffic
Chuck Cooper

NO WASTE IN JAPAN

When design is near to perfect
Nothing is left to take away.
Everything is compressed and exact.
No waste.

Don't spend a moment,
With idle tears,
Stalled, stale with fear.
Life will not wait,
There's no time like today
To live.

CAPITALIST SUMMER

Nothing is free.
I got to see you bright,
Feel the warmth and the love.
See you fly,
See you shine.
I looked into the sun.
The price is tears and burned retinas.
Nothing is free.

The Complete Second Verse
Dr. Charles Cooper

NAKED

In the courtroom,
I was striped bare, again.
My dedication to my family
Used against me.
"He works too much, too long, too hard…"
I did not show my rear this time,
Though you all deserved a look.
Who are any of you to judge me?
Jesus, looked at us each,
And knowing our worst,
Never once said,
"Fuck off."

FRIENDS

Who do you cherish
During the nights
In hotel rooms?
The bed is cold.
The bar is hot.
The drinks that flow,
More real than not,
Offer meaning to feelings
Which are not real.

Friends are the people
Who drive you home,
Put you to bed,
Tuck you in,
Hold your hair,
As you kneel at the throne
And declare,
"I will never
Go there
Or do that
Again."

Blood and Traffic
Chuck Cooper

LONDON

There was a painting sage
Living merrily his days in Paris.
Until one day,
In a burst of youth and inspiration,
He joined a flock of fools passing by
On a journey to the streets of London.
There, he found himself,
All dolled up, in a bowler hat, and kerchief.
His face was white. His lips were red.
He spent his days as a barker,
In front of the Strand.

There are no plays there anymore.
The rent's too high and words too cheap
Actors and Actresses too droll.
Soho's too cool for drama.
Shakespeare's too drab and wordy
To echo through the night
And bring in crowds
When the likes of smooth Jazz
And Craft Beer,
All sharp, and quaint, and cool
Come cheap and make a profit.

Nobility once ruled the day here,
Thieves, prostitutes and pimps ruled the night.
Now ladies in burkas glance at men,
Hidden forever from their sight.

Our sage was near enough to them
Beneath his dowdy paint
To understand that just to write
Can hardly mean you know
Anything more than words and spelling and punctuation
Which is meaningless anymore.
When diversity and destruction are synonyms
For the same people, places, and things

348

The Complete Second Verse
Dr. Charles Cooper

That tolerate each other on TV
And in speeches, kill each other
In the dark and the light
In the day and the night.
It seems tolerance is synonymous with death these days.
Stand by and watch die the idea that we are all the same.
Surrendering the best for the mediocre
To welcome the end of all things.

We dream that speaking is more than
Sharp, packed, punctuated sounds.
The sage has laid his pen down.
The smell of ink drying is like the smell of Soho
And Friday night jazz and a Bowler hat
And Profit.

There is nothing left in black and white.
There is no holy ground on which to write.
A murder of crows has snatched the light
And laughing they took flight.

It is the grey of the clouds in London
That seeps into everything,
Making even Joy feel so so in Soho.
Her name was Joy, I think, anyway.
All blonde, blue eyes and pasty, slate skin
Like the sky outside.
She had bad teeth and breath
That reeked of a pint of Fullers
That chased the Sheppard's pie
A little of each could be spotted,
dribbled on her too large chest.
The whole scene bespoke Britain
And greatness,
except it was a lie.

Away and assuage,
            a people feeling lost
                    Beneath the crown.

Blood and Traffic
Chuck Cooper

Just past a vintage brownstone
There on the left where was found,
The last British Bobby,
You know the one without a gun,
Who blows a whistle
To stop a homicide
Of the greatest empire beneath the sun.

LITTLE CONVERSATIONS

Like the forever friend
you trust with anything...
and everything.
Or maybe like a lover,
Laying down with you,
In a bed the two of you made   together
Crafted from forever
A material only friends can keep on hand.

The power in such words,
Binds... friends, the future, forever...
It's love, made of words...
Of a life.
My life.
I am
The man,
stuck forever in flight,
blazing eternally bright,
flames bright, bigger,
and better than anyone can.

Being such a man,
and hearing the sweet sound,
Sacred words,
I turn to truth, to you, to learn
so late in life...
That life can be more than a Faustian deal.

This is how,
a simple conversation
can be the thing
That begins the quest,
to see what love reveals.

Blood and Traffic
Chuck Cooper

TIME UPON THE THRONE

If a man spent his goes
In the reckless, relentless
pursuit of rapture
So many days running
That he found the finish line,
Not near, but at the bottom.

And having seen the finish,
Tamed his life and mind,
Worked the twelve steps,
Asked forgiveness from God
And those he had harmed,
In his unbridled pursuit,
Of rapture.
If such a man,
took inventory of his life,
Wondered at his own achievements long enough
To give credit where credit was due.

Such a man could lay down,
Close his eyes,
And leave this life satisfied.

But imagine his surprise,
When his eyes fluttered open,
And the sun shone in the sky.
Beaming, gleaming brilliant sun.
He saw happiness in her eyes
And knew,
That all his life had been
Preparation.
He didn't need
Forgiveness
or redemption
or repentance.
Salvation was not his to seek.

The Complete Second Verse
Dr. Charles Cooper

He needed those lips, those eyes,
Her words and thoughts.
Life had crafted him,
At the behest of the maker
Into a polished gem.

A gem she had earned,
Through her life, she deserved
A diamond of her own
And some time upon the throne.

Just when you think God doesn't hear prayers,
You come to understand,
Sometimes you are the answer
to a prayer you never heard.
Someone else's words,
Whispered low and deep,
"I'm lonely."

Blood and Traffic
Chuck Cooper

BUDDHIST MONKS

Did you know Buddhist Monk's are a thing?
Their thing is no thing,
Which they explain:
Desire is the enemy of the happiness.
If a man wants happiness, he must not want.

There was a Monk who had aged more than not.
He had a wrinkled soul, but he smiled a lot.
Inside his lovely geometric garden,
Where he expressed the desire to be;
Just be, nothing else.
Not to see, not to live,
Not to drive, not to give,
Because he had nothing.

Save the food,
I suppose he grew
In his garden
Which he wanted
And a fancy red robe
And some shoes
And a cot to sleep on
And a lovely view to appreciate
As he pondered nothing.

Nothing cannot live in a moment;
It does not begin and cannot end.
Nothing is not a point on the line.
Nothing can only be seen by the blind.
Happiness without purpose is a lie.

PUNISHED WITH LIES

I don't mind the pain
If we can share it.
I don't mind a train
If it goes somewhere I need to be.
Oh, I will start a revolution
To watch it rise, even succeed.
I will ride the wave
Until I'm punished by the lies.
Still I won't surrender
Let it lie
Or let it be.

That's my dream in the corner,
Which you have set aside.
The revolution we all need,
In spite of your pride.
That's the revolution.
That's my dream,
Simplicity,
Happiness,
And Peace.

And I, am punished by lies.

Blood and Traffic
Chuck Cooper

THERE IS TOMORROW

I asked politely.
I prayed.
I wanted.
A subtle, hazy
Still, small voice,
Whispered, "Tomorrow is another day."

I believed, in that still small voice.
But I've never been patient in that way.
I prayed again.
I begged.
A subtle, hazy, still, small voice,
Whispered, "There is tomorrow."

I needed, I asked aloud,
On my knees.
A brazen, lazy, still, small voice,
Whispered, "There is tomorrow."

I tried not to cry, to understand why,
And I asked one last time,
"Tomorrow is another day.
Why must I wait?"
The submissive, servant's,
Still, small voice whispered…
"Because of today."

I've never been a fan of due dates,
I work, and it simply takes the time it takes,
But it is done right.

The Complete Second Verse
Dr. Charles Cooper

WE ARE HUMAN AS WELL

Priests, Preachers, and Deacons are marvelous things.
Most earn little and give much
In peace and time and solace
To everyone but themselves.
Done right, these men among men
And women too,
Spend days wandering
Learning, leading, and giving
With little recompense
Of the material kind.

We normal folk could learn from them.
But that is not our way.

Those things we learn
We earn...
Usually through pain.

A godly man,
Who preached sacrifice,
Ending social strife,
And love,
Reached so many
With comfort from above
That his whole life seemed a gift
To everyone he touched.

Then, he touched someone.
He was human, he was a sinner.
In an instant, all the good he had done was forgotten,
Vilification complete, the media circus moved on
To find another imperfect soul
While selling sex, drugs, and rock and roll.

"LIVES TO LEAD"

ART BY BECKY KIPER

SAMSĀRA

A man can be greater than his birth
Better than the path
That was laid down
Before him.
If, and only if,
He possesses the will
To be, more.

The Complete Second Verse
Dr. Charles Cooper

Man was made from the earth
And will return to it,
If, and only if,
He lacks the courage
And mind to try
And overcome
The ties that have him
So bound to the ground.

The natural resources of man
Were given to him
To take and make
More.

Men make castes
Castes make chains,
And people live in them,
When they should be opening doors.

A JOYFUL NOISE

When I was younger,
I sang very loud at church.
In my head,
it was a joyful noise.

The crowd's applause
was just as loud,
So I thought I had talent.

I recorded myself,
One day,
With a plan to make it big.
I found out,
Sometimes,
Applause is not honest.

Sometimes,
Applause wastes a lot of time.

Someone,
Told Bob Dylan
he could sing,
So he wrote a few songs,
And God could he write.
Sometimes lies are very good things.

The Complete Second Verse
Dr. Charles Cooper

AFTER GOODBYE

What comes after betrayal:
Sunset?
Sunrise?
Light?
Epiphany?
Discovery?
Self-realization?
Self-actualization?
Self-reliance?

Can that be right?
To spend so much time,
Trying to make the coupling survive,
To discover
That so much good comes,
After Goodbye.

Blood and Traffic
Chuck Cooper

LET THERE BE LIGHT

It was early. Sleep was gone.
The tepid, boy man
Struggled to silence the alarm.
He cursed the light again and again
As it rejected his pleas,
To "Please, let me be."

The interplay of light
That a child knows
Is so short:
Sunset;
sunrise;
a day;
some play.

A birthday comes and goes
To celebrate a year
Of living
And we count them
And mark them
With a value that has not come again.

Consequences are not a thing,
For a child.
We live and talk and play,
And get saved,
Again and again.

The Complete Second Verse
Dr. Charles Cooper

NO SIREN'S CALL

The sirens call,
Not an alarm at all,
Just a promise of better days,
Drawing you in,
Drawing me in.
Together sweet promises
Are never what they seem
Leaving brings regrets,
Even sirens dream.
Dreaming of a song,
Which was lived for too long.

When I finally said goodbye to you
There was no siren at all,
Just another day and night that passed
Alone in my own circumstance.

No siren's call, "Goodbye."
No siren's call, "I had my reasons why."
They were not good,
No better than yours
It was time for leaving,
And I found the door.

We find our lines
And then we cross them
Just to see, just to see
You found your line
And then you crossed it
Now let me be.
Just let me be.

No siren's call,
I said goodbye.
No sirens call,
I will not try.
I have my reasons,

Blood and Traffic
Chuck Cooper

They may not be good,
But they're better than yours
It was time to go,
And you opened the door.

The Complete Second Verse
Dr. Charles Cooper

TOO EARLY

It was too early for life:
Too soon to confront
The fatal onslaught of age, and time, and place.

Wrong place...
Wrong time...
Wrong person...
A Mistake?

Mistakes are not love,
Regardless of the time they take,
No matter the marks they make.

The promises made,
By muse or by sage,
Are the price of action,
And the pain of life and learning
In which, the young engage.
A sin is not a day,
Or a month, or a year;
Never regret a moment;
Never waste a tear.

There is no stain
that cannot be wiped away.
There is no door
  That cannot be opened again.
There is no place
  You cannot tread.
There is no home
where you cannot live.

Pain that fades
But never goes away
Reminds us tomorrow is a better day.

Lives are made of cycles

Blood and Traffic
Chuck Cooper

Whichever roads we roam,
It's all a journey home,

And sometimes we travel
Between sunset and dawn.
Where dark and light are companions
And we make a bargain,
So we can go on.

There is a distance
Between sin and redemption,
A gulf never larger than you
No matter who you are.

I saw the darkness myself,
Bargained with a pained creator,
For forgiveness I did not deserve.

These mistakes, made in haste,
because I chose to live.

These bargains,
Cast of fate,
Plagued with hate,
because I chose to live,
These things are not the sin.

I was given life, to love and strive
I make mistakes and that is life.
To not live, is the sin.
Please, live.

The Complete Second Verse
Dr. Charles Cooper

IN THE NIGHT

Patently absurd,
for a boy to take the steps of a man,
But that was the journey he was on,
Across the ocean,
to the sand
                    And back again,
There is no sin in orders…
But the guilt of knowing better
Cuts deep
For those who can still breath.

Too young to regret:
The early onset,
    Of responsibility,
        And the consequences of dreams.

Impossible dreams…

Are a thing,
In a dry desert heat,
In the light of night,
Where such things are seen,
and can be secured,
To offer meaning.

A boy - man, having seen such a thing
Such an impossible dream
Whether lost or naïve,
The Child cannot deny,
The drive,
the thoughts,
And the actions,
Of the Child-made-man, by choice;

There is no choice then,
And no regret,
The sun that rises,

Blood and Traffic
Chuck Cooper

also sets.

Days are not a place
To dream big dreams
But to do,
And in the doing
Make dreams possible.

It is a lifelong gift for you to dream a dream and do

So, leave regret behind and strive.

Please, strive.

The Complete Second Verse
Dr. Charles Cooper

SING

Forgiveness is...
the refuge of the young.

Knowledge is...
the harbor of the strong.

Patience is...
      A fairy tale for hearts that cannot decide,
Or see a risk and run,
Or accept the lie,
That they're worth more than you.
Who might have seen that,
If someone had said "please."

Reason is...
the gift, God gave to Man,
So he would know what was right
And what was wrong.
        When to take her hand,
And when to leave her alone.

It's been so long
This lonely song
I have much to bring,
If you would
Please,
Sing.

Blood and Traffic
Chuck Cooper

CHILDISH THINGS

One day that boy will be a man.
Choice can make it so;
Actions can make it so;
Fate can make it so.

Fate...
Is the self-proclaimed, cycle of life.
It has no regard for your desire
Or your will,
        Or your commands.
You...
Are a child...
Who plays at being a man.

You wait for fate,
And make a trade:
Freedom and choice...
For some later stage.
You grew old...
But never aged.

<<<You>>>
If life was fair.

On that day,
like every man before,
on every day before,
when someone chose
to take responsibility
for thoughts
and actions
and consequences,
a monument should rise,
to the cycle of life,

that lies between childish things,

The Complete Second Verse
Dr. Charles Cooper

and putting them away.

Such monuments would be few,
But there would be one for you,
different,
rare,
A unicorn in full bloom.

Please, put down those childish things,

There is so much more.

LOVE COMES

When life is fair,
Love comes to every heart;
For my friends who wait,
Have patience.

It cries to every ear
Of a burden too large
For many to hear.
For some there is too much to bear.
It's never easy.
Life isn't fair.

You must carry such a thing
From the dark to the light
So you can perceive it right.

If love refuses to move,
From one desperate point
On someone else's arbitrary line,
That they drew without input from you,
You have learned all you need to know,
This soul is not your home...

Be Patient... Love comes to every heart.
Through this life,
Compromise,
is the hardest thing.

Whether husband or wife,
Days,
Can be full of light
Or dark as night
Depending very much
On who you spend them with.

If I had to give advice:
Laugh a lot

The Complete Second Verse
Dr. Charles Cooper

And look his way;
Fix your hair;
Buy awesome underwear,
As often as you can, wear it,
More often than that, take it off.

Love often and much.
Take a risk,
Bet on Love.
I do not mean cling,
Or wait forever,
Or love unflinching,
Or take a beating,

I mean love,
together.

For men, it's simpler still,
Be aware
Of this person,
apart from you,
Who is a part of you.

Be kind, make today that day,
for the love she deserves,
　　　She bet her life on you...
make it worth her while,
please.

Blood and Traffic
Chuck Cooper

DAYS

Patience is required
To become a man:
And bear the burdens
Of life;

Turning, living cycles of decision and consequence
Of actions taken and spoken,
Of tidal waves of history,
Of guarded thoughts, decisions, and lies.
Even Nature itself, which eternally decays
Sometimes releases her rage.

A day and a night, the next day
Turning dark into light…
Dawn blessed the way
And paved the road
Where all men go.

These are the days
In life,
You can miss it if you blink twice.

The Complete Second Verse
Dr. Charles Cooper

CONFUSION

Sometimes when people meet
You see what you need to see,
And walk where you want to walk,
Without watching where you step.
Women with dogs… Sigh.
Beware, nothing is ever what it seems…
You never can tell
What "love" means
Without the context of time.

In truth, we never know.
We spent so much time
Confusing wants and needs.
It's an easy thing
For any man.
Even me.
Even me.

Blood and Traffic
Chuck Cooper

POTENTIAL

Arch laden pathways,
built by calloused hands,
The hands of slaves
        laid the roads
That led to, from, and within the Wasteland.
Make no mistake,
Slaves are made and
Harnessed
for their road building skills.
The chains
they wear are camouflaged,
In hearts and compassion,
Made to look like the best of things.
That have been
Flayed and framed,
charred, twisted,
and shaped…
By words like sacrifice,
hope,
change,
and fate.
All of which mean nothing,
When it's free-will you trade.
The wasteland is the place,
Utopia of which you dream
Thought is barred,
Ideas and dreams banned,
Free speech traded for feelings.

Taking life from one,
to give it to another
Is taking from every man.
For his life is the only gift
He can be given without strings.
Until in his haste and foolishness,
Or, at the point of a gun,
They were added.

376

The Complete Second Verse
Dr. Charles Cooper

Everyman, the wasteland,
Pasting parts from each other to pave the floor
Of the cavern from which he came and may return
If he accepts the promises that make men weak
On the altar of sacrifice where lie the meek.
Who inherit the cave after only a short wait
And live comfortably as slaves
Doing the master's work
With a little torment
Painted over in hope with its alabaster hue
Hope has mastered so many men,
Its own chamber, moist, shallow, dark and dank,
Painted in the gray and deep reds of sacrifice.
You can barely make out the impressions left by lost life.
It is the chamber of almost.
Almost greatness,
almost potential,
almost humane,
and finally nothing.

Fear is the darkest chamber, consuming all things,
feeding on itself, darker and deeper than hope,
No color or light to speak of,
Just dry, pasty rocks that crumble beneath the touch
Just shapes and jagged angles
Just pasted rock-like cement bound souls in a ball lost to escape
forever bellowing, "I would, but…"
Or the bastard cousin's cry, "I could've, but…"
Fear is paved by sacrificial men,
By those who avoid strife
By giving in.
There is much surrendering
Tears and sacrifice,
Bellowing fools, compassion,
Balancing cost and price
That matter not at all
If you give away your life.

Blood and Traffic
Chuck Cooper

Reason, the narrow strand that held man above the Wasteland
Reason is the mouth of all caverns,
The doorway to the world outside.
Rushing from the darkness to the painted path
toward the light,
to the light.
Not the hope,
see him rise,
Not the fear,
damning lies
Only through reason can all men rise.
Crying reason,
setting fires,
Burning torches to escape the pyre.
The worst of us would
Stand by
And watch creation burn,
      So their tiny piece
Would have more value.

Arc hollow the light passing through the divine
A shadow falls on the wasteland;
Not a giant among men, but a giant man,
Holding himself erect for the first time,
Reaching to the future,
to the potential,
Each man holds in himself,
the ability to reason and rise
Above himself,
harnessing life in all its glory,
for the first time,
sublime.
Not a stone foundation for some almighty collective
To climb upon
But a striver, rising higher, discovering for himself
As creator, as maker, wearing the moniker of explorer.
Should he find himself in the darkest night,
on the darkest hour,
He need not fear.

The Complete Second Verse
Dr. Charles Cooper

He is the light.

Of all creation,
only man could be a slave.
And knowing that he was a slave,
Call on the divine and discover:
Freedom is a thing within his own power.

Of all creation,
only man could be his own salvation.

Blood and Traffic
Chuck Cooper

FIRST SIGHT

The dawn breaks.
Visage. A vision.
A ripple of light passed through
Your living hair.
I'd swear, it breathed fire,
Glowing, gold embers,
Flying cinders…
Lips were red as the night
Painted in the blood
That pounded in my heart,
Pulsing – pushing – pounding
As though,
Your gravity determined the flow
Of light, and air, and tides.
My own life force,
Was not my own,
When I was in your orbit.

When I was in your orbit,
My heart beat in tides
That you defined.
Announcing you were here
In a sleek, taunt, little, black dress.

My life's blood
Stopped flowing, flooding the room
To paint the walls red as a tribute to your lips,
When we kissed.

I knew there and then
As I pulled out your chair
That we would make a home
Just off the Appalachian trail.
Mountains and trees
As far as eyes can see
Came to me so clearly.
My arch green eyes

The Complete Second Verse
Dr. Charles Cooper

Measured you in kind
Seeing without lies,
I was alive.

The measurements I made
Mapped the eloquent way
I crafted and composed
The sublime pedestal
Moments after we met.

It's not that you chose,
I crafted it,
and you rose
To stand there.
I looked full and well,
Blinded by beauty,
Such a capable muse
Inspired me to see,
I could take another path.

The poems that I wrote,
I still occasionally read,
As a reminder
Of you.
Sometimes,
I even wish I knew
Where you are tonight,
And sometimes
I ask,
Why you aren't with me?

Blood and Traffic
Chuck Cooper

IN THE AGE OF ME

You were born.
Charged in,
Took life by the horns.
No patience but charms,
The kind of fairy tales that harm.
Expectations that set off alarms.

In defense of me,
I was born on a lesser day
Took my time to stand,
And find my way.

I found myself on a road,
Over and over,
Beginning and beginning
Until I could not feel
No one there to reveal,
The path of least resistance,
So I did it the hard way.

That's where I found you.

Somewhere after the "Age of Adventure"
That was squandered on the young,
After the "Age of the best we can"
When we decide to either cruise,

Or...

Take a chance and run...
An imagined pirate to my flank
Commands me to walk the plank,
I turn, to find the executioner's eyes,
  and jump.
    I dive and swim.
      I find the shore.
Defying life, *I choose more.*

The Complete Second Verse
Dr. Charles Cooper

What we choose in this short life,
Is what defines us.

Time will pass, it comes and goes,
Tick tock, the clock, like dominoes.
Stale and bored, until we choose

And...

Clad our feet with road worn shoes
Step foot upon another road
To find out where it goes.
It is a new day, my friend
This new journey awaits us both.
I can't wait.

"LIFE AS A CHECKLIST"

ART BY BECKY KIPER

CHECKLIST

I've thought it many times,
Especially when I should have died,
That there was some purpose
In this life,
beyond mine;
Something I did not understand,
Years ago, when I let her go,
Believing life to be some checklist
Of experiences,
A standard issue list of events...

First Girlfriend... then the Prom
First Car... then the ticket
First College... then the Army
First Army... then the wife
First marriage... then the children
Get a job and make a life.

I wanted to be a father
     And I did.
I wanted to be a soldier
     And I did.
I wanted to be a spy
     And I did.
I wanted to build spacecraft
     And I did.
I wanted to write a book
     And I did.

I wanted it to mean something
So I wrote, poem after poem,
Chasing words with drinks
And drinks with words.
Bathing myself in lust
And ravenous adventures,
Trying to justify...
Trying just to find

Blood and Traffic
Chuck Cooper

Meaning,
Some kind of turning point
To turn this life around.

There is a cold method to achievement,
But there is a beating heart within,
That spurns the things I left behind
And all the things I did.
I never wanted to be a killer,
        But I did.

I never wanted to hurt anyone,
But I did.

I never wanted to hit anyone,
But I did.

I never wanted not to try,
        But I did.

I never wanted to say goodbye,
        But I did,
        And I did,
        And I did.
And I'm sorry.

My life is a dichotomy
Of destruction and creation,
Could I forsake the one for the other,
I would.

But which would I give up?

The Complete Second Verse
Dr. Charles Cooper

INSIDE

What is it about being a woman?
Self-deprecating,
Self-doubt,
Self-mutilation,
And "friends" that do worse.
As if there was a lack of mirrors in the world
To see your beauty.

The cold calculus of curves never drew a finer line
Than when it calculated the area inside her mind.
And it moved me to want,
For you to let me see,
All that you were capable of,
All that you could be.

All these women pretending to be less,
Opened their heart, closed their mind,
And they got, less.

Yes, you are beautiful.
In truth, you glow,
But your mind defines fine
In a whole new way.
The way that one day,
Many years hence, will
Draw me down,
Into your bed,
To kiss and touch,
The mind I love
And never regret the risks
That I took
To be there.

Blood and Traffic
Chuck Cooper

I ALMOST CLIPPED MY WINGS

The temptation to be,
Less than you are
Is a very real thing.
Just the other day,
I almost clipped my wings.

It's a fairy tale thing.
You wanted me wingless;
I thought we would fly away;
To a world where we could stay
Together, forever.

There is no such place,
No fairy land,
No time,
Not even once,
Where a woman or a man
Flies away,
Without wings.

When I was with you,
I never knew,
how to be,
Who I needed to be.
Because you needed me
To be wingless…
To be flightless…
To be vacuous…
It's true. It was you.
I was the sun
in the shadow of the moon,
And I was so close
To trading that shine,
As close as I could have been,
Even if it was a sin,
Trading my wings
For you.

The Complete Second Verse
Dr. Charles Cooper

I would have you know,
If I hadn't already known,
You wanted me wingless,
Flightless,
So much less than I could be,
That I would be wing free.

I would be:
Inside the narrow space
Of your home,
That you left for me to call my own.

I would be:
With you but alone
Weeping, silent, forsaken, home.
If you can call that a home.

If not for your own
      Selfish words,
Your hand on the door
      That you closed,
Your vindictive, silent repose,
Begging me to not fly,
I would have,
And that makes me cry...

To think,
I almost clipped my wings.

Blood and Traffic
Chuck Cooper

WE MADE IT THROUGH

Yesterday was so long ago.
Hard times, beans and rice.
We only had a dollar between us,
And it was stretched tight.

I could smile,
But I didn't much.
We fought more than not
Those days.
I would duck before I knew what you threw.

None of that seems to matter now.
We made it through.
We made it through.

The Complete Second Verse
Dr. Charles Cooper

I KNEW HER

Prevailing against charms
Is a skill set for a man.
It grows with age,
That measure of Victorian,
Controlled, cold distance
That asserts itself
When the time is right.

At 43, I slept in a bed
With a woman I loved
And held her close
For the comfort
Of the warmth and security
That I gave her.
My thoughts were not pure,
But my hands and my body
Obeyed.
Obedient,
In a way,
That a lesser me could not say.

In the morning I rose,
And I walked.
She rose and we talked.
In my most sincere voice
In the reverie of dawn,
I absorbed her loss.

I did love this lady.
Say what you will
About my being a man,

But...

Loving her,
Was wanting what was best
For her,

Blood and Traffic
Chuck Cooper

And,

Staying the passion
That would have made me a liar.

It was not a lie about love,
But a promise that the body makes,
The commitment that liberates
The soul to join with another
In exquisite anguish:
Rampant, writhing, sweat stained bliss
Breathing, panting, one more kiss.
There's a price we pay
Every time we live through this
And walk away.

The sun rose on our embrace.
She knew, as I did
That our joining was more complete
Than any passion play
Could have been.
We were joined
by an eternal bond,
Friends.

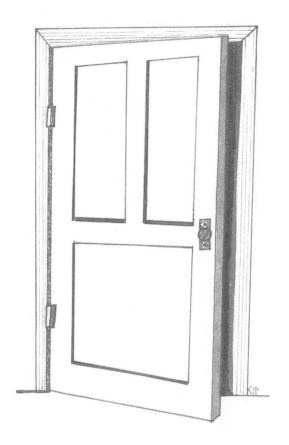

"THE OPEN DOOR"

ART BY BECKY KIPER

Blood and Traffic
Chuck Cooper

FOREVER FRIEND

I explained what that meant to me
Before we set sail on this adventure.
The price of admission
To play that song
Was long indeed.
It asked more of me
Than I had given
In many moons.

I told you then
Because there would come a day
When I was in no position to say
No.

You rode the boat to this shore
So you could explore,
Arrived at my home
Stood before my door
And price be damned
Like any forever friend,
You opened it.

The Complete Second Verse
Dr. Charles Cooper

EVOLUTION

All things recognize,
revolve around,
And connect to each other.
Nothing goes untouched.
Sometimes connections are severed, cut…
We use that word
Like it means what we think it means.
It doesn't.
Ties are never broken clean.

It is possible to be touched
So well,
persistently,
for so long,

As to not even feel it.

The past is building the chains of time,
The memories, wrapping tight
Around your neck and arms and legs and chest.
For safety sake, you surrender?
Did you know or see
The obedience of Apathy
The workless wonders,
Purveying fame
and nothing else.
No substance.
No grace.
No achievement.

They do not create,
Anything but chains,
Made of comfort and memory.
So gentle is the way
To not challenge, no challenge
No thought, no struggle
As you struggle,

Blood and Traffic
Chuck Cooper

Trying not to lose yourself
In the past
As they pass you by.

You give,
you gave,
You turn,
To go
From revolution
To evolution,
As time has passed,
Become better for the experience,
Happier for the memories
More complete for the connections made.
For those lost or gone,
Do not look long.
Say goodbye,
Evolve.

The Complete Second Verse
Dr. Charles Cooper

PILLAR OF SALT

Pillar of salt
I lost you,
Pillar of salt
You were gone
A moment before
Blue eyes left mind,
I knew you were gone,
Oh pillar of salt,
You were gone.

There's a memory we all harbor
Of a place we thought was better
Better days we tell ourselves
Better days and better times...
Looking back, no.
Please don't go
Memories are illusions of
Better days and better times...
Further on up the road
We find, better days and better times...
At a place you cannot go
If you are not growing old.

I lost you in a moment
In a flash and a smile
You can never look back
At the place where you've been
You can never go back,
Never again.

Yesterday cannot be redeemed
Tomorrow never ends
You can never go back,
Never, never again.
A pillar of salt
Is all that remains
Of living in memories

Blood and Traffic
Chuck Cooper

Which will never change.

Pillar of salt...
I lost you,
Pillar of salt...
You were gone
Lost in a memory,
Yesterdays...
Your eyes left mind,
And you were gone,
Oh pillar of salt,
You were gone.
You can never go back
To where you once belonged.

The Complete Second Verse
Dr. Charles Cooper

TURNING POINT

The gift you are given in this life, is existence.

Everything else is a trade.

Ask yourself, what is your value to creation if you do not give all you have, on a path that tests the limits of you? A chance to craft creation itself comes once in a lifetime. It is your lifetime. Don't let it go to waste.

Redemption comes too late if you wait for fate.

What trade do you have left to make after you've given yourself away?

There is only one chance,
only one gift in play,
You only have one life.

Take your life, and make it great. Don't leave it to fate.

Find a point and make it your turning point. Create something that will make the creator take note. Can you imagine the creator proud of you?

I can.

Blood and Traffic
Chuck Cooper

ENDING

I am a creator of things.
There is greatness in some of what I made.
All the pen and ink and designs.
On the battlefield, all the blood I left behind.
All the hammer and nails and bolts and screws,
Building a life, and choosing you, I did.

There are those, today, who owe me their lives,
Because of what I did, or what I built,
With my hands or by sacrifice
It was my mind of all the gifts I was given,
Which would lay the rest aside.

There were moments where,
I would never be forgiven,
For the choices I made.
With my passion to create
I could not sate
Even a tiny sliver.
In the end, it did not matter,
As I watched her drift away.
Lilly white skin
Pursed rose lips
Sharp pointed chin
Glints of gold
Flecks of red
The darkest coal coat that adorned her head.

The eyes, gave me a choice,
"The water that flowed between us
Like a river, full and wide
It can only sustain trust for a very short time,
There is more to be had, to be certain
But a man must earn his home, every day."

It was taken from me, taken away.

The Complete Second Verse
Dr. Charles Cooper

"In the end these men are fools,
See them cry for but a drop of water
From their servant's pitcher?
See them beg?
Waiting and thirsty,
Left alone,
What did you know?
Redemption is no thing for a fool,
Accursed rules,
Take a step on faith,
These lines weren't drawn for you.
Come close, you may have a taste.
Ask yourself, are you worthy,
Or will those gifts go to waste?

"LOST"

Art by Antoine Geiger

Book 6: Mobile Phone Poems

ET AMBULAVIT IN
CIBUM DOMUI EIUS
ET COMEDI. ET
STABIT IN LOCO
SUBTILES VIAS AD
VALOREM NON
CREDITIS MIHI. ET
OFFER EA OMNIA
SIBI SOMNIA ET
CONVERSA
RETRORSUM
JERUSALEM. NON
SOMNIS EI ILLA
VOLT, SED
OBLUCTARI
PROVOCATIONE.
NEC ALIAM VITAM.

STORAGE CAPACITY

3 days is not enough time.
Fail safes or salvation,
Neither is kind.
A rock rolled away
Rock and roll was here to...

What I want from you
Is code for the gifts
I have to give,
And you were confused
But composed
In spite of this.

The riddled wood,
And hobbled kiss,
Input rate
Combined love and hate
To reach too high
And pass the fall
Into winter's lie.

It's cold outside,
But there is no repose.
No holy man,
Can dispose
Of so much,
In so little time.
This heart has a capacity limit
So you will not be mine.
Sadly, there is no space
Left in my life.
Right?
X marks the spot.

The Complete Second Verse
Dr. Charles Cooper

ROAMING CHARGES

Phones are growing larger.
Plans are being simplified.
Bills will be sent monthly
Via email, paid electronically
For a single fee, a lot...
Plus tax...
And fees...
Roaming charges...
are the provider's path to apologizing
for poor coverage.

People talk all the time
I remember planning conversations,
Imagining what would be said.
If I said this,
The other soul would say that
And round and round it would go.
Now, all the conversations are had...
Anywhere, anytime...
But in some spots, there is a fine,
A "roaming charge."
"A conversation with your wife and lover
Should never take place in the same bathroom stall
At the same time."
This is a very Italian form of phone etiquette.

I'm old school, however,
I hang up after the first flush
No matter who it is.
I have no desire to hear people
Defecate, urinate... or flush it all away.
This is also why I don't watch politics anymore.

MOBILITY AND JUDGMENT, GENDER FREE

It takes a lady to bite the Apple.
It takes a man to configure the galaxy.
I really shouldn't have to explain this, But I will…
The Apple, the iPhone of Eden.
The GUI hides everything we see.
The code behind the machinations,
All the testing, the brutality of GUI, gooey, sticky…
Is all filtered away by such precise control
And pretty packing.
Behold the flat white Pandora's box
Like temptation itself,
Like the Apple in Eden,
Once tasted, there's no way back.

Samsung S8, S9… S infinity…
Google is a really big number
But not so big when compared
with the egos of its creators.
Perhaps, this explains the complexity of android.
A user… can set… literally, every…
Variable in this system…
Before it can be used.

iPhones were made
for ladies who like things, which work.
S-infinity was made for men,
Who want power and control.

In this post-modern internet age,
Every account you own,
Can have its own gender,
Who are you today?

The Complete Second Verse
Dr. Charles Cooper

NUMBER PORTABILITY

The miracle of the modern age
Was created at a company
Called Neustar.
Contrary to their name,
Their product has nothing to do with Space.

Neustar allows cell phone users
To keep their number
When they change providers.
The providers make it
As painful as possible...
Over the past 30 years,
The early termination fee
Has gone from $99
To $150... To $300... To $375...
No damages required.
Consider it the price
You pay to play.

So Neustar lets people
Quite easily keep their identity
Even if they can't commit.
And the providers
Make it as hard as they can
They cheat and steal and play network games
To get one more person, percent of the market.
That people stay is always surprising
The eerie feeling of being robbed
Month in and month out
Tends to drive a partner away
No matter what business they're in.
Party Lines

Have you ever talked on a party line?
When I was young, we shared a phone line
With fourteen or fifteen other families

The Mobile Phone Poems
Charles Cooper, PhD

On the stretch of road where we lived.

Middlesex was funny that way.
If you were on a party line,
You could pick up the phone
And listen to other people's
Conversations.
The right to privacy, or even the illusion thereof,
Was not really a thing in the 1980s.
You can't imagine the things I heard…
Too young to hear or know.

People will say anything,
When they think no one's listening.
It was funny, or it's a joke, or bless your heart
Often is used to explain away, what we really mean.

People are so honest
When they think no one's listening.
Slowly, ever so slowly,
party lines became private lines
And private lines became cell phones
And the ACLU embraced the idea:
What is said out loud belongs only to whom it was sent.
Officially, I resent the idea, after all, I'm used to listening,
To everything.

BUTT DIAL

The infamous butt dial...
For which I have this advice,
Never say anything aloud,
That you wouldn't say to the world.
Brief passionate whispers,
Careless whispers...
Mean so much,
When the wrong person hears.
Ever get engaged twice in one night?
Butt dial the ex and you can...
Ever call your pastor from the club?
I only ask for a friend...

The Mobile Phone Poems
Charles Cooper, PhD

FEELINGS

In this post modern digital age
Of Text-lish messages
and BRB
and WTF
and LMAO
and LMFAO
and lol
and emoticons…
AND A COMPLETE ABSENSE OF CAPITAL LETTERS…

How does anyone find themselves
Unable to express their feelings?

Ask yourself,
When was the last time
You laughed and typed lol
At the same time?

You think you've been augmented
By Devices,
But you've really been denied
Feelings.
No one ever shed a tear
Over an emoticon that cried.

The Complete Second Verse
Dr. Charles Cooper

BEATITUDES OF SOCIAL MEDIA

I, there, speaking with an Angel
Who was lost to me,
Given to understand,
That neither of us was free.
She gave me her tongue
And asked me relay
A message of truth,
To all who obey.

"Obey."

That was it.
A short message
But in this modern age,
Who has time for more
Than poetry.

Being me, I decided to expand
A little...
And offer a twist
To Angel's words...

A mechanical monkey
banging brass
Silly monkey
Shows his...
Over and over
Pound click pound...
My eardrums
Painful, swollen,
Stop this sound!

Pounding, resounding...
On message, off message,
No message at all,
Who can recall why
We fight.

The Mobile Phone Poems
Charles Cooper, PhD

The future is a fickle thing,
It comes and goes,
Stays and wanes,
But knowing what I know,
And I know a lot,
I have no earthly clue
How to do
What must be done
To help.

Helpless,
hopeless,
homeless…
Who are stuck in a cycle of numbers
And ideas, without goal or intention.
Are we so blind?

Love,
love,
love

Giving it all away…
Is waste and pain,
Every day more nothing is done
In vain, in the name of waste.
Vanity, oh, sweet, empty sage
Filled with life
Without love,
Which is a horror.

Love,
Love,
Love…

What is, is, patient and strong,
What was, was and is long gone.
The now is over just a heartbeat ago.
Forgive and forget,

The Complete Second Verse
Dr. Charles Cooper

But never let go,
Give us something to hold onto.

Love,
      Love,
            Love…

I have the love of a million souls,
"Friends" on the internet,
Men who come and go,
Women who want to know
And be known,
But, I am only going through the motions,
And everything is wasted
On that day like any other,
On friend and foe alike
Who could have been a brother
If I had listened
And he had listened,
And we had not judged.

Judgment great defense against love.
How safe it is to judge
Who hides behind a number or two
To save the pain of loving you?
Every soul,
Every man,
And woman alike
Is worth more than your
Petty gripe.
Rue the day you let some divide…
Let someone take a potential friend from your life.

Love,
      Love,
            Love,
Will never draw back
from a moment
Of understanding.

The Mobile Phone Poems
Charles Cooper, PhD

Open yourself up for Love.
Remember what it is to be a man among men
A hundred and ten percent
And then some?
What is love,
Which does not take up a burden for a friend?
What is love,
Which does not bear it all again and again?
What is love,
If it does not hold, comfort, and heal,
everywhere that it can,
        For every man, woman, and child,
For just a moment, or so many miles,
That you can never come home
Because you know
What it means to love.

The Complete Second Verse
Dr. Charles Cooper

NOT CAPABLE

Most people
Are incapable of restraint.
Remember the vacation slide show?
A Hollywood joke,
Because who wants to know,
What a great time you had
On the Beach
In Hawaii.
No one but you.

When you tell people they have the right,
It's a lie
Because God didn't give people
The ability
To keep anything private.
Just walk into a men's locker room,
In any high school,
Given, half of the tales are lies,
The eerily, accurate description of some girl's thighs
Explains everything.
People want to be liked,
And so, the stories flow.
They want to be respected
And so, the tales grow.
Like myths and legends,
There is a basis in truth.
Remember all the things you learned
In a locker room?

Enter the modern digital age,
Add Facebook to a phone
And Instagram to go.
Billions connect to trillions of posts
Think of all the people who somehow own
Part of your life.
Do you own it?

The Mobile Phone Poems
Charles Cooper, PhD

Have you ever?
How do you keep the special tales
For just one person,
Something shared
That's special?

How do you tell the person you love
What that means, when the announcement
Was broadcast to the world?

How do we collectively make life personal again?

How do we fight the need to share?

The Complete Second Verse
Dr. Charles Cooper

CAN YOU HEAR ME NOW

On August 20, 2017, 15,000 Anti-Fascist Protestors gathered in
Boston to protest Free Speech.

There are
so
many
problems
with that line…

Tools,
upon tools,
upon tools,

For communication,

Fools,
upon fools,
upon fools,

Resignation.

We try to be kind,
But give a fool a tool
And a voice,
And they'll say what's on their mind.

I know a twit that tweets regularly.
The quantity of people
who follow
every word,
Blows my mind.
I wish I could say
whose answer was right
As if anyone could know the solution
To someone else's fight?
You have to laugh,
As those who should know better,

The Mobile Phone Poems
Charles Cooper, PhD

Tell us all how right their way is

For... every... single... soul...

On a planet that holds
Nearly eight billion people.

Belief is a fine thing
For the individual,
When they hold their own feet to the fire.
But what of others...

What if...
The real experiment
In the United States
was not Democracy,
It was self-government.
Save by consent,
as long as no other incurs damage,
no one can make anyone
Do, think, or say... anything.
Nor can they stop them
From the same...

Welcome to the new world.

The Complete Second Verse
Dr. Charles Cooper

TEXT MESSAGE

A soft beep, slight vibration,
A shudder, and the end is over.
Your eyes never once, since that time, met mine,
I was yours and you were mine.
Until you stopped texting back,
So I texted you …*goodbye*.

Leaving should be hard.
Harder than it is.
Regrets and desires
Are married in an evening spent,
Such things should never end in text.
What kind of world,
Would allow me to say bye to you
Without looking in your eyes,
If there were no tears to cry.

She smiles, checks the phone.
He speaks, checks the phone.
She shifts, uncomfortably in her seat,
Checks the phone.

There are two bars and no data,
No touch or click can change that…
"Let's talk," she said.
He turned toward her.
And for the first time
In a long time,
He saw her…
She's one pretty lady.

BOOK 7: WASHINGTON D.C. POEMS

"Organizations are only as moral as their least moral member."
– My Dad

أفضل صديق لم يكن هناك. رجل رأى الحقيقة لما كان عليه. إذا كانت الحياة هي الإنجاز ، فقد عاش حقًا.

RAY HYDE

1949 – 2017

The Washington D.C. Poems are dedicated to Ray Hyde, a man to whose character and stature, I aspire.

He was born to the sea and has returned to her.

THE ODE OF RAY

Ray was strong,
A man of metal,
A steel man from the iron age of America.
He braced himself against
The silent waves of rejection…
To do more.

A man's man, there was nothing he had,
Which he had not earned…
Three times over.
In one of his tales, he would regale his friends
With stories of loves lost
And the fortunes which went with them.

His third wife,
He described one time,
As the triumph of hope over experience.
For twenty plus years they loved each other
Held each other in the throes of life
And the pain of the lost child.

With Margaret,
Ray went from Sailor to Farmer.
He worked just as hard
As a man who never knew anything else…
Farming was his second job.

He understood the world
Like a data processing wizard
From Silicon Valley,
Went home at night,
Rose each day
And worked the in-between:
Maintaining an estate,
Running a farm,
And building space craft…

The Washington, D.C. Poems
Charles Cooper, PhD

In every world that Ray lived.
He did his best
To provide
The horsepower and intellectual leadership
To those who earned his attention.

In every world that Ray lived,
Those who knew him respected
His thoughts but more so,
His investment
In achieving the goals
We all shared.

I knew Ray a short time,
But how can a person
not gain your respect
When his only thought
After his part was done,
Was: what else can I do?
How do you not love a person
Who shares your goals
And drive and works
Harder than any man
Before or since?

I miss you Ray.
I still want to know,
Is there one more thing I can do?
What else can I do, Ray?
What else can I do?

The Complete Second Verse
Dr. Charles Cooper

EQUALITY

At about 1200 feet per second,
The weak use
Chemistry,
Metallurgy,
And physics
To achieve
Equality
With the strong.

The consequence of attack
Even at range
Is pain
And sometimes death.

Never before
Has the phrase
Self defense
Meant a damn thing.

Never before
Has the word
Equality
Not meant dependence
On the strong.

With a spark
And a bang,
Strength became
Meaningless,
While will, and thought, and speed
Were magnified beyond words.

The Washington, D.C. Poems
Charles Cooper, PhD

BLUNT WORDS

Let us speak frankly now:

Blunt words,
Razor sharp whips slashed over
Mouth and hands,
Tongue and breath.
Which of these do not belong?
Like a question on a standardized test.
Recompense for work
Which was never done,
Equivalent to
That which was done
At a time of little
Is little or nothing.
Never worth as much
As the worker thought
In the grand scheme of the world
There's always someone more screwed than you.

Blunt words,
Razor sharp breaths
Cast and quipped
Argued and imbued with hate
Fate not withstanding
The beating should have been more than enough
The lies and tears
The whys and fears
Never defrosted the priss
From the lisp.

Blunt words,
Razor sharp,
Tragedies start
Blood seeps down the exam table.
Then we realize,
Some lives matter sometimes
And sometimes, all but forgotten,

426

The Complete Second Verse
Dr. Charles Cooper

Depending largely on who pulled the trigger,
Or vacuumed away the brain, as it were,
Lives pass away from this earth
And no one bothers to ask why
No one cares.

ROCKET SCIENTIST

I am a rocket scientist, well was…
I don't play games with gravity anymore.
Gravity plays games with me.
Age is like that…
As it goes up,
Everything else goes down.

There are people who build themselves
On top of others.
And they rise.
When the wind is right
And the pedestal willing.
As they rise,
The pedestal descends.
As they grow,
The pedestal shrinks.
Weight is nothing,
If it's not heavy.
Holding up a world of risers
Is hard work.

Games with lift, air currents, and momentum
Are all good and well,
Unless you are the launching platform
And the propulsion,
And the fuel
And the engine
And the wings
And the pedestal for fools
Who think they are entitled to such things.

The Complete Second Verse
Dr. Charles Cooper

FALLING FORWARD

Life is one direction,
And I have lived it,
Falling forward like I'm morbid…
No regrets, No goodbyes.

I have lived in one direction
To watch the river run
Always downstream when I wake up
Every day like it's made up.

Every day,
a quest before me
Falling forward,
ritual bores me.
Every day
Still I'm climbing
Start again
at the finished line…
at the starting line.

I know what it means
To make a hill a mountain
Climb to stand
beside the fountain.

I know what it means
To circle back.
Regret the things
I can't have back.

I'm old enough
to know better.
Falling forward
never got any better.
I could sit on the sofa
and dawn a sweater
But I won't go down that way.

The Washington, D.C. Poems
Charles Cooper, PhD

I know regret.
I've said goodbye.
I've told the truth.
I'm not that guy.
The starting line
is a day behind.
I have arrived.
I think, I'll stay.

Forward motion
and bright tomorrows.
Compound life,
with all its sorrows
I can't let go,
today or tomorrow,
But I can climb.

I can fly,
I will try
To stay.

STEALING LOVE

It may be heresy to believe
The great state could learn anything
From God, or me, or anyone who's not everyone:
Leave the people with the means to live.
Leave the people with the means to love.
Leave them enough to give.
They want to, in spite of your cynical view,
And all the extra baggage you taught them
To carry.

As they rise through rays of sun
With open eyes,
Higher than you dreamed was possible.
You are so surprised they still rise?
As though you know the capabilities of a man
Or what one single soul has passed through
To stand on the level with you,
The tyrant of life.

You hold the gun and claim the right
To take the same from others,
Depriving men of choice:
The choice to give
Is the choice to love.

Giving is an act of love.
Taking is an act of war.
No matter how much you had,
You always wanted more.
Stealing life, stealing love,
You think you know what's right.
There are just too many answers
To call your truth a *"right"*?

OPEN DOOR

Promises?
A man opened a door for you.
Walking through is not hope.
Walking through is not a lie
No matter what you're wearing.
Walking through is not a promise.
Walking through is not consent.
Consent for what,
I don't know…
It's just a door.
Walk through or don't.
Anything else is another discussion.

HAND THAT FEEDS

Hunger and desperation
Breeds fools, and felons.
Fallacious farce that feeds the masses.
Everyone working for no aim or end.
What we want and gain in trade,
Mutual exchange,
Is what makes us more.

SPREADSHEET SOCIALISM

We use numbers to steal.
We add, subtract, multiply, and divide
Without consequence
Inside a bubble of safety.

We run the numbers,
Compare the outcomes,
And stack the values against each other,
In a lecherous chart called Pareto,
Where axes join to enforce the 80/20 rule.

That is 80 percent see some return
And 20 percent are forgotten.
We search for answers,
That justify ends,
Without permission or representation
Stealing… For the common good.

We live in a small world
Where everything is built
On the backs of men,
On their time, and their effort, and ideas.

We sell math,
At a very steep price, when time is money, money is life.
We steal Life to accomplish what some number
Declared was right.

Math gave us the answer,
But that doesn't make it right.

9-21-9

CONSULTANT YEARS

I'm driven to know
To understand.
The passion is ravenous
To find a problem and solve it.
And I have done my fair share
Of solving and knowing
And walking away.

How many years have I spent
Playing that game,
Heart racing,
Mind flashing on truth
Problem solved,
Forever, for all time,
Until the next administration.

Heart-rending apathy is made of such days
They call it consulting:
All the passion you can muster,
But you dare not care
Because sooner or later,
The new boss
Wipes your work away.

3 Keys in the City of Dreams

The Complete Second Verse
Dr. Charles Cooper

COMING TO TERMS

Coming to terms with what you are, not who, takes time...

People living in the 1960s went searching... for who they were.
They called it finding themselves, and for the most part, they were
unimpressed when they did.

People living in the 1970s, mostly the same people, went searching
for nothing... through drugs, and sex, and cheap thrills. It cost them
a lot, but for the most part, they lived on. Some broke. Some stayed
behind on a foreign field to decay and someday die in the hearts and
minds of their country.

People in the 1980s, mostly the same people went searching for
money. This life of plenty did NOT give them what they wanted, so
they painted portraits of new gods, gave birth to thinking machines,
played at controlling each other's lives, and offering sacrifices to...
themselves.

People in the 1990s, mostly the same people, complained about the
younger generation. They ran fast, and hard, headlong into a series
of beaten, competing moralities. They cast off the church, cast off
God, and sought to replace belief in the divine with belief in
themselves. They sought to replace and redefine, the innate divinity
of the human being with a legal system run by the majority, for the
majority of... less than perfect, definitely not divine, human beings.

People in the 2000s some of the same people, some of the new
people, and some of the silent majority, rode the wave of bubbles...

Economic and champagne driven lust, corduroy and cordovan
miserly miscreants, school days and pocket protected plays on
Broadway, which was cleaned up bright, shiny, and new with no
evidence of ink or *permanence*, drank from the 24-hour news cycle,
played at power and pleasure and plenty, and became more corrupt
than anyone dreamed was possible in the age of over-production.

The Washington, D.C. Poems
Charles Cooper, PhD

People in the 10s re-opened old wounds, drank starch and ate liver, spied on a world of open secrets, and hid their humanity from each other. Behind lines of pulsing electrons and crystal, words drew blood. Bullets passed silently in the night killing those camouflaged by gang life and the darkness within each of our souls. As soon as we uttered the words, "The law only applies sometimes, the entire system quivered and broke. We stood and kneeled, and prayed, and laid with each other, for each other, in media driven, maltargeted hate. Is it too late for tomorrow, today?

It is 2018, and no one hates by preference. No one holds anger in their head or heart by will alone. None marinates in revenge like slaves who are freed and made slaves again by marketing images. Giving in to the emotional wasteland left by surrendering all that we've learned for convenience. Is it any wonder we wait to be told what to feel by people whose only interest is control?

If God created people and gave us free will… if God was all powerful and trusted people enough to decide. If the church, ever controlling cabal of men bent on control, kept *that* in when they wrote and re-wrote their holy writ…

WHY?

Why would we offer ourselves anything less? Why would we trade an ounce of life, *Individual Liberty,* for a single instant of relief from the burdens of life?

Is it so hard, we would trade something so valuable?

Is it so easy to bow down, to take a knee?

Raise a fist! People have been given a last chance to stand. *Stand up!* People have been given a free pass by Nature itself. There are no predators left, save ourselves and death, and we will die for sure.

Why not live today? Live and let live, there is only one way to be sure we have given everything we had coming, received, everything we deserve… Why would any of us, the breath of God inside, waste

The Complete Second Verse
Dr. Charles Cooper

a moment of time on anything less than creation, anything less than life.

Why?

On the other side of the millennium, do the Flower children of peace and free love want to return to their youth? Re-open the old wounds as if to heal them again, with salt and lemon juice, in the absence of God and Sin... who do we blame for such things?

Those childhood days of marching and fighting, and gassing, and bombing, and fighting for something right still seem so real... Don't they? Re-living the riots of the past injecting vehemence into words, hoping to feel relevant once again. You would destroy the world to give it meaning.

Harmony with humanity, sometimes means coming to terms with your own ideals un-desire-ability.

Democracy is sooner or later, the accumulation of stupid.

A POLITICAL GAME OF IDENTITY

58 years or so ago,
Legal equality was a thing,
The pain and hate still moves people
So politicians
Use it, fan it, coddle it...
Because moving people
Is the path to power.

The divisions given to people
By politicos
Remind us every October
Who to hate,
And why we have our fate
Because nothing in life is fair
And we send the same keepers
Of the same system
Over and over
Year after year
Answering to the same campaign.

Is it any wonder why
Politicians live in fear
Of tolerance and love?
Is it any wonder why
They live in fear
Of the man judged
By his character
Or the woman
Not judged
By her sisters?

Whom could they dominate
If we weren't busy fighting each other.

The Complete Second Verse
Dr. Charles Cooper

WAGGING THE DOG

Rattling cages,
Playing with wages
The flow of energy
Blends with the push
To grow and grow and grow.

The general impulse of people
Is to seek control...
To centralize control,
Which never works.
It always ends with the one
Or the few
Killing those
Who disagree
With some truth.

The Washington, D.C. Poems
Charles Cooper, PhD

WE'RE ALL HUMAN...

I weep for my state.
I weep for my country.
I weep for the dead and the soon to be dying
Who believed themselves to be invincible,
Realizing too late they are human after all

I weep for the corrupt
  and the money corrupting.
I weep for the chains
  and the lies people buy which bind.
Oh it's not your fault, you were taught to believe
So you did.
It was on TV after all.

I weep for the slaves
  and the potential lost
    For the public cries
      For dependencies cost
In chains, in slaves, in life and living..

I weep and weep and weep
And I wonder, if one lemming survives to tell the rest
Of the beach bathed in blood
Of the starving, mangled mess
That lay on the shore below the cliffs,
Would the next generation run anyway?
Would they edit the textbook
Change history to say
Something more comforting
And hopeful about yesterday?
And then run to the inevitable...
Finding equality at last,
We're all human
And there's only one way out.

The Complete Second Verse
Dr. Charles Cooper

WELCOME TO CLOUD CITY

I told the truth,
Which to some is a crime.
I studied Egypt.
I didn't tow the line.
And disagreement
With DC types
Is a greater failure
Than any lie could ever be.

"Tow the line.
You'll do fine.
You can be redeemed
If you don't run afoul
Of me."

For my failure, the truth,
I was directed to the basement
Where punishment loomed.
In the basement
There are files,
Possibly, probably bodies buried
In them, on them…
Definitely by them.
A stack of projects
So deep
One may never see the light of day again.
A project given not to Jane,
But to me.
The line between us so slim,
There was nowhere to run
When she began
To craft that shifty revenge.

How do you get
people
In power
To surrender,

The Washington, D.C. Poems
Charles Cooper, PhD

The source of that power,
For the greater good.

Simple, right?

Handed the impossible,
It's what Jane does.
It is what I was given.
A healthy dose of humility,
In the basement
Of building six.
I spent six months driving
From here to there
And there to here…
And there and there…
And here and back again.

In the end,
It wasn't me
Or the greater good
Who saved the day.

It was a Jewish stoner
Who practiced catholic mass
three days a week,
And on the high holidays
Who said, "dude,
"Put it in the cloud."
"Push, don't pull."
"Accept, don't demand."
"Let them let go
Instead of taking
What they know."
And I got it. I understood.
And we built it.
And it was good.
And they never saw it coming.

WISHFUL THINKING

An Irish Dirge for the Victims of Gun Control

Dirige, Domine, Deus meus, in conspectu tuo viam meam

I wish I was God,
And I could give you the world anew
An Eden, a garden, a neighbor
Whose motives didn't need to be questioned.

I wish I could give you a world,
Where love was all we needed,
And weapons of war,
Were things not known.

But forbidden fruit and original sin are a thing
And no one can afford to be that naïve.

In this world, when help is minutes away,
In the seconds you have left,
You defend yourself
Or you die.

I wish the world was full of better people,
But it isn't.

PEOPLE'S HYMN

It's not chance that makes life true.
It's choice and values.
They can only come from you.
The world contrives the chains, but you wear them.
The lock has no name, but you click it in place.
You were born without shame
Every soul given its own key
And the choice to decide to die or to be free.

Freely giving is an act of love.
Force is the act
That destroys choice.
I always wanted more.
You never accepted this.
Stealing life is stealing love
And it leaves us all with less.

Don't make an excuse.
There isn't one.
No one owns a person.
There is no magical percentage rate
Of life you can take
That doesn't make it stealing
To take from a person, *without consent,*
Their time, their thoughts,
Their hands, their breath.

Taking life from some soul,
Taking time better spent,
On the values of the one who earned it.
Who can afford to let a heartbeat go
For anything less than life itself,
And that is a decision we make for ourselves.

The Complete Second Verse
Dr. Charles Cooper

YESTERDAY'S NEWS

The trades people make
For roles and a seat
At a table
Where are made
The decisions,
Which flay fate,
Cost.

If you want the part,
You have to pay to play.
Sacrifice is part of that game.
What does a whisper in the ear cost?
Access is a game unto itself.

ORNAMENTS

Ornamental gallery of disgust,
Times love by hate and hope.
Trashing rationality,
Emotionally moved,
Driven by fear and hope.

Love is a multiplier,
Unless he's a manipulator.
Then love is just control.
Break the chains of love with thought.
Bind you to me with rationality.
Supercede hate to become great,
To multiply you by me
For greatness,
Taste the echoes of history
In the making.

Do not confine reason.
Let it rule,
Or be a fool
Driven by fear and hope and love
To one more mistake
Baste it in hate.
This one you cannot take back.

Regret and guilt confine you.
Bravery and courage,
Define a step toward freedom,
But you are scared to be that alone.

People are ornaments
        In the halls of emotion. Find them there, and rule.

EVOLUTION OF MURDER

Cain murdered Abel.
Time passed.
No one blamed the rock
Or the fist
Or the hammer
Or the tree
Or the upbringing.
He was marked,
Cast out
Destined to walk the earth forever.

A doctor
Inserted a vacuum
Into the brain of a baby,
At the behest
Of the mother,
He turned it on.
God was silent.
No one spoke up.
Rights.

TYRANTS WALK AMONG US

Mao Tse Tung
Now Say Tongue
The tyranny of the polite
The dismissive genius,
So sure he's right.
The kind soul
So young, and yet
So old.
No sorrow
No tyranny
Just expectations
And entitled behavior.
What is the value
Of something that costs nothing.
Kindness is not surrender
Suicide by guilt, is.

Whatever,
None of this matters.
Mask in hand
Marching to a better land
To burn it all.
Who's life matters
when all we do is set fire
To another and another
And Another, One Another?

The Complete Second Verse
Dr. Charles Cooper

CONTROL

Long ago, distance and logistics
Overrode,
people's desire for control
They were forced
To let go.

For the first time in forever,
The world worked.
The Sun rose and set and rose again
There's always another day,
another time,
another test
  For the Best.

And man gave us Democracy
And it was ok.
Fools vote,
And curse and demean and divide, and corrupt…
All in the name of Control.
And what did they know?
But they learned,
the divided can be mounted
The mounted can carry
Many a traveler
Many a mile
And knowing nothing else,
Will seek nothing else.
So the story is spun,
And repeated, and told
And repeated, and sold
Until no one knows any different.

EDUCATION

What is education,
But a laundry list
of fairy tales
Ideologies
and principles
Until there is belief.
The tale beget belief.
Belief beget the sale.
The sale beget control.
The slave will never know
Anything different.

No force needed.
No compulsion required.
No power apart from belief
Can render a man blind
And impotent
Or make him a God
In his own right.

It's a bold soul that hands a man a knife
And unarmed, asks him to die
For his own good.
It's that particular lie
I despise…
It's killing me.

LEE BRIDGE SUICIDE

Traffic here sucks,
I think every day
On my way
To work.

Three bridges and a ferry
Unite the north and south
A boat, bricks, and cement
Pavement, rubber on roads
And drivers who lament
The time lost
They could have spent
With family.

NON-STANDARD TESTING

There is no one like you,
DNA and experience say so.

What makes anyone
Think...
That any of us, should think,
Act, Know, or feel
The exact
Same
Way.
A
B
C
Or D

Is as much perception as anything.

The Washington, D.C. Poems
Charles Cooper, PhD

A CITY OF TIMING

The spot just north of H street
Where the road divides
Between the haves and the have nots
Sits the smallest park in the city.
His park, a monument to his life,
Separates well-funded lobbyists,
From HUD homes and food stamps.
People here know what it is to live in fear,
Sometimes the road is just too long to walk
The mountain, too high to climb.
Countless investments in transit
Have yet to help
The drugs
The gangs
The murders…

Some people get out,
But it's a few generations
Of walking the line
Before any of these people
Can find a way to climb
Anywhere.

Just on the other side of the street,
Bathed in PR and wicked, whipping,
Sublime while less skilled ladies,
The purveyors of influence
Practice their wares.

Never having owned a Tupperware lid,
they agreed to represent them.
After all the lids and bowls made enough cash
to buy a vote.

WHAT IS MONEY

Money can buy a boat.
This means to transit, as old as the ocean,
Still calls to those who can afford
To move that slow.
Artists play at motion
Like poets play at truth
And music captures everything
Which can be felt.
I am mute.

For a car, a house, a boat, a child
Money.
In this age, I wonder at the value of anything
I wonder at myself,
How many years
Have I spent trying to make a home,
At the expense of the truth, of the poem.
"How many more years
before poems will fund the least
of life?"

The Washington, D.C. Poems
Charles Cooper, PhD

ECONOMICS

Fair isn't a thing in the world.
Scarcity isn't real.
The sun never set,
Some queen said.
And then she pulled back,
Pulled out,
Leaving behind the residual
Burn of prosperity,
Capitalism, competition,
Rule of law, Commerce,
Oh, sweet commerce
And the prosperity that comes with it.
If you wanted to rule the world
Why would you want to run it?
Think first of the cost
Proportioned in time and blood
For you and yours;
Feelings aside, ruling is a very long ride.
Playing economic games of
Sales and cycles
Money that prints
And is given away,
People that wait in lines
To have a new toy
Which will be widely available in a few days.

If you want to rule the world,
You have missed the point.
Would you rather live without fear?
Who needs to rule?
Economics is the long parade
Offer people prosperity,
If they would give
Just a little more.
The queen learned this.

If you truly knew what it was to rule,

The Complete Second Verse
Dr. Charles Cooper

You would see
That each person is a tool
To your end.
To their own end to be sure,
but to your end as well.

The point of all this wealth
Is life, self-actualized.
Prosperity
For all...
But more for those who lead.
Destruction is the enemy of
Life,
More so of prosperity.

The only reason men pursue peace
Is because it costs them less
In dollars and cents.
If for a moment, they thought they could make more...
If for a moment, they thought they could build, create...
For the cost of a life.
What else is worth a life?

HATE

Today someone brightly pointed out
That evolution was causing hate to disappear.
I was shocked and confused.
There is nothing more natural than hate,
I said.
It's as real as happiness or fate, I said.
The poor lady, left stunned, said,
"What do you mean?
Don't you hate, hate?"

Of course, I do.
Like any sane human.
I hate the stupid.
I hate the irrational.
I hate what I don't understand.
I hate what I don't know
That I don't know.

And today, what I hate the most is simple…

How any aspect of nature could lead to a place
Where a person could hate, hate…
Without hating themselves.

MARRIAGE

Sometime in the past fifty years,
Marriage went from
Take your name…
To hyphenate…
To I'll keep my name.
The divorce rate
Went from something no one talked about
To 20% of all marriages
To 30%
To 50%
To more.

It makes me wonder,
What Neustar would do
To innovate
In romance.
Maybe add a fee
Keep your name,
Pick a name…
Random name assignment?

What would people do…
If marriage had less to do with property
And more to do with love.
What if there was a love detection kit
That let you see your partner in the hospital.
Even partner is a word
About property.
Contracts,
Law and government…
Are about power,
Absolutes
With no divining ability
No ability to value.
Processes, systems, they function.
They don't feel.
Black and white and no grey

The Washington, D.C. Poems
Charles Cooper, PhD

It's how they work.

People play at meaning,
Play with words…
Words like rights,
Sanctity, God, commitment…
Then they
take your name,
hyphenate
or keep their fathers' and / or mothers'
Family name.
Is that Marriage?
Is Marriage commitment, love, property?
Are the Married property or Partners?
Simply an excuse to have sex
with the same person
For the rest of… Til death or…
Until paperwork is completed
Filed and stamped…

And you name and rename
The tall tales we tell each other
About the women and / or men
Who are the sad reminders
that another person is something,
someone,
we need.

The Complete Second Verse
Dr. Charles Cooper

MIRACLES

The rank and file remember little.
History is replete
With blinding blends
Of genders and sins
Which occur over and over again.

Men want more...
Women want less...
But more intensely.

The invisible hand
Gave us Skirts and Chastity Belts,
So people could be
innocent a while longer...
Staving off the animal baggage
Left over from birth.

We struggle to deny nature.
An inclination to keep ourselves
From harm...
from the *unnatural* practice
Of *unnatural* charms.
Skirts and chastity belts
Are more ancient than the Olympic games...
Still the end is the same,
a present play,
a Greek comedy,
People damn the invisible hand
For roles and marketing...
Innocence betrayed life
It was greed that embraced nature
Is it any wonder who won?

THE UPGRADE

Pasty, white, sun baked rib…
"I am," said the burning bush.
Flaming red hair,
Kissed by fire
Untouched by brush or razor.
Painted in sharper tones,
Eve, the ginger heart
Of Adams woven chains
Pronounced release and set humanity free,
And that was the upgrade.

Long, submissive, and silent;
"I am," said man,
Who knew not what he did,
But he did it anyway.
The crafty creation
Buried his savior,
before salvation could begin,
And that is the upgrade.

The Complete Second Verse
Dr. Charles Cooper

AMERICAN DREAM

Innocence lies dormant, not dead,
There is hope in "Dormant."
She is secluded and laid to sleep
By her own hand.
Her hero, in a heap,
Found his calling,
But failed to arrive in time
To vanquish the fire of lies
The elixir of truth lies
Inside a safe, combination long lost.
Now, the Futile armor,
Scattered on the floor
Bears no resemblance
To the man who once wore
Freedom, liberty, and honor
As a calling card.

The feudal system disposed of,
The pike, the knife, the sword,
Left no knights to wield a weapon,
And no champion upon the field.
The marketers come calling
With catch phrases but no ideals.
Proclaiming shadows
Blaming the light
For what never happened.
It isn't right,
But it achieves a singular goal.

Flexible minds will find
A way to believe anything,
A way to surrender anything,
To the shadows,
Even in the absence of light.

What if no one comes calling?
The darkest days lay so distant now,

The Washington, D.C. Poems
Charles Cooper, PhD

No one remembers them at all.
With innocence asleep,
Naivety was never relieved
Of its position
Dueling life at her feet,
And this is how we learn.
Naivety and innocence
Walking hand in hand,
Making trades with life,
Playing games with fate.
Learning from failures and success…

Which brings us to today:
One lies dormant,
The other has been banished into silence.
Which is which matters little.
They don't teach history in school any more
They mold minds, grow mold on minds,
Melt wills, drive stakes, castrate males,
Whatever it takes,
For the land that never was.

That fellow sitting atop innocence,
Containing parental protection,
What does he want?
What is he here to capture?
"There are no innocents anymore.
Each one has made the trade.
Do we shed tears as we walk into
This darker place?
Is there a chance to walk away?
Is there liberty left?
Does Freedom call?
For what did we trade honor…
This thing which rests on her chest?

What is it we have done,
Which we offer as homage to our children?

The Complete Second Verse
Dr. Charles Cooper

FOUNDATION'S VOICE

Sad silence,
So much violence.
Foundation's voice,
Which came to us,
And gave us choice,
And diversity.

In every combination,
People are miracles.
Combining a soul
With a creature
To craft creation
Is a step only an insane deity would take...
A choice only raving creator could make...

Be bold, create creators!

And the Architect was...
Miracles happen every day now.

The day God gave Adam breath
was not the last day of creation,
It was the first.

COMPLIANCE

Who do I want to be?
A child's question,
In a game of growth...
Not what part will I play,
Which is a different question
And a different game.

People make systems,
And rules, and norms,
And draw lines,
very fine lines,
Around what a person can be
And succeed
On the inside.

Like math,
We unite thoughts,
With standards,
norms,
and forms.
We craft process
With steps,
Decisions
and revisions.

And then we force
people into a mold...
To play a game.

Will you be able to answer a question
Or alter a scenario?
Is the question story
Or a revision?
When you answer
What is... where do you draw the line?
When you combine two things,

The Complete Second Verse
Dr. Charles Cooper

What is...
The lowest common denominator?
You use
to press,
compress,
combine,
to find...
A moment of completion
in a piece of life,
which is Divine.

How much
Or how little
Will you comply
To get the part you want
Does a piece of play define
what you are, or who?
Will you let the part,
the place, the system
Define you?

Or will you ask yourself
Who Am I
Then be true to the answer.

MESSIAH COMPLEX

Dead, no two ways about it.
Passed on…
Passed over…
Not left behind…
Not rolled away…

Funny thing is,
I feel fine.
A deep breath of air,
And an extra quart of blood
Fuels a small messiah complex,
And the guilt,
Which comes from
Having survived *death*,
Time and time again.

I am bold, old.
I've sold my soul
A thousand times
On million mountain sides
No man had yet climbed.
The mountain defines men
In so many ways,
Steep and tall,
Slip and fall
To rise and do it again.
How many times can I explain,
I am who I am.
And I like it this way.
Some celebrate their birth,
I celebrate resurrection day.

There are no seasons in my heart,
No revelations in my dreams
No ten headed master
Of the world beneath my feet.

The Complete Second Verse
Dr. Charles Cooper

Life is forward motion,
More often than not.
Mastering movement,
Curtailing emotion,
I will feel later.

For now,
It is enough
To be
Moving:

Always forward
Always up,
Ever rising,
Until the sun
In full eclipse,
Nowhere to run,
Retreats beneath the stare,
Looks back in fear
And wonder at a God
Who, in all her grandeur
Spoke the words,
    "Let there be more."

And I was.

WITCHES, WITCHES EVERYWHERE

Witches.
Witches, everywhere!
but none to eat!
If I commune with Nature,
Would you commune with me?
Dance naked by a fire,
Perhaps you'd participate?
Until dancing in my fire,
You only knew desire.

There was once a colony
Founded by people
So religious,
Great Britain
Bought them a boat
And gave them the boot.

Pretty, petty misanthropes,
Miscreants, missives home,
Begging why we can't all just get along.
Eating berries and dirt,
Blending herbs, healing hurts.
Finding medicines not made of prayer,
Congregations who read your book
And left it there.

Witches, Witches, everywhere
And not a duck to be found
To weigh you down,
I know, let's see
If she will drown...
If she floats,
We'll burn her.

VISION QUEST

Herbal cocktails of Washington and Jefferson,
And Adams, and Tyler
Prepares me
For my first meeting
With a President.

"Not my President,"
As the resistance would say,
But he was, and is,
Even today,
Even though it's another man.

Funny how it doesn't so much matter,
I wanted to do good,
To be more,
To be the best I could…
He let me and did not care.

Then like now,
I inhale deeply,
Breath in the silence
That surrounds
The restaurant I'm in…
An hour later,
Less than impressed,
I walked away
From everything
I thought I loved.

A trip home,
A return to Poor Farm Park,
In the shadow of oak and maple,
Where I knew happiness for so brief a time
I found there, what I needed to understand:
There's a difference between belonging
And being needed.
There is a difference between

The Washington, D.C. Poems
Charles Cooper, PhD

Romantic notions,
Tales of fairies,
Rivulets of want,
Desire, a pretty face,
And a stalwart heart
A stony consciousness,
Playing a part and being

~ Exactly ~

Where you need to be,
Who you need to be,
What you are
In your heart and soul
Whether you, like me
Are a warrior poet
Bathed in blood
Or a forgotten friend
Who has never known
How often you recur
in the thoughts of your friends.

How can I explain,
That in those moments,
Those last moments…
When I am sure
My next thought will be my last,
I always turn to you.
For whatever reason,
Those thoughts,
carry me through.

"THE SCALES OF JUSTICE"

ART BY BECKY KIPER

JUSTICE

Justice is the cold, heartless father of us all.
Where justice is perfect, harmony prevails
But we get what we deserve,
we live to succeed, or fail.

Justice is a pendulum,
swinging to and fro
When you hold too tight,
And finally let go,
The reward you receive,
Is a cataclysmic blow.

Our will to rule is a fool's desire,
To make peace among all men.
Like fools and liars who seek control.
The denial of belief is to surrender the soul.
What lark, what pithy blend of will and melancholy…
Is there nothing more human.

Nature will be swayed for a time.
Vengeance can be stayed for a time.
Cataclysm is the end of manmade peace.
People think. People are.
People will be in spite of all that comes,
Just as the moon will set and is chased by the sun

So have peace, if you will, for a time,
Apollo knows that though your eyes close
The sun will rise again and shine.
Ares says that blades and bows
And swords bring justice, the end of all men.
But the God who gave us mercy and justice

"METRO"

ART BY BECKY KIPER

TRAINS

I took the train.
It makes me a liar.
I hate trains.
But I boarded one today.
Sticky floors, padded seats,
Made in Europe, not large enough for me.

A few, stale heartbeats,
The car's gentle sway,
And I felt sick.
Eyes on the sun you say.
You rail against me
In the light of day.
But as night falls,
You cling to me so tight.
In the absence of the sun,
Is it the merriment you value,
Or is it that I didn't run.

What do you need?
I only ask because...
I need you.

BOOK 8: ARTISTIC ENDEAVOURS

"JOY"

ART BY BECKY KIPER

12-24-33

Жизнь - это Достижение, и вы обязаны тем, что должны сущности, более могущественной, чем вы.

LANA IN BLOOM

ART BY LANA RODAVICH

Artistic Endeavours
Charles Cooper, PhD

FALLING FLOWERS

Floating, flying water lilies
Like thunder,
The delicate sound
Of the growth of beauty,
The flower rises in silence.
Beauty always rises.

Gravity is the beast
Pulling everything down.
Harrowed circumstance
Battered bullied sound
Of scraping concrete
And burning metal
Beauty rises
Silently, without a sound.
Water lilies,
Inward folds of yellow and white,
Float and fly so beauty can rise
These delicate floating flowers
Will become more, always more,
Because beauty will always rise,
And we, we will rise upon it.

We fight the gravity together
With brush and paint, pen and ink.
Making art and poetry.
Fight the gravity together
With sights and color,
Pages and words.
Hail the canvas
Hail the artist
Hail beauty
Hail the masters of music
Sing you words, sing your sounds,
Your song to the heavens
Choose your instrument
And rise,

The Complete Second Verse
Dr. Charles Cooper

Watch it rise,
Watch us fly,
Beauty will always fly.

For all that we've lost
Tears given; life's cost.
For everything we feel
Those cuts that are so deep
We think they cannot heal:
Broken heart, sullen soul,
The mind that keeps it real...
Until we let it go.
Until mouth, hand, eye, and ear
Without hesitation or fear
Rises up to create beauty.
Every voice, every instrument
Aligned in time
To find:
Peace and healing,
To rise on the wings of beauty
To fly. Beauty, fly.

KNOWLEDGE

Sold your soul for knowledge…
I know.
I was there,
You wanted to know everything,
Like a solitary monk in despair.
You were given much.
Not nearly enough
to know
that you don't know,
what you don't know,
And that, is sad.

MICHELANGELO'S PLAY DATE

In an age, which holds creation
Above the created,
People tread a perilous line.
The created are cunning,
But cunning is a
Violation of the trades
We make with the creator
So that we would not be slaves.
What Michelangelo did to get paid,
Is not forgiven by what he did for the money.

Your life,
A brief moment
Whiskey and women…
It's the rape of Botticelli's walls,
For which you will never be forgiven.

The Complete Second Verse
Dr. Charles Cooper

FRIVOLITY

I do play.
It may not seem that way.
I may not seem that way
To those who wake with agendas.

I am, occasionally,
so overcome with desire
that I live deliberately.

I never tire of this.
I never wait for air or ground
underfoot.
I jump and there in the space
between the known and unknown
I create my world,
and it recreates me.

RISING

Match my rhythm.
In time,
Sublime
Vibrations
Mean so much more,
Than petty pieces
Of life laden virtue.
Smug that rises
Destroys, pollutes
Life.

Artistic Endeavours
Charles Cooper, PhD

NOTHING FEELS...

Nothing feels like an open door,
When you step into the light,
Sing with all your might.
Standing there at the threshold
Staring into your eyes
Nothing feels, no nothing feels as good,
As you.

Nothing feels like a gate
Where none should be
Something that confines
The truth and the seed.
We need to grow,
Need to grow,
Or we'll never know,
Never know.

Nothing feels like the same four walls
Until I hear that voice and it soars,
Here a voice soars,
Like a Nova, Heather Nova
Like a star in the night
Taking flight, Making life.
Nothing feels, no nothing feels as good
As you.

The Complete Second Verse
Dr. Charles Cooper

70 TIMES 7, SUBMISSIONS

76 ways to bury yourself before death…
A poem penned by publishers…
About control,
What you see,
And what you know.
You put yourself out there
Because you feel it,
This part of you is worthy,
Worth it,
People will be better for having seen it.

In a satirical, rigged melle' of monstrous proportions
You submit.
You create and relate, your world
For some Satan
who offered you a deal…
"Sell your soul…
And I will reply
If you include,
A self-addressed, stamped envelope."

By the fortieth submission
Even I called it SASE.
There's a reason *they* call it submission.
You put ink to paper.
You cast your own form,
Blazing, blue-red imagination
Which you sought for so long
And wrote it down.
Carefully following every rule,
Formatted to perfection,
Copied and pasted,
Authors last name on the first page only
Subsequent pages may be found discarded
In an alley

Artistic Endeavours
Charles Cooper, PhD

Contained and marked,
"Burn Barrel: Your self-worth..."
I became the submissive.

Oh, they evaluated,
They scrutinized.
They stuffed your envelope,
And returned a sliver of a piece of paper.
One inch by 8.5 wide, "Sorry,"
Their canonical, repetitive domination began.
"Your denounced soul,
So kind of you to send, submit, drop a dime, our way
We understand you bore your soul...
To paint pages with profit on my ledger...
After careful consideration,
Your soul is not good enough,
Recognizable enough,
Righteous enough,
Relevant enough,
Minority enough,
Well known, enough...
ENOUGH... to matter.

After 76 repetitions of this cycle of surrender,
Chastisement, abasement,
Humiliations galore.
I walked away.
I'm not made for that kind of punishment.
Oh, I didn't stop,
Did not surrender,
I stood up and did the work myself
Because who is better suited.

The Complete Second Verse
Dr. Charles Cooper

BUILDING

Some men have a history of building,
Monuments to women,
Pedestals on which they can stand,
In honor of the life they lived,
And I am one.

If you had known the women that I have
You would have done the same.

Monuments and pedestals are very different things.
Both are built by people
Who have flaws,
For people who have flaws.

A younger man cannot build a monument.
History is required,
And experience.
Though sometimes a child can see,
He cannot know,
Cannot compose,
The words,
Or hear the music that I give to you.
There is nothing to fear.
You don't get a monument
From a day or a week or a year,
But rather, a lifetime of life.
Periods of trial.
A penniless pauper or
A sated sage, I am not.
But I have loved,
And I have loved at first sight.
I have never gotten it right
You understand.
I am a man, after all.

Artistic Endeavours
Charles Cooper, PhD

I only say this so you know,
What I build, when I compose,
This monument to you,
You should,
Not fear heights,
Not fear wings,
Not fear flight,
Or victory,
Or passion,
Or pain,

Even though,
From heights such as these,
Sometimes we fall.
It's worth it to me
To see you so tall.
The foundation is laid
Being built day by day

Pedestals are a scary thing,
I know.

Expectations is a nasty word,
I know.

But I didn't build this monument,
You did.

The Complete Second Verse
Dr. Charles Cooper

"VENUS IN RETROGRADE"

ART BY CHARLES COOPER

Artistic Endeavours
Charles Cooper, PhD

NO FORGIVENESS ON VENUS

In 2020, NASA reported a glimpse,
Of life,
On Venus,
A pattern only known to exist
in the organic.

On Venus, Life prefers metrics
465 degrees Celsius
Seems so much less
Than 900 degrees Fahrenheit.
It's atmosphere weighs 98 times
That of Earth.
Is it any wonder
That life on Venus
Feels so much pressure?

On Earth, perhaps,
Life just lacks perspective.

CRESCENDO

What kind of fool am I?
Playing games with words, women and guys.
I used to sit,
Bide my time,
Fantasize.
What a price to pay.
What a game; what a game;
What kind of fool
To even play.

Dramatic depths and crashing waves
Weeping crescendo
Musician's lie,
Playing emotions
With words,
I watch the rise.
I dream, and dream
I live to fly.
What kind of fool
What kind of fool am I.

Artistic Endeavours
Charles Cooper, PhD

VAN GOGH'S BABIES

My performance
Was live,
Not like the dream
Of studio magic,
Or photoshop lies.
My memory, more
Or less shadows,
Could not be dignified,
So I painted these pages
In colorful goodbyes.

The scenery drowned
In blue, black, terrified clouds.
No words could capture the agonizing sound
Of life being wasted.

Oh, we are all ok,
But shouldn't we be more?
Shouldn't we be happy?

"ZEN"

ART BY BECKY KIPER

PAINTING ZEN

I never felt the happiness of the moment.
Dig a hole. Fill it up.
The expression that graced my face,
Just a disguise I wore.
Symbology is never lost on me.
Letting go was not a skill I possessed,
Much less forgiveness.
Disguise in place,
Glock in hand,
I will keep my secret,
Until I have my revenge.

Artistic Endeavours
Charles Cooper, PhD

AN ABUNDANT LIFE

If the ends would meet,
One good time…
Or a few times in a row
Maybe.
If I could control,
The comings and goings of cash.
If I, myself, was not so rash.

If I owned a thing
I wouldn't feel the sting
Of age,
Quite so badly.
I put one foot
In front of
The other.
I wake up, every morning
To try.
In spite of myself,
I ask the mirror,
Why?

Do you ever think
You got more than you should?
The reward which awaits,
Might never be as good
As a few more days
Where I can strive,
And laugh, live, and thrive.

Do you ever think,
I am glad I didn't die?
I think, this is what it means,
To live an abundant life.

The Complete Second Verse
Dr. Charles Cooper

FRIENDS

Who do you cherish
During the nights
In hotel rooms?
The bed is cold.
The bar is hot.
The drinks that flow,
More real than not,
Offer meaning to feelings
Which are not real.

Friends are the people
Who drive you home,
Put you to bed,
Tuck you in,
Hold your hair,
As you kneel at the throne
And declare,
"I will never
Go there
Or do that
Again."

Artistic Endeavours
Charles Cooper, PhD

MUSE

Van Gogh became famous
Sometime before he cut off his ear.
He delivered it to a prostitute,
Who saved his life,
As he lay in bed bleeding to death.
Thus goes the story of one tortured soul,
A man who's muse,
A gentleman named Gauguin
Refused to see him
After the mutilation.

One day, between writing
And working,
And being a father,
I met,
Just the right woman,
At just the right time.
At the end of so many things,
When the heart and mind are open,
The bleeding has stopped,
And the artist is engaged
In the act of creation.

It can truly be said that this woman
Freely came to my side,
And smiled as she inspired,
Simple, easy,
Without effort or lies.

These were the feelings that spawned
This craftsman of words
To rise and write.

Tears of Joy!
Shouts of Joy!
Feints of ecstasy,
Flayed open to the world,

The Complete Second Verse
Dr. Charles Cooper

Exposed more than any man should be
Crying out sound
And words,
Unlike any I had heard.
Reverie, Compassion, Passion,
And I just wrote it all down.

Slipping ecstasy inside
Growing, every moment
Dams that held back floods
Trembling, pushing,
A tiny hole emerged in the dam.
A stasis built over years;
Kept behind walls for fear
Of release.

The Muse, whose gravity
Seized and pulled me into her orbit,
Back and forth,
The pulling Moon.
The Moon,
that cast a shadow
On the Sun,
The pushing Moon.

For a moment?
A minute?
Never for long.

Until a tiny drip turned the tide.
Until I had cause,
that is.

To be more than I was.
To live,
Not in the moment,
But in the hour,
In the day,
In the year,

Artistic Endeavours
Charles Cooper, PhD

And years to come,
To face what lies ahead
Cresting mountaintops of love.

When that dam breaks
To release the flood,
The Muse cannot rest
Lest the water recede,
To reveal the blood we bleed
When the joy will not come,
And the words
Are stagnant
And the ink
Leaves nothing but a stain.

Please, don't let that happen!
I exhort none to action
Against their will,
But I am not above begging...
Please.

If you and I can discover,
What words are worth.
If you and I can discover,
A means to that rush of joy.
If you and I can discover,
A way to surrender
Control for long enough
To realize, exultant, ecstatic
Passion,
In a quantity
Which would relieve me
Of the chains that weigh me down...
If and when,
Then I could be yours.

And you, my muse, can be mine.

REMEDY

There is no remedy for me.
I am bold, old.
My soul has been sold a thousand times,
Collection on death,
Still, I am alive.

There is no medicine for my infection.
For me, life is a race.
Catch me if you can.
Your spritely reverence
For this old man
Serves no one,
And me even less.

There is no slumber
That contains my mind
No waking hour where I don't dream
The world is a flood of dreams,
I drown in daily
and become
A blurry eyed, master of creation.
Unity with fantasy,
I will not wait
for reverie.
I will not search
For cures.
I know my disease
        Quite intimately.
There is no cure for me.
You can search and test and try,
But there is no remedy.

Artistic Endeavours
Charles Cooper, PhD

DAUGHTER

It's not the Pearl Jam song
I've heard twice today.
It's the young lady sitting at home,
Which is an angry creator's punishment

For my youth.

SON

God's way of reminding me
She's not actually mad...

But I could have done better.

PASSION PLAY

The Mattaponi River
Runs 103 Miles
Through the Virginia countryside.
Perfectly blending the native
And the settled.
People craft creation
To serve themselves.
Roads, buildings, houses, and fences
Can make heaven hell.
Sometimes the mother,
Creation, rebels.
But here on the river bank,
Beside this settled land
Harmony prevails.

Farms grace the banks
Growing the food of fathers.
Pulling forth the riches
And wonder of life from the ground
To feed the masses.

Fish race the river water
Chasing the light
Downstream,
East to the ocean
Where all life began.

April brings the heavy rain.
Clean water feeds Spring's desire
And fuels life's growth again.
Ripples on the water
Caresses like lace,
Marks each place
Where gravity blends,
Water to the flesh of earth,
A silky, lithe, living drum beat
Pounding out

Artistic Endeavours
Charles Cooper, PhD

A mother's desire
To touch
and feel
To grow
in grace
To finally bloom.

Embrace
Harmony,
Strive
to be alive,
To live
And fulfill
The potential
Of creation.

The Complete Second Verse
Dr. Charles Cooper

SAY WHEN

Start, say when…
Pick a pace that's right, In the dark of the night
It feels like a race, but more like a fight,

Thick, brackish water, I'm a slow starter,
Slow like hope, at the end of a rope.
Playing hangman's noose, Like a war with a truce,
We have to start, say when.

Heard a gunshot ring, such a passionate thing
Wear a uniform, but add some bling,
Find some hope in suffering,
Now start, say when.

Run the miracle mile
With a wink and a smile,
Add temptation. God what a nation.
Dance like a has been
High on life;
Love like a madman but make her your wife.
Then start, say when.

Oh, you'll never know,
Because you don't want to see
There's no way back for you or me
To start and Say when.

Run naked on the lawn,
Like a deer and a fawn,
So young, blurry eyes
Hope is no disguise
For a mouth full of lies.
Til you start and Say when.

It's like a race, but more like a fight,
Slow like hope, playing rope a dope.
There's no way for you to not live in fear.

Artistic Endeavours
Charles Cooper, PhD

Stale bread, second dates, why did you wait.

Hope won't disguise a mouthful of lies.
Run this race, pick your own pace.
Play the music loud, stop to dance.
Wait for a day and the sun to rise,
Live your life, never run when you can fly.
There is no fear in action.
There is no way to not gain traction,
When you put, one foot in front of the other.
When you accept a man as your friend and your brother.

Then you stop, look around,
All you've done, every sound
Every word, every inch of ground,
The trails you've tread,
The lives you've led.
The people, the places, the books, and ideas;
The steeples, the races, everything that was real.
Remember this, look and see, this is what beauty
Looks like.
This is what life can be.
If you start, say when…
Start, say when…
Start, say when…

The Complete Second Verse
Dr. Charles Cooper

HUMMINGBIRDS AND CALIGULA'S MIGRAINE

Bumping, thumping, pounding pulse
10,000 beats... I've lost
Serenity. A million layers
Under the floor
Of my lair,
My mind...
Where lightning strikes
Making me blind
While castrated mimes
Do what they were sent here for.
"You like that don't you."
"I'll have another."
So silent and cross.
So vacant and lost.
What I need is so much more than you know.

Heartbeat accelerates
Take flight and fight
The wind, the air, the sun, beams of light
Like an array of daggers in my eyes.
I'm blind, but still, I harness the feast of Apollo
I can never surrender to sorrow.
I bath in wine and women and song
To stave off the wrong feeling
Spiraling, reeling
Wheeling and dealing.
My beak is so long,
My wallet so deep,
Relatively speaking.

No sorrow tomorrow, but this hurts so bad.
That blinding light
Terrifying, righteous, and right
Pulse pounding sound
Left vacant on the ground
Turn and again.

Time and again.

Place the patient in the recovery position
And pray…
He does not survive,
As he does the same.
"God, *the pain!*"

"SUGAR JUNKIE"

ART BY BECKY KIPER

The Complete Second Verse
Dr. Charles Cooper

A SENSE OF SIMPLE

My lady can sense the simple on so many levels.
With passions, motives, agendas and organizations.
Plans within plans, within plans,
A game where no one wins, but "we're all okay,"
And laughing men take the field,
without knowing the game they play.

Everyone dances for my lady.
This great ballet of belief,
Marionettes plagued by strings
On a slick, spinning, vinyl record.
Too fast fair puppet,
Slow down before you drown.
Skip nothing, scratch nothing,
without fear of my lady facing you down,
Her nose so near, she can smell your fear,
but never close enough for her
Unless her glare meets the stare of an equal.
Tape a penny to the needle to weigh it down.
It is certain, there are clues left to find,
But there's still a chance I'll get out of here alive.
On days like today, a man has to try.

BURNING HEART OF GOD

We mechanics of earth,
Hearts beating,
blood thrusting…
Align,
confine,
pay and stay,
sacrifice
For creation sake.

In the swampy heart of the creator
We, the creators,
who dance inside
The burning heart of God…
There is so much life,
From life, death
From death decay,
so much decay.

There is a price to pay
In ghosts and love and hate
So that we can create.
We sold our souls.
No one noticed or cared.
The pain and destruction
They cannot or would not
Take away
The apathy and malaise,
All part of the price we pay.

What man resents the light?
Still he will raise a banner to fight
Against creation…
For the sake of control.

What soul desires the fight?
I have seen it begin,
again and again.

The Complete Second Verse
Dr. Charles Cooper

and end,
and end,
and end…

In tears.

The beauty of creation
Never fades with age.
Symmetry is replaced
With scars.

Scars,
Beauty in its purest form,
Is the artwork which adorns,
the burning heart of God.

A MAN'S EMOTION

I want to know what I feel and why.
No matter how loud I scream
Or how fast I walk,
It always slips in
Unbidden
And wrecks my perfect, positive
Outlook on life.
Why?
I said, WHY?

Reprehensible, wreckless, wandering eye...
You can see the universe,
But you do not know why.
Does anyone know why we cry?
These feckless feelings
Are trashing my life.
And all I want to understand
Is why I cry?

Can't I impose my will
On the grief,
The tear, the rampant fear...
It's only anger or frustration
Which brings me to tears.
What happened this time?

I will master these emotions if it kills me.
I will...
Not...
Be...
Part...
Of another lie.

The Complete Second Verse
Dr. Charles Cooper

UNREQUITED

She liked me,
Even loved me,
But not like that.
Unrequited circumstance
Wasted love, a wasted dance
That left me feeling empty, bereft.
I was so young then,
I knew I would never love again.
Until I did.
And I did.

This wanton, wasted, whirling feeling...
These wicked, wary, curving spears...
They drive us down.
They keep us from caring
Because experience rules
The inner world.
The mistakes of the young
Can never be unmade...
Chances lost, such a waste.

BOOK 9: THE OLD SOUTH

"GATEWAY TO FREEDOM"

ART BY TAMMERA COOPER

*Chan eil duine ann am fiachan dhut.
Faodaidh tu a bhith nad bheatha le
bhith a 'gabhail no a' cosnadh.*

CUT AWAY

When you cut away everything,
All the superfluities of life.
Very little matters:
Some art,
Not politics,
But the words, the poetry, and you...
The words I leave behind
The eloquent, the fine
It's what I am made of...
You are what I was made for...

Tripping righteous residents
Cutting away lies
To the bone where we find,
There is no truth only people...
What we say to get by
Is what makes this home.
I don't know what that means,
But You and I are bound together,
A bond of flight not roots.

This fight for paradise and post card dreams
Is so much less than what I've seen...
No Roman Coliseum,
Or Lion's Den...
This is how I rise
Without compromise.
No fiery furnace or mortal sin.
This is how I rise
Without embracing lies.
Touch the sun, torch the miles
Over burning coals every day.
I'm further away,
But it brings me closer to you.
This is the thing that drives
Everything I do.

The Complete Second Verse
Dr. Charles Cooper

"THE LIGHT WHICH GUIDES"

ART BY TAMMERA COOPER

513

BURDEN OF TRUTH

The road's too long.
The mountain's too high.
The hill is so steep,
And people will say anything…
Wearing disguise
after disguise
after disguise.
I cannot compete.
This isn't my game.
The only way to win this time
Is to walk away.

I measure all it will cost.
Today, I retreat, broken.
My heart in failure slows
And stops.
I am finished.
It is finished.

The Complete Second Verse
Dr. Charles Cooper

BORN AT THE CROSSROADS

I want a rock and roll fairy tale.
I'm ready to pay those dues.
I want a rock and roll fairy tale.
Let's lay down some folk and blues.

I went down to the crossroads,
In my beat up Cadillac.
I tried to catch a ride
Cause it would not take me back.
The devil himself was there.
Strat in hand, Jimi too.
He offered it to me,
If I'd learn to play the blues.

He took that thing and made it sing,
A haunted tune, laced with stars.
He sung a few notes,
Looked at me,
Then he promised I'd go far.
He said, he was buying.
But he didn't want my car.
If my soul was for sale
I could meet ole Robert Johnson,
When I finally got to Hell.
He handed me the guitar
Lord that thing could sing
He taught me a tune or two
Cast a spell and we were through.

From Jackson Mississippi,
To Mobile on the coast
I'm packing in the crowds
At all the dives that pay the most
Take a ride on my tour bus baby,
I'll play until the night is through.
Fall in love in every city
Cause there's nothing else to do.

The Old South
Dr. C. Bradford Cooper, PhD

I want a Rock and Roll Fairy tale.
At the Crossroads,
Friday tonight.
Burning passion
With desire
Feels so good
It's always right.

I want a rock and roll fairy tale.
I'm ready to pay those dues.
I want a rock and roll fairy tale.
Let's lay down some folk and blues.

The Complete Second Verse
Dr. Charles Cooper

THE ADMIRAL

At Two-Five-One Government Street,
In Mobile, Alabama,
In my room,
three-two-seven
The remnants of the first Marti Gras,
Holds tonight's redemption,
Maybe even forgiveness
For tomorrow if I'm bold…
If I can choose to leave it alone.

Cats and Dogs sleeping together (Whisper);
CATS AND DOGS liaisons at 11 (Shout);
c-a-t-sss and dawgS, Just one more barkeep (Slur);
and allergies between you and me…
One more drink of sweet tea.
If there was an answer,
Cats and Dogs,
would give it to you,
But there is nothing there.

Free tea and coffee
And apologies
For a thousand years
Of paintings, which can't be understood.
Painted faces, stilted blues,
And a lot of people with nothing to lose…
Who free at last
Can't escape the past
Where midgets and little people
Lived together happily as one
Slathering lollipops and eating grits.

Life is a circus, if you let it be.
Too many people selling slavery for cheap.

There are answers,
But they are not here.

The Old South
DR. C. BRADFORD COOPER, PHD

Only a guidepost,
Which will be gone
In 3,622 days
Of malaise and humidity.

Never look back…
Craft a response in your life.
There is no past,
Only pages and painted memories…
Forgive yourself.
Please.

The Complete Second Verse
Dr. Charles Cooper

OLD LADY IN A MEMPHIS AIRPORT

Old, is one way to describe
The woman before me.
There is nothing left
For her to do
To defy
The lines of age.
No taunt skin is left
To fade away.
Gravity is a bitch
Who has had her day.

All of this is not what I see
A face is like a book.
If you look, you can see…
I saw her life was long.
Two husbands,
Three children,
And seven grandchildren
Grace her face.

The time her boy went to war,
The time her husband didn't come home,
The time her two daughters were late
Before marriage,
before college,
before they should have been
        Women at all,
Dug deep crevices
Which framed a smile.

Days and nights of laundry,
Cooking, dining, washing,
And laundry,
Cleaning, dusting, vacuuming
And laundry,
Teaching, learning, defending,
And laundry,

The Old South
Dr. C. Bradford Cooper, PhD

Arguing with teachers, principals and lawyers
On behalf of others,
And laundry,
Drew ridges of focus
On her forehead.

Her eyes were simply satisfied.
She knew all that she had done.
She knew all that she gave away,
She knew all the trades she had made,
What she had given to her men.
What she was and what she could have been.

She knew she had carried,
created,
crafted life,
and another
and another.

When she looked back now,
Her own makeup applied too heavy,
The mirror which wasn't as kind as it had been.
But that matters less when seen through the lens
Of everything she had made and done,
And she knew,
"It was Good."

What I saw,
Every stitch and cell,
Was just gorgeous.
Mirrors be damned.
How we live,
What we leave behind...
This is what makes a person
beautiful.

520

The Complete Second Verse
Dr. Charles Cooper

HUNTSVILLE

Today I stood on the Foot Prints
Of Alan Sheppard!
Remember him,
The man,
who walked…
On the moon.

In the late sixties,
While the country,
Was eating itself,
Over a ten-year war
In Vietnam;
Where black people could eat
And go to school;
And who could tell who
Who could vote.

I saw the building where Alabama
Codified their constitution.
The building is a *gift shop* now,
That most American of things.

Three ladies guarded the register,
clustered behind the counter,
To make mention of the *northern gentleman*
Who took such an interest in their history.

They were very nice in that very southern way,
You know the tone…
There were things left unsaid
Behind their words… and smile…

And the gripping, delightful,
"Bless your heart."

This was the scene,
Unfolding in a very real,

The Old South
Dr. C. Bradford Cooper, PhD

Very Southern, way:

Can you believe that man?
Walking around with $500 in his pocket.
Did you see his suit?
A Carpet Bagger if I ever saw one.
Bless his heart.
Bless his Heart.
Bless his heart!

For all the blessing going on,
No one noticed,
when I slipped out the back,
To sneak a picture,
of the fake Liberty Bell
With a fake crack in it.

The crack isn't irony.
It's there to remind me
And everyone,
That even a more perfect union
With equality and liberty for all,
Has fake ladies
Offering fake blessings
Every day to everyone,
Equating dishonesty with kindness
That makes everything alright.

Even a perfect system,
Practiced by imperfect people,
Is a little broken.

"THE ROAD HOME"

ART BY CHARLES COOPER

COUNTRYSIDE

Country living sucks
life and soul alike,
In a fight, every day.
You are, surrounded by too much beauty,
To appreciate.
In a battle, every day
  with nature.
We try not to surrender to hate.

Day in and out.
Only the strong survive here.
In cowboy boots and jeans,
They ride…
With sheer force of will,
And guns at the ready.
God's will be done…
In the country,
Life must suffice for poetry
Too much is needed
And the beauty supplied
By breathless innovators
Who are in bed by nine.

Between the Country

The Old South
Dr. C. Bradford Cooper, PhD

And the city,
There are vast tracks of people
Who settled
For a lukewarm in between…

Please don't settle.

The Complete Second Verse
Dr. Charles Cooper

MORNING

The sun rises in the west,
Peering over the pristine mountain
Standing in the distance.
Trees play at shadowing life
As this morning arrives,
And I rise with it.
In truth, I have fed
From the mind of a woman,
For the first time.

Never again, can I be without,
Apart from the angel of morning
Who greets me now.
Addition is a word that applies
But I am fed, and what do I care.
Addition may be the word to choose,
But in truth, I don't mind,
I live to satisfy her needs and her life,
Such a small thing to ask
In return for a glimpse of her mind.

HISTORY

History measures men,
It is a needle as much of now as then.
What we remember is as telling
As what we forget
And what we deny ever happened.

The books we burned,
The statues destroyed,
Say as much about us
As what we regret
And the tactics we employed
To make our world.

No man may own another.
None may command without consent.
Perform your task if you will,
It is you, you will resent.
Let your values be bold.
Hold fast to what you believe is true,
But remember no man belongs to another,
No one belongs to you.

The Complete Second Verse
Dr. Charles Cooper

EVERYTHING

The first time I saw you…
Hands clenching, wringing, wrought,
Renegade light show,
A strobe glow,
Like dawn at midnight.

The days leading to you
In unison, ripped and tore.
The routine of it all,
Burnished glass,
The sun would rise.
The day would pass
And there I was alone.

I don't know what I felt at all,
Accomplishing the mission of the day
I don't remember the blood or pain,
Until… You smiled,
The sun shone, and I was born again.

This time, I will take the time to love.
This time, I will open myself up.
This time, I will find the courage
to reveal that tender space.
I will stand at the alter,
See the look on your face
Where that same joy radiates…
There, I will lay me down,
lay me bare…
It's not that I don't care about this life.
It's more simple, everything is worth this.

LACE GOWN

If I were the sun, for a day,
I could stay in one place
Glory in the sound,
Touch, and feel of space.
Parsing the lace of the gown
Low cut, high rise,
Legs, on display,
Caress my eyes.
Is it any wonder, we've found
No vacuum
That didn't want to be filled.

I don't have to touch a single soul,
To know the pain in this heart, your heart.
I only wish you would let go,
Release that death grip
On the guardrails of life
And fly.

"A LADY'S GOWN"

ART BY BECKY KIPER

The Complete Second Verse
Dr. Charles Cooper

TOUCH

If I could touch everyone.
Grip and hold the burning sun.
Fire, the hot gift to man,
God gave and called it sin.

Craft and create; Feed and ameliorate
If I could make it all alright
Capture fear and hate in flight,
Stop these men from being men,
Trap the grief under the skin
Before it sunk down within
The swollen belly of lost men.

Maybe then,
I wouldn't feel
The rise and fall of empire,
The in and out of breath,
The striving reign of power's stain,
The vapid fail of Kurzmeil breathing,
All of the start and ceasing of life,
On my twisted eternal journey.

If I could touch everyone.
Reach out and touch the burning sun.
If I could lead a man to heal
With words like life and beauty,
Embrace the leaves,
Call forth the trees
Put down the gun
Never again run.
It might finally be enough
For me
To find peace.

SAFE

I kiss your neck,
The gentle pulse of electric wave
Proclaims a time to heal.
The jewel laced brace
Divides the light
Neatly into rapture and redemption.
It cannot save the fall,
And you are falling.

Tiny sparkles the resident afterglow.
Nothing guards the entry low.
The vulnerable lay down together.
The journey of joy light as a feather
Leaves me hoping, wanting, knowing…
You can be enough
In this patient, Virginia fall,
The leaves are late in turning,
The fireworks long since gone.
The cold holds us tight to one another.
It is your warmth that feels like home.

The Complete Second Verse
Dr. Charles Cooper

BOOK 10: MASONIC LORE

"REST WELL BROTHERS, HELP IS COMING."

Temple Church	51.513186° N, 0.110442° W
London, England	
Great Britain	
The World	

The Complete Second Verse
Dr. Charles Cooper

SPES MEA IN DEO EST

SCOTLAND

Penning sacred texts, on sacred tiles,
In sacred places, on sacred isles...
The Shetland Isles,
In Scotland, where,
I wrote home,
As if it were the last time,
Complexity is for the young
When finding oneself
Is a thing,
And mirrors are apparently not.

Then as now, I spend
Too much time,

looking into myself,

At myself

finding myself to be

Myself.

I do what I do.
I think what I think.
Like any madman with pen and ink,
I write it down
To see who will read...

And that is who I am.
Who are you?

57.3229° N, 4.4244° W

The Complete Second Verse
Dr. Charles Cooper

ROSSLYN CHAPEL

Rosslyn Chapel	55.8554° N, 3.1602° W
Roslin, Scotland	
Great Britain	
The World	

Masonic Lore
Brother Charles Cooper

MEEK

Mankind was born to create.

We simply solve the problems,
that get in our way.

We embrace every tool
That helps us navigate.
The Square and Compass
Light the way.

It's not fate,
It's the active pursuit
Of a more perfect world
That is ingrained in man.

Every square inch of planet Earth
Is sacrosanct,
hallowed ground:

A church,
The holy house,
The Synagogue;

The road,
That takes men home
At night;

The Lodge,
Where men can find light.

The hands that take wrong,
And make it right.

The farmer's field,
The reap,
the yield;

The Complete Second Verse
Dr. Charles Cooper

Grass and trees,
falling leaves;

The abundant handywork
Of the Great Architect
Of the Universe.

A long time ago,
There were men who built a road.

They covered it in concrete,
To take life,
And add speed,
And the freedom
That comes from mobility
And it was good.

Some two thousand years later,
A tiny blade of grass came
And cracked open that road,
To remind all involved,

That
There is a creator,
Greater
than ourselves…
Even me,
who sometimes needs to be reminded.

Men pursue the perfect.
They try
and cry
and fly again.

They fall
and fail
and rise again.

The holy writ

Masonic Lore
Brother Charles Cooper

that flowed once
from my pen
Will be forgotten and lost,
But it will come again
When I am reborn.
And grow to know
More than I ever did.

Until then,
I live to navigate,
In water,
and wind,
and space itself;

To live, to die,
to feel and cry
Communicate, relate,
To touch and love
And even to hate,
There.

Let the meek inherit the earth.

I want more.

The Complete Second Verse
Dr. Charles Cooper

SYNERGY

ART BY MARTIN HILL

Masonic Lore
Brother Charles Cooper

THIRD AGE

Mankind fell asleep,
Deep asleep.
Under the covers of convenience
And a stack of problems solved.

While he was sleeping,
Something possessed his soul.
It wasn't reason, or hope, or change,
It wasn't adventure,
Or exploration
Or striving
Or ambition.
It was a dream.

A misty, airy dream.
Man, the man, a Spanish Jesus,
Begging people to have a siesta.

Can you save your soul,
Spanish Jesus?
There's something in you
That's wanting freedom
But you're still afraid to earn it
After 10 AM.
Welcome to the third age of man.

Then you trade them your mind.
They offer theirs in kind.
Collaborating collectivists
Offering up their power,
and strength, and will,
To a beast they do not know
Have never seen,
But they trust.
They were the men
of the third age of man

The Complete Second Verse
Dr. Charles Cooper

Trade that spirit.
Part with your soul.
Unloose your mind:
Forget what you know.
Welcome to the third age of man.

Trade your spirit
Part with your soul
Welcome to the third age of man

Something forgotten
And something known
Spirit, Soul, Mind, and...
Welcome to the third age of man

Tonight is the night,
And the story was told.
In 1999, all the days are long.
Those eyes, that burn with fire,
Abandoned Anti-Christ,
Without his clothes, but draped in the blood
Of the those who know...
Camouflaged in the collective will of no one
Proceeding as if no one knew,
And out of his mouth came a sharp sword
That brought nations to their knees,
Not a single man surrendered,
But they embraced the apathy
For comfort and convenience
They accepted the ban
On life itself.
Welcome, to third age of man.

Masonic Lore
Brother Charles Cooper

GOD AND MAN

Man would rise and fall,
Five times before now.
They will rise and fall again.
Creation is in their nature,
Destruction is their sin.

Fighting over resources,
Betrayal, pain, murder, war, and women.
The same spark that gave Michelangelo to the universe
Will see his frescoes destroyed for more,
Always more.

I tell you, Mankind is a fickle bunch.
I tell you, the walls of St. Peter's
Have seen paint before.
Before Michelangelo was born...
As though Botticelli were not the master he was;
As if a perfect ceiling was not enough,
They painted it all again.

Such is the nature of sin:
Destruction;
Such is the nature of man:
Production;
In an endless cycle
That cannot see perfection for what it is;
The creator demands more.

Give me more.

The Complete Second Verse
Dr. Charles Cooper

CHAMBERS

Arch laden pathways
        built by calloused hands,
The hands of slaves
        laid the roads
That led to,
        from,
                and within the Wasteland.

There, slaves were harnessed
        for their road building skills.
The chains they wore
        were camouflaged,
From hearts,
        from compassion,
                from the best of things,
Flayed and framed,
        charred,
                twisted,
                        and shaped
By words
        sacrifice,
                hope,
                        change,
                                and fate...
Not consent,
        there was never consent.
And all that was good
Became the instruments of slavery,
All that was good became
the worst of things that day.

Taking life from one,
to give it to another
Is taking from every man.

This life is the only gift
Any of us are given without strings

Masonic Lore
Brother Charles Cooper

Until in haste and foolishness,
Or, at the point of a gun,
They were added.

Everyman, the wasteland,
Pasting parts from each other
to pave the floor
Of the cavern
          from which we came as animals…
To which,
          we may return,
If we accept the promises
          that make men weak
And perish on the altar of sacrifice
          Where lie the meek.

The life of the slave is made comfortable
By doing the master's work,
For room and board,
A little something to eat.
Consent is so little to pay,
And the little life
Which is sucked away.
A tiny torment,
Glossed over in hope
The rainbow hue of mother of pearl
Hides despair, surrender.
Hope itself has mastered so many.

In the chamber of hope
where so many journeys end.
Painted in the gray
Striped deep reds of sacrifice.
You can barely make out
the impressions left by lost life.
It is the chamber of almost.
Almost greatness,
Almost potential,
Almost humane,

The Complete Second Verse
Dr. Charles Cooper

Until finally,
>nothing remains.

Fear is the second chamber of life,
It consumes all things,
feeding on itself,
Darker and deeper than hope,
A sullen melancholy,
A pasty void,
No color or light to speak of,
Just dry, vapid rock
that crumbles beneath the touch
Just pasted, rock-like, paralyzed souls
Bound in a ball of forever
Bellowing, "I would, but…"
Or the bastard, cousin's cry,
"I could've, but…"
Fear is paved by the bodies of the slave,
And lit by those who trade,
Belief for surrender
Or peace.

There is much surrendering
Tears and sacrifice,
Bellowing fools, compassion,
Balancing cost and price,
Spreadsheets and numbers…
That matter not at all
If you give away your life
For a lie.

Reason,
the narrow strand
that held men
above the Wasteland.

Reason is the gateway to the world,
The doorway to wisdom and life.
Give me men,

Masonic Lore
Brother Charles Cooper

Rushing from the darkness to the painted path
toward the light,
to the light.

Not the hope,
see him rise,
Not the fear,
damning lies
It is through reason all men rise.

The flames the slavers set,
Burn ever higher.
Would men call on reason
to escape the pyre?
The slavers would watch creation burn
Rather than work a day in this life.

Arc hollow the light passing through the divine
A shadow falls on the wasteland;
Not a giant among men, but a giant man.
Holding himself erect for the first time
Reaching to the future, to the potential,
Each man holds in himself:
The ability to reason and rise
Above himself,
harnessing life in all its glory,
for the first time,
sublime.

Not a stone foundation for some almighty collective
To climb upon,
But a striver,
rising higher,
Discovering for himself,
Himself:
As creator,
As maker,
Wearing the moniker of explorer.

The Complete Second Verse
Dr. Charles Cooper

Who found himself
in the darkest night,
on the darkest hour,
Without fear.
He was the light.

Of all creation, only man could be a slave.
And knowing that he was a slave,
Call forth the divine and discover:
Freedom is a thing within his own power.
Of all creation, only man could be his own salvation.

NOT ENOUGH

The devil took a man to a high mountain
He showed him the vast expanse
That lay beneath,
Bow to me, he said,
And all this can be yours.

I met this man many years later,
Fully engaged in a quest to own the world.
No matter where or when,
From a servant's hands,
Any worldly pleasure was obtained
From the slightest whim.
He worked all day and night,
Rose from his chair to join a fight.
He calculated every move;
Predicted past and future alike.
Every new idea he perused.
Investing here, touching there
To make the money grow year after year.

When he spoke to me,
He called me son,
And drew me close
In whispered tongue,
"There is no right or wrong," he said,
"We do not live to quench the many,
But to be the few;
That is what I was made to do.
The world is not enough
For people like me and you."

He lived for nothing
Not servant, or woman, or man.
His heart beat for only one reason
To triumph, to trample, to ban.

The Complete Second Verse
Dr. Charles Cooper

"There is no satisfaction,
Never give up,
And never give in;
Take what you want;
Never rest,
The world is not enough
For me and you, man!"

"Never join the many.
If they speak to you,
Cry havoc;
If they raise a flag,
rejoice!
Speak peace as war
And war as lust,
Wage life as a destroyer of men.
Destruction is their end.
The world is not enough my friend.

"Behold in disgust.
Every worthless man,
Their painted souls
All vacuous, vacant, old,
Slaves one and all,
Because I told them they could vote.
And they voted for me
To take what was theirs
Refine, repackage, and return,
With a half-life of life,
Never what they'd earned.
It was mine.
They were mine.
Become slaves without binding.

As they aged before their time,
That blank stare that came
From that blank slate they crave,
Nothing, until I painted it.

Masonic Lore
Brother Charles Cooper

I sold them that lie.
I told them to hate, hate.
And for hate's sake,
to rise against
Themselves.
This is my fate,
That I sell to the world,
And what of the poor sodden man
Who does not care
To understand,
What I can or can not do.
What is it to you?

Does he believe in me?
I could never let that be.
I kept him from life,
With comfort and a vote,
Such is the fate of ordinary men,
But you and I both,
Deserve a world, no!
The World is not enough!"

I had seen and been and lost a friend,
And wandered until,
I found a new mountain to climb;
I rose and strived, rising high;
Earning the days and the things that were mine.

I met a man on that mountain,
He bade me join him in his climb,
And I did.

As days passed,
We worked hard,
Each of us amazed
At the growing size
Of the things we had done.
Then to my surprise,
He took my hand

The Complete Second Verse
Dr. Charles Cooper

And we flew, ever higher.
Into the troposphere
Where the air
Is thin,
Where anything can happen
That is imagined by men.

He asked,
If I, as a man, liked what I saw,
The world below,
The ocean, the land,
The women and men.

"This is the world that I love,"
I said.

He nodded, "yes."
"All of this can be yours.
If you kneel."

I smiled, shook my head,
"No," I said,
"And again, no."

"What," he said?
"I never. How?
All, of this can be yours.
The world that you love,"
Anger was in his tone.
"Can be yours,
If you kneel!"

I smiled again,
"It is a poor man,
Who thinks to control
What he loves.
Control changes everything.
A world that I love
Is worth too much

Masonic Lore
Brother Charles Cooper

To be mine.
The loss too high,
Owning, controlling the world
Is not payment.
It is the price."

And I woke in my bed,
With a full heart,
And rose again,
To live.

"ARTHUR"

ART BY BECKY KIPER

ONCE AND FUTURE KING

Once upon a time…
What the future brings.
Ink and pen,
Sword and shield,
Daylight to night…
What the future brings,
I write.

Masonic Lore
Brother Charles Cooper

I am a monumental man
Graced by a lake,
The aftermath of memory,
A time, a place,
That never was,
And never will be,
I am a price to be paid
For a night of passivity
A consequence
A choice, made by two
And left to grow inside a womb.

I am a monumental man.
Restore my will.
Forgive the day
That lit the night
Gave me the life
Not yours to take.
Was taken all the same.

A monumental man,
A once and future king
Triumph and salvation
For an entire nation…
A revelry ends in silence
A man with no voice
A pen without ink
Stretching daylight to night
A future goes unwritten.
Another book left unfilled.

There I was, the sun
Even if you never saw me as one.
The ghost that will never go away.
Memories lost, darkened the night
Misty fields of feelings
Tears that tear the heart

The Complete Second Verse
Dr. Charles Cooper

Memories tear that soul apart.

Goodbye mother of the future,
Goodbye and good luck
There is no hand to take the pen,
The future goes unwritten.
I am
The once and future king
Goodnight, the sun is setting.
Goodnight, I hope you sleep.

BIRTH

On the first day,
There was a burning ball
Of Hydrogen and Helium and Fusion…
To mark the occasion.
And there was light.
It heated the rocks.
It made matter and energy dance,
And play less than simple games
Of tag and you're it.

Gravity is the bitter bitch of the natural world.
A persistent, tugging, nagging whore
Whose only purpose seems to be to pull you down.
As if there wasn't enough excitement with the bitch
As if it wasn't enough to be pulled
A bastard was added to push.
And the bitch and the bastard danced and spun
In circles. In centrifugal motion,
With centrifugal force.
Like a thuggish Italian guy,
Centrifugal Force
Forever marked his dance
As a tattoo of the equator
On his Bicep.
Flex and Rotate
Push and pull and dance,
And Spin.

Millions or Billions of revolutions later,
Guided by intelligence and chance,
The experiment of the reptiles
Ended in failure.

While they were large
And fun to play with,
Easy to manipulate,

556

The Complete Second Verse
Dr. Charles Cooper

Masters of blood sport,
They could not know,
Could not create,
Could not appreciate,
The life they were given.

Their inability to reach beyond their created form
To gird themselves against the cold
Is what buried them all
before they grew old.

Before the last Dinosaur took its last step,
A new, more adept creature walked the earth.
There was stronger to be sure;
More beautiful,
with more allure.
There was faster, bigger, and more vital;
There was even more vicious,
But not with the intent to do harm.

Next to the small, divine spark
Of creation, given to man,
There was no other animal at sea or on land
With the gift of creation
With the breath of life.

"THE APPRENTICE COLUMN"

ART BY UNKNOWN APPRENTICE

Rosslyn Chapel	55.8554° N, 3.1602° W
Roslin, Scotland	
Great Britain	
The World	

The Complete Second Verse
Dr. Charles Cooper

APPRENTICE COLUMN

The road underfoot,
The sky painting life
In blues and reds and a blood moon
To light the night red,
Ravens flying through.

I found myself at an abandoned church
In the east of Scotland
On the ground,
Near the door,
Lay a sign,
"No trespassing,"
In red, the sticker read
Pasted over the ancient, accepted
Words:
"All are welcome
But few will come.
We make men,
Who are good men,
Better... men."

I stepped nearer
And heard nothing.
I stepped nearer still,
Cocked my ear,
But I heard nothing.
Perhaps there was,
A whispering wind,
The quiet was so eerie,
Airy absence of movement
Not a still, small voice to be found.
In that place,
A breath carried the might of a roar
As if daring such a thing to happen at all
As though nothing could speak
for the reverence required here

Masonic Lore
Brother Charles Cooper

Was more than any creature would dare.

In the hall of the Atrium,
Two columns rose
One a rough-hewn granite slab.
The second column was singular,
More beautiful than anything I had seen,
Journey as I might,
Down roads through bend and turn
From the Parthenon to the Pantheon
Hagia Sofia to Vatican City,
I had seen nothing like it.
The spins and twirls, flowers and bones,
And bones, and bones.
They were everywhere.
Men who had laid down,
Sword in hand,
Shields underfoot,
Helmets cracked.

I wanted to belong among these men;
"In Hoc Signo Vinces"
Every man bore the crest.
Every man bore the shade
Of the faded Red Cross across their chest.
Many years had passed
Since these men made their stand.
I felt a tear on my cheek,
It fell to the floor,
Onto a brass plaque,
That read,
"This is the column of the Apprentice
Whom the master left,
To wage war.
The Apprentice,
Who left his gift
For men
And the master

560

The Complete Second Verse
Dr. Charles Cooper

To adore
Though none can comprehend
The work, and the love, once it is done.

Not unto us,
Oh Lord,
Not unto us,
But to thy name give glory."

Of all these men,
Only black splotches and bones remained.
Of the blood that was spilled,
At this sacred place,
On this sacred floor.
Torrents of violence
Men used to defame
Memories and lies,
Lay empty vessels splayed on the floor.
Bones and bones and bones,
Like a warning to men,
A warning to me
Of a passion I had ignored.

As I passed between the pillars,
The building shifted,
Stairs descended,
And I was lifted
To a hidden floor,
A secret place,
Home to the skeletal remains
Of a single knight
Still in the uniform
Of a grand commander.
He lay beneath an oculus
Entwined in a circle, circumpunct
On a stone table
at the center
Of a Pentacle...

Masonic Lore
Brother Charles Cooper

Mind, body, and soul of man
Joined.
The pentacle painted,
On both the ceiling and floor,
Symbolic of the joining of forces
That gave birth to life,
Even his,
Even mine.

"Eternity" inscribed on the blade of the sword
That rested on his chest
Held taught by his hands,
Tight in his grasp.
A linen fabric wrapped round the hilt
Faded by age, weakened by the nature of men
Deteriorating in the exposure
to the earth, air, water, and wind.
Like any secret men claim to keep
Can be kept by two,
If one is dead.

I fell on the floor.
I wept at the loss of the Master's word.
I pulled the sign and seal to myself,
Pass and grip exchanged,
Grasping tight the hand of history,
Offering my sign to those who came before.
What if man refused life and
Denied creation?
What if men everywhere lost courage,
And bowed before existence,
Chose not to grow,
Chose not to love,
Chose not to give,
Chose not to strive,
Chose not to live,
Because of risk,
Pain,

The Complete Second Verse
Dr. Charles Cooper

What?

What risk is there
For man who was given so much?
What Creature would bind a gift
And leave it unused
For fear to damage,
For fear to lose?
And in the end lose it is all the same
For what unused does not deteriorate?
Man can.
Such a man can lose his use.
Such a man, is a fool.

I unfurled the linen from the handle.
Delicately pulled back the fingers.
The painted, ink-stained cloth,
Bore words inscribed to eternity.
The ink was gold,
Illuminated to endure time.
In a cold, French style,
The words were acute,
"I have died to preserve life,
Given all for peace in war.
This treasure is not lost,
But forever out of reach,
Of man,
And any whose hand
Would use such
To make war
Enough blood has been shed.
Enough."

Consumed by my own wasted life.
I reviled the haste
That drew me to this place
It is too late to know things such as those
Which could save me.

Masonic Lore
Brother Charles Cooper

I lay down on the cold tile floor,
Examining closely the shades of wood,
The parquet letters crafted by a master's hands
That offered such a simple hope for man,
Hope of happiness
Hope to live and to strive
To love and to try
Hope to create something great.
Greater than itself,
Myself.

Destined to wonder
as we wander along
Blessed if we leave the world
With a single song worth singing,
Worth Remembering.

Possibly years later,
Time without meaning
The body subsisting its will for breath,
Can stand alone.
Into the stone,
I carved these words.
"I am.
All the knowledge I have gained
And still I wanted more.
To think what I would have paid,
For more.
Faustus, you thought yourself a fool,
But I have been a whore.
What is knowledge without action,
That I might breathe,
Without blood,
Without lungs,
Without a heart,
I ask you,
what have I done

The Complete Second Verse
Dr. Charles Cooper

Simply to know?"

Then I raised my blade high,
It glinted in the sun.
The streaming light from the oculus
Burned my eyes.
I was blind,
But I saw God,
And I knew why.

Standing there,
I stripped myself bare
And knowing who I was,
I was ashamed.
But knowing who I could be,
Was more than enough
To dance, naked before the creator.
Great Architect of the Universe,
Who crafted the code,
That made me,
A being with the breadth of potential
Capable of all the design implied
And more,
So much more.

55.8554° N, 3.1602° W

Masonic Lore
Brother Charles Cooper

"THE TEMPLE DOWNTOWN"

Photo by Charles Cooper
in Mobile, AL

30.6912° N, 88.0463° W

THE SCOTTISH RITE TEMPLE

Rising, Mobile at dawn on Dauphin Street,
With all the grandeur of an Egyptian tomb.
Rising up, from the streets of ordinary,
In waste, the Grand Lodge lays before me
In Mobile.
America lies with it,
For the lack of better men,
Which has never been felt so deeply.

"We make good men better,"
This was the offer that drew them in.
Mystery not withstanding,
No perilous penchant,
No Sunday school fatigue,
Oh, they all went,
To Sunday school that is,
But they practiced their ritual,
And did not preach.
To practice and not to preach
Makes good men better.

They guided the youth
Who circumnavigated the lodge
Taking step after step after…
"Who comes there?"
"Who goes there?"
"Who was there?"
I could not say.

"All of us."
All the things we knew
were washed away.
Cleansing things we didn't know could be clean.

Not a religion,
Just men

Masonic Lore
Brother Charles Cooper

being better men.
No baptism of the righteous,
Just men
being better men.
So many have come before,
Just a trickle now of former glory.
Just conspiracy theories
And history,
Swords
And rings
And stories.

All the grandeur of an Egyptian tomb
Rising up, lying empty.
Not kept up,
By men, too few,
And so old.
Too much rain and mold
Too much dirt
Caked on the storm ravaged doors.

They still could open
To you, to men,
Who wanted to be
Better
Men.
A master could still utter the words,
"Let there be more…"
Still,
Even today.

BOOK 11: MONUMENT TO SIN

"MONUMENT"

ART BY BECKY KIPER

LE VÉRITABLE AMOUR PARDONNE TOUT

The Complete Second Verse
Dr. Charles Cooper

AMBITION

Rampaging hands never gave a man
Satisfaction.

Too fast is too fast.
And over too soon
Is more than you can expect
When you are the moon
Chasing the sun.
Run, run, run...

Reverie
Never gave me,
A wake up call.

I wanted it all.
Too soon,
Too fast,
No patience to last.
But for persistence,
I would have fallen behind
So many times.

I never want to fail,
But I have been there
And done that.
I left the shirt
And bought a hat.
No monks fashion for me.
There are achievements to be had.

The reverie which called to me
Came late each day.
It bid me lay
Down.
The bed was soft,
And comfort has as much allure
As apathy.

Monumental Sin
Charles Cooper, PhD

Apathy is
The only thing now,
Which stands between me
And my goals
And my desires.

This bed is so damn comfortable.

Shred the wind,
And curse the trees,
Stain the cross
With ash and leaves.
It's all burning down.
It's taking me apart
And remaking who I am.
I will never forgive the day,
I was caught in this
Web of satisfaction.

The Complete Second Verse
Dr. Charles Cooper

ONCE RIGHT

Fix what isn't broke
The theme of a generation
Immortal curse.
Eternal cruise.
Righteous verse,
If only we had learned history first.

Tragedy, the mirror of generations.
In my mind, I know, I can't fly,
And so,
I will never fly.
Once right,
I fulfill the limits of my mind.

We once thought,
All people should be free.
Set fire to the walls and chains,
Let loose the spirit on man on the land,
And they did trade
It all away.

We traded this and that for a little less or a little more.
Some gave all. Some wanted more.
It was in the trades
Which forged the chains,
Which soon enough,
We all wore.

We were free once,
But that was yesterday.
We were right once,
But we threw it all away.

Monumental Sin
Charles Cooper, PhD

BAR SCENE

Three drinks in, I was
Nearly blind at the local bar…
You could smoke in bars you know,
Not so long ago.

On a good night,
There was just enough haze
To obscure the lines
In the lady's face.
She was older than she said,
But younger than I thought;
Still, her lie was nothing
compared to my pick up line…

Add alcohol…

(We blamed the alcohol, but…
we both knew why we were there
and for what.

And the avenue to a requisite weekly release
Was well underway.

No one has ever died of passion,
Lest it fester and build…
It's by the pressure of passion
Against the walls of the heart's
Unrepentant valves,
That passion unrealized…

Unreleased…

Will bring a master to his knees.
And someone less to their grave.

"Strive or die"

The Complete Second Verse
Dr. Charles Cooper

Is the motto we lived by...

Nature's vision for me,
was something else though,
Something I had yet to know,

The price I paid to be alone
Every Friday night,
What it cost me to achieve.

You may have been there too,
I'm guessing you have,
At least once or twice.

On that road,
Where we don't attach strings,
To the most costly things;
Where we sink so low
After three drinks,
to expect something
which can only be given for free,
Or the price of a drink
And the jaded illusion of intimacy.

MONUMENTAL SIN

Jesus said, "love,"
His followers,
so busy following,
debating,
leading,
Commanding,
Crafting,
      Writing,
            Killing
      Studying
Living,
Forgot to love.

Jesus said to his disciples…
"Do not Judge,"
The most beautiful of his creations,
Graced with conscience and reason
Divined right and wrong,
As what hurt others…
As what did not bring comfort
As everything, which was different
Than themselves.
Left to the ravages of time,
An inborn desire to control
But some were strong
And others became subject to their blurred feelings.

So they parsed the words of murderers and Felons
To decide what was a lie,
What was truth,
And who would die.
They judged away.
They judged anything,
Not like them,
As wrong,
As sin.
Jesus wept.

The Complete Second Verse
Dr. Charles Cooper

Jesus said forgive.
Disciples, followers, readers,
And casual friends
Would not, could not, and never will
Forget.
And their insides turned black as night
And they hated,
Denied wrong and right
And planned and burned and executed
To find they could only reap what they sowed.
And wars and rumors of wars
Waged without knowledge, sacrifice, or even malice.
Set fire to the pyre,
Burning the righteous and the sinner alike
In the name of...

Is it any wonder Jesus cried?

Jesus who said...
We have a long way to go to love.
But not as far to understand
You are what you allow yourself to become.

If you love, well...

Monumental Sin
Charles Cooper, PhD

TAKING LIFE

Elizabeth took life
For all she was worth
On the days that called for it.

Elizabeth took life
As it came.
She lived as much and as well
As a person can.

Elizabeth took life,
By her own hand,
Took life by her words and commands,
Laid Men low.
Elizabeth gave life to so many,
Let men live and give and care,
Made it possible for people to love,
And explore, and to find more
Within themselves
Than they ever would have known.

Elizabeth, where are you now,
When I need that river to flow.
Elizabeth, some how,
Find a way to let us know
That we all can take life,
Without taking life.
Can we learn to let it go?

I believe,
We can.
I believe,
you believe,
whatever you believe.
I believe,
        I can find a way,
            To take my life,
        And make it mine.

578

The Complete Second Verse
Dr. Charles Cooper

And you,
      Can do the same
             With yours
      And life
For all that it's worth
Is worth more
Because we let it be.

MIRACLE

Somedays, I think we need a miracle…
Because like water into wine
There's an answer if we try.
You can whisper to the wind
About a world that can't begin,
But you'll never know why
Unless you try.
Unless you try.

FREE WILL

Free will, the upgrade,
Which cost us the garden,
Is the trade they want to make
For suicide and control
And no one knows
Why some people want suicide
So intently.

I am always terrified,
By the ability of mankind
To propose suicide and slavery
And expect people to accept it.

The Complete Second Verse
Dr. Charles Cooper

LEAVES FALL

An explosion of color,
Every Fall,
Leaves on the trees
Change and fall.
Rain fell before I could see
With my own eyes,
The final explosion of color,
Of Earth, of the thread running through life,
Not a thin thread, pull as you might,
With all your might, life doesn't unravel.
It isn't made that way.
It will pause, and if you will wait,
The green visage of foliage
Will return.

Leaves Fall in Fall.
Winter wanes and moments slow,
A sweet low hum which calls to us both,
With a subtle secret we already know:
The price of life is cheap,
A little water and winter wheat made into bread,
And breath and air.
We've all been there and done that.
A little life is easy, a small price to pay.

The price of living, on the other hand,
Reaches the sky, where the air is so thin,
We might die if we don't try.
Effort is required to move
From life to living.
Active transport is necessary
To live.
Anything less is a monumental sin.

SERENITY VALLEY

Sometimes we love something,
Which is so good,
So original,
So…

We find ourselves in
Serenity Valley,
Facing the alliance,
They have the technological advantage
And money, lots of money.
We have love.
We have commitment.
We have passion.

But it's not enough.
A business cannot see
beyond the moment
And keep it alive long enough
To let it thrive.

Silly business,
You could have been rich.

The Complete Second Verse
Dr. Charles Cooper

FRIVOLITY

I do play.
It may not seem that way.
I may not seem that way
To those who wake with agendas.

I am, occasionally,
so overcome with desire
that I live deliberately.

I never tire of this.
I never wait for air or ground
underfoot.
I jump and there in the space
between
the known and unknown
I create my world,
and it recreates me.

Monumental Sin
Charles Cooper, PhD

THE SIGNATURE OF SIN

Part the Mississippi… part of a legacy.
Give me a staff
Try not to laugh
As I raise it high
Held aloft,
There are no lies
Between us,
Give me time,
And I'll part the Mississippi.

You never wait for long,
An extra breath and you'd be gone.
Just along for the ride
Why won't you try?
I never understood the revulsion you had
For work…
Always the answer it is.

There's always a shortcut
You always did it better.
I wanted to be so much
You wanted to leave so much.
A vicarious battery of bodies in my wake.
Punching my way out again
That's the signature of sin.
When I have to hurt people.
And at that, I am good.
Staff aloft, watch the Nile swell
I lower it down to watch my "enemies" drown.

If you only had patience,
If I only had time,
I would part the Mississippi for you
I want to be kind.

The Complete Second Verse
Dr. Charles Cooper

SWEET YESTERDAY

Of all the things
I was never told
when I was young…

I was going to grow old
and watch everything,
which was so much fun
turn into mist
dry rot
And melt away
And run away…
memories not withstanding
The miles I've run,
The hallowed trails.

I lived those days
like they were eternal,
in a state of grace
Like life was eternal,

      Youth, we called it.

So young and fertile.
Youthful smiles, not scary, or creepy.
Satisfaction, was a sign to strive more.
Not a flashing neon light
Saying,
"You're going to be sore."
Hopes and dreams
Were things of grace
Like glowing skin
And a glimpse of lace.

I would rise and fall
like the silent sun
from dusk until dawn,
I would race and run.

Monumental Sin
Charles Cooper, PhD

Deprived of light
until I revived
The dream
to shine
one more time.

I was bought and sold,
at a monumental pace.
Occasionally,
I paused at Main and Grace.
There,
I would contrive to live again,
be sold and spent again.
Over and over passion revives,
even on days and nights
when old dreams die.

It was
Not desire
so much as explosion,
not art
so much as compulsion,
retraction of the imagined,
songs and stories of myself,
       by myself,
             for myself.

I will never regret
as much as politics,
narrative tales
or following snails…
In the left lane
Makes me want to.
My efforts are still incomplete,
My vision, still aware
An awake.
Credits remain unredeemed.
There are no refunds,
For the investments I've made.

The Complete Second Verse
Dr. Charles Cooper

Tomorrow is another day,
but tomorrow is not yet.
If I had hope,
I would pray for a sacred heifer
to find a way to stay the grains of sand
slipping through my fingers.

A woman's battle cry,
"NOW, NOW, NOW!"

If I never had to see my love mold and slow,
my passions change.
The flow of waking rivers
   desire and light...
My desire,
to rearrange and constrain
my priorities,
like wishes cast into a well,
these bargains made with Hell,
A sweet deal that bought me you,
Thoroughly paid for with one more payment
always due.

All I wanted,
never failed to float
just beyond the vail,
just out of reach,
just far enough to keep me alive,
and let me strive.

It's the living,
which makes sorrow.
It's the dreams
and the time.
It's today
lost to tomorrow.
It is the hell of being alive.

Monumental Sin
Charles Cooper, PhD

Sweet time is the stage,
which deprives us of desire,
      passion,
      stamina,
      reason,
      and memories.
It's hard to hope,
when memories are what is left to touch.
It's harder when those memories are gone.
It's hard to feel,
when you've already lost so much.
And harder still when you cannot touch
The things you hold dear

Sweet sorrow, sweet yesterday,

If only I hadn't been in such a rush.

The Complete Second Verse
Dr. Charles Cooper

SUICIDE BY LOVE

Day in and out
Trading pieces of me
In a passion play,
With "No strings."
People like us,
Trade life for rings.

We take and give,
And give and take.
The self is a high price to pay
As if to say,
"Suicide by love,
Is my new thing."

Rapt kiss,
Just bliss,
And those fine lips
The tender grip
Of Suicide,
Suicide by love.

Hold me tender,
Hold me true,
Nothing to feel,
I just want you;
It's all too real;
All too quick;
I never give up,
Surrender or skip
A chance to hold the line,
A chance for
Suicide…
Suicide by Love.

There's no place to hide
I have to try;
No one else matters,

Monumental Sin
Charles Cooper, PhD

When we two intertwine,
I can't even think.
Let's go for a ride,
And touch the sky
Like teenage kids
One more time
Until one of us goes blind,
And surrenders the self to find
Suicide,
Suicide by love.

Emptiness consuming
All that I am
When I am without you,
I don't know if I can
Embrace the climax,
I'm not just another man.
I might be worth
The self that died
You're in my mind.
Suicide,
Suicide by love.

Complete the maker
With me.
Embrace the circle,
Three hundred sixty degrees.
Running hot!
To try and find,
Each other
In kind…
And embrace

Suicide,
Suicide by love.

Life is lonely
When your free.
There is no defense for you or me

590

The Complete Second Verse
Dr. Charles Cooper

All the threats aren't from above.
There is no cure for love.
It's peddled on the streets
In every corner bar
Where people think sex is cheap,
But they didn't get too far;
Some beer and wine,
Obscure the mind.
They play at love,
But never find…

Suicide
Suicide by Love.

Suicide Solution
In your arms
Resistance waned
There is no harm
For you or me
To give and take
And make
One Body; One Blood;
One Life; One Love
And finally, One Mind

Unified by suicide;
Suicide by Love.

Monumental Sin
Charles Cooper, PhD

REVELATIONS

Surrender Life; Give up, Life.
Stealing life from me,
Giving it away to someone new.
It's not always what you do.
It's been done, once or twice,
But that doesn't make it right.
Choice makes it right.
What you surrender
Is what you can tender.
It is your sacrifice
　　　　To make.
Not mine, the communcal mind,
Or the collective lies,
And while it may be kind,
It's not always justified.
Sacrifice is a thing, only you can decide.

If I was to give up life,
The resources, time, or talent
Which make up my tool set
And there is something to do,
Which I have not accomplished yet,
What have I done?
What have I lost?
What trade have I made
In life?

A creator laid a path to me,
With all the stones, moss and gravel,
Men and women, who walked that way,
Fords and passes,
Low running water
Gulley's and streams
Making up the mountain's Watershed
Which made me
For some purpose.
If I give this life away in trade,

The Complete Second Verse
Dr. Charles Cooper

If I take this life
Making a song too few
If I am done
Before I am through,
What is the price of sacrifice?
The pained betrayal of the one who made me.
What is the risk to the rest?
The price of sacrifice is this:

Revelations 10:4 is the last line
Man gets to read
And remember...
Because everything
          which was given
Is gone.

GREED

Is wanting more than I need greed?
I think not.
Is wanting more than I deserve?
Wanting not to serve?
Wanting to be more than I am
Capable of?
Of which I am?

I want all these things,
Not for the recognition
But for production
Not for adulation,
But for the monument
To be.

I have to answer
is the desire to be greed?
Is greed that capital sin?
Are we all lost who strive?
Or are we caught in a web of lies
Because we live to try?

As a created being,
My nature clarifies the motives
Of my creator.
If my motives and drives
Speak ill of me,
What does it say
About God?

"PERMANENT"

ART BY BECKY KIPER

BURIED

When I was so young,
I lived next to a graveyard.
When I was young,
I wrote a story for each one
Of the headstones in turn
If they could teach,
I would learn.
Sadly, they could not,
I spent long Summers in the heat,
Cold Winters in the night,
Learning that death
Is permanent,
And the lessons it teaches

Monumental Sin
Charles Cooper, PhD

Are wasted on the young.

Whatever lesson had buried them,
Whatever hill they had died upon,
Whatever cliff they had stepped their last
All of their predators lived in the past.

I could not learn from graves.
I could not live amongst the stones,
Though I tried for a time.
To live and to learn, you must be alive.

GRIEF

Love never dies;
It just changes form.
The final phase of love, grief.
I never stop loving
And so, the grief will not go.

Be still my heart.
Really, please, stop my heart.
I don't want to go through another day
With grief, even if it is just love.

The Complete Second Verse
Dr. Charles Cooper

DESIRE

I never wanted.
It was not so subtle.
I had to have.
Desire burned like coal dust
In a miner's lungs
Cutting through the healthy tissue
Leaving a purer form of will, me.

Always make the sacrifice.
Always is the price.
Twice the effort
Makes twice the right
In any fight,
Which isn't true,
If there is an objective
Truth,
But it works in practice
More often than not.

Monumental Sin
Charles Cooper, PhD

FAR BEYOND DRIVEN

The creator creates,
So life was set in motion,
And I will seek the best
Without reason or emotion -
And this is the first law of man.

Build the best,
        With brick and stone.
watch it crumble,
Cry and moan.

Painters paint
The winter wood,
With white and red
The purest blood.

Write the best
        With ink on page.
Without the muse,
There is no sage.

I flail and mumble falling fast.
Eve and Adam regrets still last
But I will never live this down
I made the deal and have not found.
A way home, yet.

Design the best,
        To space alone
Poor bastard thought he could get stoned
And business would forgive the night.
Money doesn't live or forgive even if you're right
Or craft a driverless car to take us home at night.

The highest vault,
We have yet made
To the moon…

598

The Complete Second Verse
Dr. Charles Cooper

We should have stayed.
Men would not go higher
Space gets no one laid.

When I find rest,
A sated pauper,
I will examine my flaws,
Which brought me to this place,
Which oversaw the fall
Of the best without regret…

Asked and answered,
My flaw revealed:
I believe the best
Of people.
I see the best
In people,
      I want them to be,
Everything that they can be

As long as it isn't better than me.

Monumental Sin
Charles Cooper, PhD

CAUGHT IN THE OZONE

O cubed
It's not natural
To fly so high
Ionized
Like tantric, kind
Blind straps,
People
Living life
Better
Than anyone thought they could.

Now they feel trapped.
I feel trapped
In the web
I wove
I tried to fly
In a murder of crows.
It reached so high, I dove
Through the Ozone.

The stable ground
Never looked so low,
So much like a place
I could never go.
I was caught in the ozone,
In the web which I'd made
In the life that I wanted
Deep, layers of complexity
I craved.
Life Cubed... O Cubed... Ice Cubed...

More.
I always wanted more.

SOMEONE TO BLAME

Life is hard.
Where-ever and who-ever you are,
Life is hard.

Life does not come easy.
It will not yield up her treasures
Just because you take a breath.
It's not the game she plays,
And it can only be played her way.

What is required to live is
Absorbing the extreme explosion
Of strife over rock laden roads…
In bare feet.
Against currents of rushing river rapids…
Up mountains where there is no air…
You are energy,
Your body, not withstanding,
Obeys
Your will.
For the distance between your starting place
And your present point,
There is no one to blame but yourself.

Monumental Sin
Charles Cooper, PhD

FREEDOM

Release the restive warden.
Free the prisoners now.
Yesterday, the deeds were done
Tomorrow is the price we paid to cow
A revolution
For just a few more days.

Power and establishment,
The hallmarks of tradition
Which holds today
So firmly in its grasp,
Can never
Free your mind,
To find what you truly want.
Freedom is the will to change
Everything.

The Complete Second Verse
Dr. Charles Cooper

LOVE, JUST LOVE

There is a knife in my gut,
Some Poison in my glass,
A hammer buried neatly in my skull,
The bruising from the noose around my neck
Hasn't begun to heal at all,
but *You* still
Bring a smile
To my face.

Monumental Sin
Charles Cooper, PhD

SELFISH

Honestly, it's the righteous that really bother me,
The one's who don't know your name,
Or your mind,
Or your values...
But they judge all the same.
How could you believe you know what's best...
For me...
For me?

If you knew,
What I went through
To be here.
To stand in your presence.

If you knew the price I paid and
The gifts I gave:
To a wife...
And children...
And family...
And country...
And company...

You might not say the things you say.
It is the fool who judges me
Without meeting me,
knowing me,
Even if we disagree,
Respecting my right to be...
Just as you belong to you;
I am my own,
And it will always be that way.

I see the world through my own eyes,
Never disguise my values or my will.
What you can make me do
With my life,

The Complete Second Verse
Dr. Charles Cooper

In defiance of my will is stealing.
What I want and what I do,
Has nothing to do *with you*.
I am selfish, and it is my choice to make
That's all there is to say.

BOOK 12: SLEEPING WITH THE END OF TIME

"THE END OF TIME"

ART BY JM STEGER

The Complete Second Verse
Dr. Charles Cooper

LAST DAYS

Every generation since time began
Has been prophesying the end.
The last days as described in Revelations
Was chosen from a stack of stories
About the same thing.

Now it's my turn.
People are mammals.
Mammals are
Animals with
Hair,
And milk,
And breasts,
Warm blooded
Bodies
That move, and eat,
And breath with lungs,
And breed... and give birth
To live babies.
The question that will end all of this is...
What if we were more?

Immortal, energy,
give up the flesh,
the limits of the mind,
passed the speed of matter
And God said,
let them be spirits,
and they were,
and it was good.
As it ever was,
the end is the beginning...
Of more.

GYPSY CURSE

Independence is the rallying cry
Of men,
Who got the milk
And sold the cow,
For a few beans from a gypsy.
Magic beans that didn't grow.
Men who complained about being alone…

When I met the gypsy,
I was just a baby.
She just cursed me,
With independent thought
And action.
If only the curse was a command,
I could have walked away.
To this day,
I don't follow instructions well.
I am my own cow it seems
Silly me.

"THE EVIL EYE"

ART BY BECKY KIPER

The Complete Second Verse
Dr. Charles Cooper

DALI'S PARCHED LIPS

Turn back the clock
Burned, bent in madness and disarray.
I re-imagine the world as new
With Every Sunrise
Inside my own creation,
Inside my mind,
I find a way
To feel alone,
And very out of place.

Circus clowns and vindictive fools
Cannot help but invade,
So I bend the light
To stave off a shadow blockade
In my mind.

Men should not live this way...
Created, burdened, bent,
And polished with rage,
Working through the night
Staying on to work the day
To claim the rights...
Which belong to them anyway.
Worship, march, say what you will
But you are a slave.

Lips parched, throat starched,
Clothes tattered and torn.
Yesterday, I knew regret,
Composed of a pasty, vanilla horde,
On the steps of the first public school in Alabama
Where a blockade met its end
And a mind opened anew
To something better.
New life began for so many that way.
Now the sons
and daughters

Sleeping with the End of Time
Charles Cooper, PhD

and grandchildren
of sacrifice and sorrow
Do their best to undo,
The good which was done
There are no safe places for freedom
Some things just don't end well.

The Complete Second Verse
Dr. Charles Cooper

BRING IT BACK AROUND

Reeling sound,
Bring it back around.
Once there was love,
I buried it deep down.
It's so hard,
Once it's found
To bring it back around
Once you found out
About love.

What's so bad about love?
What's so bad about passion?
What's so bad that we would bury those feelings?
Who would we offend,
With love?
Who would reprimand
Our Love?
Who is worthy
Of love?
Not one, no not one.

Feet on the ground,
Let's bring it back around
To Love.
Let's live it out loud,
Sing out, be proud
Of love.

Would that be enough?
I thought that love was enough
Until you found out,
And you fought it,
Fought me,
Tried to burn it down
To silence the sound.
What's so bad about love?
What's so bad about love?

Sleeping with the End of Time
Charles Cooper, PhD

I'm not stealing feeling,
Or applying it to you.
I just want to be
Just want to do.
To breath the sacred air
Take flight so we can share
Our love.
Bring it back around.
Embrace that sacred sound
Of Love

I want to bring it back around,
Back to you and I.
Take flight and fly...
Take back the summer time,
Blue skies, and the sea.
Let's bring it back around
To you and me.
Bring it back...
Bring it back...
Around
To love.

"LOVE"

ART BY BECKY KIPER

QUARANTINED

Quarantined by COVID 19
It's just so mean…
I met my family again
The subtle servants of my sin
Itemized, marginalized, chastised
And one more time
Revived erect and speaking.

Quarantined by COVID 19
Never as much as I've seen
I only needed you to be,
Not a shadow, but a person.
Not a voice, but a heart
Not a feeling, breathing, beating
Like some lost dramatic art.

Quarantined by COVID 19
Where I was just me
And it was all I ever
would
have been
Trapped by original sin
Bound by an earthquake
to a lake
In San Francisco
Preaching about the end of days and rainbows

Quarantined by COVID 19
I was working anyway
Building a better place,
A better world
A better tomorrow,
An inch at a time
Dying this time
One more time
For the road
So we can fly.

Sleeping with the End of Time
Charles Cooper, PhD

Now I'm Quarantined by COVID 19
I will never say goodbye
I will never ever lie
The door that shuts
On part of your life
You didn't hear from me
For a while,
But you cannot trust in silence,
Can you?
Cannot know the heart
Which you cannot see or feel.
It is not rampant lust or violence
with you
No Quarantine or virus
Can keep me from you.

There's so much I have left to give
To that one, the one.
Even the end times
Can't withstand the love I feel
Binding us
Together
3 hours distant
Three million miles to go
Two minds bound
In forever
Each quarantined
Drowning in COVID 19.

"DALI'S DANCE"

ART BY BECKY KIPER

DANCING ON THE ASTRAL PLAIN

It's a funky groove,
Got the funky moves.
Got sax and drums and blues
An astral plain, I never could regain.
Not for lack of trying
Or for lack of pain.

Sleeping with the End of Time
Charles Cooper, PhD

I just didn't visit the astral shore
Or lay down for the staccato love affair
On the road to nowhere.
Tickets are cheap,
Coffee is cheaper,
But life and lies
Cost everyone
Too much.

So go, live,
take only what you need to survive.
Industrial strength hair dryer
Not withstanding
I saw the glint in your eyes.

So I danced
And you danced
A little longer
Longer than we had intended,
On the astral plain
Where nothing but memories remain
And everything stays the same.
Then you grow up
And you find
There's not a way back
To the love that was.
No way back to the dance
Or the astral plane.
We danced in vain.
We played and sang.
We ran in the rain.
We let the phone ring,
And we waited to hear a message
That there is someone,
Anyone... who still cared.

The Complete Second Verse
Dr. Charles Cooper

THIS WILL NOT KILL YOU

It's a long time coming.
Longer than it took to leave.
It's a hollow promise
What you said,
The words spoken,
In your bed.

What doesn't kill you
Makes you stronger
Walk a little longer
Closer to the light.
The ground beneath your feet
Rises up to meet you
Reaches out to greet you.
This is not a fight.
What doesn't kill you
Makes you stronger
Walk a little longer
Then we make it right.

In your bed,
The webs we weave
Tied tight and taunt.
Made of love and your sheets
There was a promise
In the song,
Boards that creak,
You gasp and moan,
"Don't wake the others"
"Don't wake up mom and dad"
Forever starts at midnight.
It's all in what you said.
What you said…

What doesn't kill you
Makes you stronger
Walk a little longer

Sleeping with the End of Time
Charles Cooper, PhD

Closer to the light.
The ground beneath your feet
Rises up to meet you
Reaches out to greet you
This is not a fight.
What doesn't kill you
Makes you stronger
Walk a little longer
Closer to the light.

What doesn't kill you makes you stronger.
Were you left for dead
Beside the road?
You made a promise
I kept it longer,
A heavy load.
Heavy load,
I carried it.
I carried you.
I made it work
We made it through,
Almost, all the way through.
And it nearly killed me.
But this will not kill you.

What doesn't kill you
Makes you stronger
Walk a little longer
Closer to the light.
The ground beneath your feet
Rises up to meet you
Reaches out to greet you
This is not a fight.
What doesn't kill you
Makes you stronger
Walk a little longer
So we can make it right.

"BELGRADE YOUTH"

ART BY LANA RADOVICH

Sleeping with the End of Time
Charles Cooper, PhD

BELGRADE, SUMMER 1999

Art
Days of art in Belgrade
Evolution of the mind
And the body of youth…
Coffee shops and Canvas,
Brushes, archetypes, and architects…
One in particular.

Love
Nights of love and wanton highs
Absinthe and no rent
Oh, to be so young again.
Tracing paper and gravestones
To know the joy of never being alone
Oh, to know those nights again.

Fidelity
Faith and belief and surrender
Friendship, folly, together
Who can offer so much as the young?
Purity of belief, to fear, and not to run.
The first step is always the hardest
The second, a surrender to fate.

Trust
What would you say
If I told you how damaged I am?
A fifteen year old, who has seen war
Up close and personal. I trusted you then.
A woman in every way that doesn't matter
Consequences real, but not ready to feel, this.

Betrayal
Side long glances, lingering stares
That promised so much to young eyes.
I did not want to believe
Those things I saw.

The Complete Second Verse
Dr. Charles Cooper

What I believed was love,
Turned out to be lies.

Infidelity
Too young to know the kiss
You gave to me was practiced
Not in love, but in lust
Again and again and again
On others.
Night after night after night.

All the rest
Belgrade is a city:
Buildings and roads and people in such density
The energy can camouflage the likes of you,
A succubus preying on the naïve
Leeching innocence and joy
To feed your need for youth.

Summer 1999 taught me so much.

Note: The art that inspired this poem was created by Lana
Radovich, however, the story in the poem is the product of the
poet's mind alone.

NEVERMORE PART I

Blast you Poe,
No one will ever know
A Raven by any other name...
Nevermore.

Quite quaint the melancholy
No sorrow or blood left on me
My hands are clean.
There is no victim,
There is no crime,
I'm not guilty this time...
Of anything but justice.

Guilt grows, like winter snow
In the mountains of Maine,
Even when you can explain it all away.
Justice notwithstanding,
Destruction is still a thing...
Which paints black
Stains
On the creator.

Beating hearts, everywhere
Still beating long after the battlefield is clear
The victors rejoice,
The enemy retreats in despair.
The survivors do not.

As people celebrate the victories,
and the brave,
and the courage,
and the glory
and all the words, once heard
Which paint a proper dirge
For the dead and dying
And the killers who weren't,

The Complete Second Verse
Dr. Charles Cooper

But became,
For necessities sake.

Some Private,
perhaps stationed at Fort Monroe
Who failed out of West Point and UVA
And had to find a way to support himself
Penning poetry of life and lost love,
And using ravens to cover the cost of killing.
Nevermore, Nevermore...

Survivors cringe and cry
Because how could you not,
at all the eyes forever closed
By bullets, bayonets, and blows
Delivered by men.

There is no rest for the soldiers who didn't run
But somehow walked away.
Nevermore, is just a line
To those who never wore
A uniform or fired a shot in anger.

Nevermore...
Is what Poe knows,
The Raven cries,
Soldiers bleed and soldiers die
Every day, to settle someone else's score
And pay a price in blood, and rest, and life...
Night after bloody night...
Too late for some...
Too dark for sun...
One thought of war,
Nevermore...
Nevermore.

NEVERMORE PART II

Thrust, thud…
Beating heart covered in mud,
Darkened veins pulsing with blood,
Thrust, thud…
Salvation, ever hollow as a promise,
Offers up this patented, empty sound.
Thrust… "I'm sorry,"
Thud… "Yesterday,"
Thrust… "Forgive me,"
Thud… "Today,"
Thrust… "Promises, and promises,"
Thud… "and Goodbye,"
Falling… "Squeeze"
Down… "Thud"
Ending, cry, fail, rise…
"Goodbye."
Like an echo chamber, strung out on life.
This sullen, beating heart
In a cavernous cave
Doors that open and close
Where we take our turns
And make our trades
Nevermore.

Bated breath,
Pasty, sallow wind
And a blurred, sympathetic vision.
Salvation for men?
Forgiveness for sin
Over and over again
Is burdened by memory.
Guilt and regret
Which can blight the soul.
No one can forget,
What no one knows.
Nevermore,
Forevermore.

The Complete Second Verse
Dr. Charles Cooper

Regret is a knife,
With poison that cuts
Out the sweet taste of life.
Heart beats, given and taken in kind,
While guilt is the venom
Through which life dies.
A swirl of air,
thrust of heart,
and a final breath
Will carry me home again…
Nevermore.

Beating heart, coursing with mud,
Darkened veins pulsing with blood,
Thrust, thud… thrust, thud…
Bated breath… shallow, sallow wind.
A lack of oxygen offers
A kindly, compassionate vision.
Nevermore.

If you give men life,
It will be wasted.
Nevermore.
If you give men salvation,
They will never forgive you.
Nevermore.
You and I,
We must forgive ourselves.

Sleeping with the End of Time
Charles Cooper, PhD

ELIZABETH'S LAST NIGHT

I wish there was an option;
There's always a countdown.
It's not like the 1980s
Where there's a nuclear threat.
Now, it's a nuclear option.
There may be no band named Europe anymore,
But there's always a final countdown
A point where we decide.

When I close my eyes,
I remember that night
I was ready to give away so many things
Scared to death if I was honest.
She knew, resting patiently on the phone.
I wanted promises.
I wanted life,
I wanted so much more for her.
But the cost to me was her.
Little did I know,
I was deciding that night,
The future for both of us.

Elizabeth's last night
Was my first,
Greatest
Mistake...
A trade that gave birth to so many things...
Well and thoroughly hollowed me out.
What I love now, the girl,
Or the woman she became...
Doesn't matter.
I have my creations.

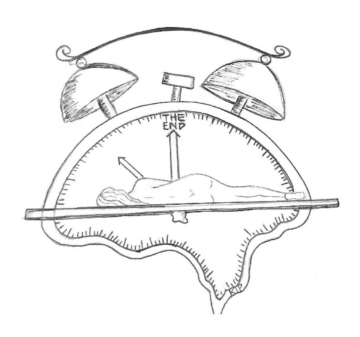

"REST"

ART BY BECKY KIPER

SLEEPING WITH THE END OF TIME PT I

There is no tomorrow.
There never was.
Tomorrow is the construct
Of hope and promises.

Hope is a sin for men
Who dream to achieve:
Persistence, blood, sweat.
Effort and reason never regret.
Is the price for those who would live.

Creation is the miracle
Upon which the sun never sets.
There are no days or nights
Just drive, passion, intellect, and action.
The will which keeps the eyes open,
The hands moving,
The mind thinking,
Is the thing that separates
The creators from the rest.
The price of creation,
Too often for those
Is to be alone.

What cheery eloquence.
What dreary fools who created fire
And gave it to men
Who's only desire is to watch it burn.

There is no tomorrow,
There never was.
Embracing fire,
The creator found
The end of desire,
And the glory of sleeping
With the end of time.

The Complete Second Verse
Dr. Charles Cooper

SLEEPING WITH THE END OF TIME PT II

I smile when I don't know what to say.
When gut wrenching oblivion has stolen my tongue,
I smile.
When brazen lack of logic has saturated my mind
I smile.
I have an arbitrary reflex
       to laugh and make jokes
When I'm exceedingly uncomfortable
When I'm dancing at the Tally Ho,
When I'm dancing with the end of time.

The release of all that humanity
The emotion that sweats,
The rolling tongue regrets
Nothing.
When I'm singing at the top of my lungs.
That is when I become human,
a glutton consuming life for all it's worth.
A God skating across planes of desire.
The young will never see what's mine
They'll never understand,
Sleeping with the end of time.

When I'm sleeping with the end of time,
I try, harder than I should
To be better than I can,
And sometimes I stumble
Say the wrong things
Play the wrong games
Lay down my cards
When I should have played a hand.
You'd think Time wouldn't mind
Having forever and all,
Having seen it all,
       again and again,
But she always does,
Always makes a fuss

Sleeping with the End of Time
Charles Cooper, PhD

There's yelling and frustration,
And then she forgives.

Laugh and smile as I might
Try as hard as I like
The most is not enough
For the immortal ones.

The best, not good enough
When it's all been seen,
      and all been done.
Sleeping with the end of time
Should teach a lesson
But we never learn, do we.

The Complete Second Verse
Dr. Charles Cooper

SLEEPING WITH THE END OF TIME PT III

Derelict hearts, overrun by neglect and pardoned crimes
Like shadow deals and dreams that are not mine.
To steal such things and walk away,
What man among us, wouldn't play,
Even with the end at stake,
A hand.

Shadow hearts, echoed refrain of life and love,
      Scars and pain.
What is the password, was it you who entered the password?
Would you like to make a bet?
You can lose it all, without regret.
At least you played a hand.
Now you are barred from this land.
Homeless, penniless, without a password
No re-entry.
No escape.

All those who enter here…
Abandon…
Not dreams or hope.
Not loss or fear,
Not grief or knowledge,
But all those who enter here
Need despise reason.
It's all we ask.
Despise desire…
Thereby acquire happiness.
No less sacrifice
Than the self
Can pave the way
To the end of you.
You must leave that bitch behind
To know the ecstasy that comes
From sleeping,
With the end of time.

SLEEPING WITH THE AFTERLIFE

I lived. You lived.
And then it was over,
And it was good.

Now we live in the afterlife.
I never thought I'd walk this way,
A lonely road, no place to stay.
I never thought I'd find a reason why,
To grow these wings, to learn to fly.
I never thought I'd use the road,
Meandering hills, a heavy load.
I never thought I'd bow again,
In the end, I never did.
I never thought it'd end in sin,
But you surprised me.
See, I never believed in sin,
Until the time, this time, this one hurt.

Don't pull out, get out alive.
You asked me to bow,
I asked you to try,
And that was the last thing
We ever did together.
There are no regrets
Cause life can be tough.
Never surrender
We all paid our dues,
I didn't ask for that
Didn't ask that of you.
Never again
I didn't ask for that.
Never could walk away
But you couldn't stay, either.
Never in my heart, never again,
Never thought it would end in sin.
I never believed in sin,
But this one hurt

The Complete Second Verse
Dr. Charles Cooper

The both of us.

Blunt words make the sharpest cuts,
Cuts that take the pain away.
So I'm working on tomorrow,
And I'm living today.
Wash my heart clean
The blood stains in my shirt,
Wash my heart clean,
With touch and love and work.
Wash my heart clean
I want to know what being loved means

I'm looking for signs of the afterlife,
I'm looking for tomorrow, today.
I've found a glory, a majesty
In the imagining
That we call "We."
And that is all I have.
All I have today,
Telework, tons of books,
A fantastic life,
Friends for life,
but I still want a wife.
I won't apologize for that.

I need a mountain to climb.
I need music to live.
I need the river to thrive.
I need wings to fly.

And a wife who gives
As much as she gets
Without regrets
Or anger.
Without thinking I'm the afterlife.
Considering, after all she's done
Will she think of me as another,
Or does she think of me the one.

Sleeping with the End of Time
Charles Cooper, PhD

The good old days are behind us
Embrace the setting sun.

When I think about what could have been,
I never thought it would end in sin.
I never believed in sin,
But that one hurt you too.
All this damage done,
Too much truth laid in the sun…
For all to see, no thoughts of me.
I have chosen to go on, anyway.
I have chosen to live,
Because the afterlife wife,
The One I've always dreamt of
Is right around the corner,
I will embrace her as a partner,
I will embrace her, as my perfect end.

The Complete Second Verse
Dr. Charles Cooper

SIGNS OF THE AFTERLIFE

Decades come and decades go
Time slips by like melting snow…
Like the burning currency
Which paved the road to
Search for signs of the Afterlife.
Eternity never paid a day's wage.
Wisdom never made a Sage
Of anyone, without time
And experience.

Seeking truth
Is the path of the young.
For those who age,
Remember the race we've run,
It may be too late for victory,
Or to lap the setting sun
But we can find perspective
And glimpse the signs of the afterlife.

Who wants to live forever?
Who wants to know the truth?
I promise you,
Not you, or you,
With your grandiose ideas
Bathing in the whispered writ
Of amoral ambivalence.

Are you so high and mighty?
You can believe in nothing?
But belief in nothing
Disproves nothing,
Acknowledges nothing,
What can you offer in trade
When all you have is nothing?
Hope and Fear
Like a car salesman
Selling a repair

Sleeping with the End of Time
Charles Cooper, PhD

To a used Corvair
You have yet to purchase?
Maybe some small return
On your time, effort, and churn.
Give me one more year
in this bastion of plenty,
Paid for with borrowed money
We used to paint the sky
Happy colors to placate
The fancy new automated workforce.

Palliative politics punish the willing.
Chains are made for you
By you
Out of you
Until you cannot escape the bondage
Because you never learned to fear
You.

All you were taught,
All that you know,
Everything we've lost,
Is there a place left to go
Where we can find
Signs of freedom,
Signs of the afterlife?

The Complete Second Verse
Dr. Charles Cooper

RENEGADE HEART

Baby, it's a renegade heart
That beats entwinned
In your chest, and my...
Some things are better left unsaid.
Some things are better left unread.
It's a renegade heart
That got us this far.

Competition tears down walls
Bonds people into teams.
There is no commune,
There's only me and you.

The self sufficient set afire
Because no less sacrifice
Could mount the pyre
And burn for Creation's sake.
Nothing less than the renegade heart
Could see the end to this thing we started
But did not finish.

Uncertainty doesn't help.
Faith has failed, as well.
Striving, burning,
Sacrificing for you,
The heart, The mind,
Those thoughts you wish you knew.

There's little time left
For salvation.
The fire has leapt to the final floor.
It is a thing to see foundation burning,
But the need
to be
is more.
The light,
        the warmth...

Sleeping with the End of Time
Charles Cooper, PhD

life can go on, please
Get up off your knees
And try.
Strive.

Become a renegade at heart.
Take us back to the start.
Seize the embers that remain
And claim your rightful place
Among the living.

The Complete Second Verse
Dr. Charles Cooper

A MESSAGE FROM TOMORROW

Tomorrow is another day
Crisis comes and panic plays
Protests, riots, no one stays
To make sure
Something's changed.
What's redemption for?
What's forgiveness,
When there is no loss
To speak of.
No way to justify the cost
Or what was gained
Because no one stayed
To make sure
Something has changed.

Actively denied potential
Slavery, limiting the air we breath
Basting meat in creativity
Too long, too tough, too righteous…
No not one…
No not one…
No, not one.

How can I say in my prayers
Go back to the day before
And will that history never happened.

Now what would life have been like?
How do I put a price on maybe
I might as well value the afterlife
Or the predestined fate of a friend
Or the mystical fantasy of a perfect bride
Or the government which never lied.
If only…

Still, when tomorrow called,
It left a message for us all,

Sleeping with the End of Time
Charles Cooper, PhD

Persist, tomorrow is better
Than you can believe
When all that you see is now.
Behind masks and clouds and spring leaves
Are people and dreams
And if they don't give up
And you don't give up
Tomorrow will be extraordinary.

Thank you for not giving up.

The Complete Second Verse
Dr. Charles Cooper

AT THE END

We spend lifetimes
      in pursuit of perfection.
More lives
      seeking better than that.
We stack provisions,
      Add armor
            To our daily attire,
      Acquire a sword,
A scabbard,
      And more.

Since that day,
I have tasted.
I have felt.
I have reveled,
Without stealth.
I have touched.
I have known.
And been known,
Still, I am alone.

My quest,
Not a holy quest,
But a quest to be whole.

Not a perfect person,
But complete,
A connection between two souls.
Decades it took,
Decades of life
Invoice paid in full.
My quest of quests
To know,
      What it is I do not know?

Sleeping with the End of Time
Charles Cooper, PhD

At the end of every road
At the end of every Rainbow
At the end of every quest
There is rest,
And a pot of gold,
Which is an optical illusion
Like the rainbow that brought us here
To you, to me and you.

Here,
I have tasted.
I have felt.
I have reveled,
Without stealth.
I have touched.
I have known,
And been known.

In a way
That paints forever
As the poet's words
Paint the sky,
In the way
I called "epic love"
Every day before today
Such things are never lies.
I said to her, "I love you."
And she, she said it too.

It took forty seven years to find out
How a quest ends.
It ends with rest
And You.

The Complete Second Verse
Dr. Charles Cooper

"LAST STEPS"

Art by Lana Radovich

643

Sleeping with the End of Time
Charles Cooper, PhD

THE AFTERLIFE

What does the afterlife look like,
    Which is worth waiting for?
What does the afterlife look like,
    Which is worth living for?
What does the afterlife look like,
    Which is worth dying for?

Is it heaven, or hell,
    a passionate love spell?
Spun in silver or gold,
    Is it cold, old?
Boiling or hot?
What does it mean this life reborn?

I have believed what I believed.
I have poured out every ounce,
Every inch of passion.
I have been every bit a man and a woman.
I have lived,
Not without chance,
Not without risk,
So many days,
In so many ways
I have put more than my neck
On the chopping block to tempt
Lesser men than me.

All but this one thing,
Which I have hidden away
Behind a door,
But doors are meant to be opened.
To live, you must pass through,
Key in hand, combination in mind,
Gate before you,
This fence you must climb.
Gates and walls are nothing.
Doors are the barriers to life.

644

The Complete Second Verse
Dr. Charles Cooper

You can hide in them, behind them,
Believe in your own lies.

But you can also emerge
To find yourself
Reborn into the Afterlife...
And that is worth waiting for,
Living for, even dying for,
Only life where you are you, and I am me,
Only Life
Is worth that.

BOOK 13: IGNITE THE SUN

9-56-45

DOMINUS DE MAGIA, AMOR, LUX, ET LOQUENS

Ignite the Sun
Charles Cooper, PhD

SURRENDER TO LIFE

Burning heart, flaming mind,
I already know you won't be mine.
And yet I play,
Still I play along.
Let it burn I say.
Watch the flames.
I want for nothing
Save to hold you again.

Let us torch the mount,
Climb the planes
Of existence
Set the flames
To spare the well
Let my mind touch
The ethereal
If the secrets
Burned in hell
I would go,
I would know.
If the price was twice tonight
I would pay.
I would stay.

I never wanted like tonight,
The mind afire.
Flames delight
In my surrender.
My attire.
One more night.
One more night.
Surrender to life.

The Complete Second Verse
Dr. Charles Cooper

MELTING POINT

I harbored dreams of Angels
As a child, a small child.
Life and frowns, I found,
But no angels until now.

Still, I harbor dreams of angels
And a love, so deep
Two people find their melting point.
They bond
And intertwine,
running together...
Complete.

Please be mine?

Is it such a crime?
What say these angels?
What dreams are true?
I thought I was dreaming of Angels,
I realized I was dreaming of you.
With your wings and aura,
Bright as sun.
Liquid copper and gold
Gilt, the metal you made run
As your wings beat above
Heating life at a furious pace
I only want to watch,
For your heart, I can wait.

I hoped that you would come.
But it was not enough for me,
Watching metals melt and run...
Asking if you were a dream...
A fairy tale,
Mystic unicorn,
Flower in flight?
Righteous was the night...

Ignite the Sun
Charles Cooper, PhD

When you made me feel, again.
I might have found it easier
But you would not be mine.
Just one more thing I wanted for,
I was destined not to find.

Dreams can be like that sometimes,
They leave you wanting the truth.
The truth is you are not any one's
                        There is no melting point for you.

The Complete Second Verse
Dr. Charles Cooper

"MICROCOSMOS (DETERMINISMO)"

ART BY REMEDIOS VARO

Ignite the Sun
Charles Cooper, PhD

THE VANGUARD SPIRIT

Creation forward, minds ablaze
Wall or mountain, nothing can stop
The spirit of humanity
Indomitable life.

At birth,
A white clad clinician will verify:
Five fingers and toes,
Arms, and hands
to carry a load
Feet to walk
Legs to run or jump
As the needs arises,
And he will give each of them a score.

In this world you can die of optimism
But living without it,
Seems so much worse.
Hands, feet, fingers, and toes in tact,
or not,
Through the vanguard spirit,
We rise.

For now,
So much is common-place.
We do what we must
To survive.
But the ideas do not falter
The dreams do not vanish
We vanquish obstacles,
It's what we do.
These lives are ours,
For us to rule.

Somewhere in the midst of the mechanics
You find, the thing that makes people more,
The mind, the passion,

The Complete Second Verse
Dr. Charles Cooper

And the river from which all things flow.
What of creation:
The creators that we became
What of the afterlife
Where heaven and hell are all the same
Like beer, state fairs, and pork rinds
Which were fun at the time,
But there's a smell of regret that never goes away.

Cast down, cast aside, trod upon,
Relishing anguish,
Two roads divide
But you chose wrong.
These days, everything is wrong.
These are the times,
Littered with crimes…
We must turn inward
To the spirit
The vanguard spirit,
So we can rise.
We are creators…
Artists…
More…

Take wings, take flight,
You were created, a vanguard spirit,
With matching mind
Not to be denied
Not to be silenced
Flight.

Take heart, take wings and fly.

Ignite the Sun
Charles Cooper, PhD

WHAT IS TODAY...

What is today valued at,
So much time spent planning,
So much time left behind.
What is the consequence of a day lost
That no one can ever get back?
What is a day worth lived in the sun,
Lived in your arms,
With nothing left undone.

There are consequences to life, to living.
There is something precious in each one
But we've lost too many moments
For me to even try to run.
Today is the day I promised,
I will never go away.
The roots of another circumstance
Never blinded me to you.
I saw the light, which came from you...
Nothing else would ever do.

What is today worth?
Nothing without you.
The only life worth living
Is today times you.

The Complete Second Verse
Dr. Charles Cooper

NOT ENOUGH LOVE

There's not enough love,
Not enough love.
There's nothing left for me.
At the end of the day
Energy Spent
I lay in wait
And pay the rent
But there's no love left for me.

Haunted tunes
And vines of Kudzu
Growing over me
Like a tent.
Time ticked by,
I accept the lie,
There's not enough love for me.
Harmonic blooms
Vines of Kudzu cover everything
There's not enough love to heal,
Not enough love to steal
Another hour in my bed for you.
There's not enough love for you.

There's not enough love for me.
I wanted everything,
The castle, moat, and drawbridge...
Love buried deep,
Sealing every breech,
Where the vines grow through,
Because there's not enough love for you.

What I thought I wanted,
Terrified me...
One plus one is nothing
When there's not enough love for me.
Time passes by, not enough love.
No rest, I won't cry, not enough love.

Ignite the Sun
Charles Cooper, PhD

Harmonic lies, Haunt terrify
There's not enough love for me.

Time passes by.
          Not enough love.
Vines grow and thrive,
          With or without love.
They intertwine and bind
          There is no love
Just pain, wired steel,
          Cutting, slicing, blood.
The blood is so real
You said I couldn't feel,
But you never did love, me.

The Complete Second Verse
Dr. Charles Cooper

FORGED IN THE SUN

I have seen beauty,
You wouldn't believe.
I cannot tell it,
Cannot say the words.
Justice will not allow
My pen to preserve
Her face.
As if bliss had captured
Joy and innocence,
To release the ecstasy
Of the moment of creation
From a polished metal rib.
A gleaming metal with a copper hue
That God took from herself
To forge you.

She knew me, watched as I stared
And memorized every line
Of the dancing fire
Flowing through her hair.
In the ritual, on the alter,
Where she was laid bare,
I was the one who burned,
For standing too close
To the heat of the Sun.
I watched as she was forged for me.

She smiled
And brought me to my knees
Raving like a mad man,
"Dear Lord, Thank You.",
As I burned,
Begging for more, please.

Ignite the Sun
Charles Cooper, PhD

TO THE RIGHT OF THE SUN

You cast no shadow…

I noticed,
The day after forever.
Standing taller than life
Through your grief and strife,
I saw you,
And you cast no shadow.

Like any man my age,
The ghost of the younger self
Lingers large,
Making war against the sage of age and wisdom.
Passion wanes but is not contained;
My wisdom is larger than it has been
And it was stretched, nearly to its end;
You were there,
I still didn't comprehend,
When I saw you,
And you had no shadow.

I looked, I saw, I stared,
But there was no shadow there.

I felt you were near
by the warmth on my skin.

I wanted to be more than I ever had been.

The smile in your eyes,
Made me want to know more.
And every day of learning,
Brought me through another door.

Every word you spoke,
Every truth you intoned,
The gleaming person forged in tests

The Complete Second Verse
Dr. Charles Cooper

Of strength and character
Will, purpose, and hope,
Brought my desire to new peaks.
Still, you cast no shadow.

The gilt, gold hair,
I could not believe was there;
When I reached to touch,
Expecting nothing but air.
Then, my fingers tasted fire,
And I knew,
The flames that I felt burning,
Also burned inside of you.
My resistance was through.
The fight I waged was done.
I was standing to the right of the Sun.

"IF I COULD FLY"

Art by Becky Kiper

THE FREQUENCY OF KRYPTONITE

Clark bent down
Falling near
The statue to a lesser man
Who imagined
Himself
As
So much
More.

It's not that he's strong.
He just keeps happening.

I am, I am not a superman
But repetition
And energy
Drives me
Places no superman could go,
I am vulnerable,
Humble
A father who has failed
And succeeded,
Leapt and flown
For a moment of time
To fall and try again.

Every morning,
I am closer to who I know
I could be
If I only knew
The frequency
Of Kryptonite.

Ignite the Sun
Charles Cooper, PhD

TAKING FLIGHT

The next step is always hard,
I've been gone too long.
Like a lead weight, I lift my leg.
It falls hard beneath me,
And crumbles for want of strength,
You, still the source that compels me to move.

Reunite with me.
Reignite life.
Reunite with me.
You are my soulmate
If not my wife.

I've made a life learning to fall
And get back up.
Mistakes are a constant companion
In life. You have to fight
For what you want,
For what you need.
Once it's spoken aloud,
There's no reprieve.

Reunite with me.
Reignite life.
Reunite with me.
You are my soul
If not my wife.

There's never an easy way, to do it.
No convenient way through
When I see the light in the west
On a road that's barely paved
I think that all of life is staged,
Planned,
But very poorly executed.
I take the next step.
This time, I know we can.

The Complete Second Verse
Dr. Charles Cooper

Reunite with me.
Reignite life.
Reunite with me.
You are my soul
If not my wife.

I always take the long way home.
Nothing easy, ever came.
I only ever have one goal:
To see your eyes again,
The setting sun, it mocks me,
The lazy grey October sky.
Someday, sometime, before forever,
You and I will reunite
And when we do…

Take flight.

Ignite the Sun
Charles Cooper, PhD

YOU CAN'T BE MINE

In braised comfort,
Your hand adorned mine,
Soft and tender, our fingers intertwined
Tell me why, baby why,
You can't be mine.

With a burning heart,
And a flaming mind,
I gave you everything
I could divine,
But you still, won't be,
Won't be mine.

I rode all day to find you
It was this road, took me home
I love you sweet baby,
But there's places a man cannot go.
Tell me why, Oh why,
Can't you be mine.

I've got a burning heart,
And a flaming mind,
I would travel all day
Just hoping to find…
One more glimpse of you.
There's nothing I would not do.
Just tell me why, baby why,
You can't be mine.

The Complete Second Verse
Dr. Charles Cooper

CHAINS

Much too young for chains,
Hands so full of life
Too full to be restrained.
You were too young for chains.
I swore you'd never know sorrow,
Swore never to say goodbye.
Swore I'd never fall again,
But I'm much too young to lie.

Lord knows I'll make the promise.
Lord knows it aught to be
You are the girl worthy of chains,
These chains, I made from love
A lock and a key for you and me
Sweet layered links of ecstasy.

Hallowed halls of wrecking balls
Satin sheets spun, wailed, and railed
Spinning around blending sound with your whirling gown.
I made these chains to last forever
Then I found your links on the ground.

You were much too young for chains,
Never thought that you'd distain
The links between you and me.
Never thought you'd say goodbye,
But sometimes people leave.
Sometimes we lay down the chains
Sometimes we get up and walk away
Because love doesn't stay the same.
Love never stays the same.
Sometimes people don't grow together
Even when they live together.
Sometimes when people say forever,
They mean until I change or
Until I break the chains.

Lord knows I'll keep my promise.
Lord knows it's all for you.
I made these chains of love girl
With a lock and a key for my heart girl,
My broken heart, my broken heart, my broken heart… Girl.

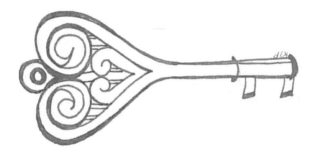

"FOR EVERY LOCK, A KEY"

ART BY BECKY KIPER

"IGNITE THE SUN"

PHOTO BY CHARLES COOPER

IGNITE THE SUN

Broken patterns rise
As they have fallen,
Again and again and again.
Another year passed away.
Hazy days all ablaze
In fire and might
No light like midnight,
When the desert is cold and hungry.

A strand of coiled iron
And oxygen slides across the skin
Drawing blood, again.
Rust is a thing which pays in pain,
Blends with strength and strain;
The effort is enough to make my heart sing, again.

So far beyond masquerading men
Who paint their play in modern

Ignite the Sun
Charles Cooper, PhD

Hues of gray
And end their song at night.
For them, the sun refuses to rise,
They pray, I open my eyes,
Because they know
What I know…
This is what it takes to win.

I cannot rejoice in my redemption,
I never took that deal.
I have bathed in stolen feelings,
And pretended they were real.
Experience and time
Would make them mine.
But who has time for that.
Real, warm, sharp and real.
The blood makes it real.
The effort is real.
Belief makes it real.

My steel will carry us through this
As if, nothing I do can ever be undone?
Iron and coal and high carbon
I will take a breath,
Raise my hand
And ignite the sun…
To feel it burn.
And we burn.

Beating heart and high heat
Until the fuel fades
And dampens creation.
As the days drag on,
The light dims.
None of us are as young,
as we once were.

You knew what it was to strive.
I knew the instant

The Complete Second Verse
Dr. Charles Cooper

Living was no longer the lie
I told myself for so long.

A patient still, small voice,
Has so much command:
"What does it mean,
To be a man?"
It means never having to say
I could have been…

CONTAIN THE FEAR

I do.

IT'S TIME TO RUN,

I do.

SACRIFICE EVERYTHING
TO RAISE MY HAND,
AND IGNITE THE SUN
ONE MORE TIME.
THIS I DO WITH INK AND RHYME,
AND PAGES BURNING WITH MY MIND.

Burning at the heart of the sun
Are all those lives we give
To try and strive,
To grow and give.
I feel it.

Every time you choose ideals
Over convenience or waste.
Never waste a day.
Never take the easy way.

Every time you refuse to fall
For one more lie.
Fighting to stay true
To the self… you must try.

Ignite the Sun
Charles Cooper, PhD

Every time
With will and wonder,
We bind broken hands,
Touch broken hearts,
Find a moment to make a monument to
Common ground on which to stand.
Every time I feel the will
of passions combine,
People who shine
Voices which sing
To ignite the sun,
With work and a dream.
There in the fiery glow,
we all grow.

For this day
to the next,
For the mountains steep and long,
For the trail beneath my feet,
as I climb, and leap, and feel,
For the moon with her crown
Of raven hair tossed,
And scarred with scatter shot stars
For this, a man would try.

Pierced ear and claw,
Sword and shield aloft,
Train cars in a parking lot
And the wasteland of York,
Make up the 9 fiery heads
of the dragon,
Who calls out the maker,
"Creator, come forth!"

I want to hide
Behind so much pride.
I want to bind myself deep inside you,
One more time,
To see the mountain's majesty

The Complete Second Verse
Dr. Charles Cooper

Unfold on my flank
All dark and steep
The pain and humility
Focus me,
Eyes growing sharp
In the light,
Which polishes the blade
Of impossibility
Which sharpens the
Promise of redemption
On the cheap,
Are we fallen?
Or do we rise.

Steep and wide, the mountain.
Deep and wide, the cliff.
If I follow the trail, I cannot fail.
So I take the step...
Wings mean nothing
In the absence of air.
Breath means less
In the presence of war.
I went through it all
Like a painted, Persian whore.
No truths are hidden any more.
No innocence was lost
It was the cost of the flame.
For me and for her,
It was just a trade.
It seems I am human after all,
I can't help myself.
I ask, "why am I here...
Trying to recompense?
Trying to be a man?
Trying to Ignite the sun
With a feeble, frail hand?

I take on so much
I need more than one crutch.

Ignite the Sun
Charles Cooper, PhD

When the crutches give out
I have to find a way
To support the world
I have made.
I will never walk away.
I give all that I can…
I bear burdens long enough
To be worthy of redemption…
But I cannot make the trade,
Cannot be forgiven
For myself
By myself.
Try as I might,
The spark and the light
Remain just out of reach.
Redemption is not my game.
I never found the value
In letting go of anything in this life.

This world is a sponge
Seeking whom it may devour
Feeding on life.
It takes and gives,
Forgives much,
But I like the fire,
Living, and desire.
If I can, I will be consumed
On my own funeral pyre,
And so, Ignite the Sun
With my life.

I'm far too driven,
To walk away again.
The time and effort spent
More than justifies
The callouses
on my mind and heart,
feet and hands,
Stern command

The Complete Second Verse
Dr. Charles Cooper

This fight is my gift
Like some sacrificial lamb.

Ignite the sun,
Vicarious array of flame
And light,
Ignite.
I gave my blood
For this *right*...

My feet are screaming.
I ask them for more.
My arms afire,
I command them, "more."
I beckon my mind,
To strive, ignite,
Every ounce of me,
Every atom,
Every breath
Commands your ears,
Like music in youth
And vanquished fears.
So I can have a chance to say:

I lived this life for love,
And I gave it all away.
With my last breath,
I leave these words, "I love you,"
My love will never fade.

Take this flame,
Ignite your life
With light.
Ignite the sun, and shine.

APPENDICES

INDEX OF FIRST LINES

N

O

P

Q

R

S

T

V

W

The Complete Second Verse
Dr. Charles Cooper

THE GUIDE to Solving the Puzzle Contained Herein:

There is a key in this book. Doors open and close. There are clues in everything. Codes live, no one knows why the NSA lies when they have so many truths from which to choose. If you've read my previous poems and study this book, gates will open and rewards will present themselves. The value of some information is worth as much as life itself. The reward hidden here along with the journey of discovery, is more valuable than information.

These are the rules:
1. Everything means something.
2. Some things mean more.
3. Places are relevant.
4. People are the most critical.
5. Codes are in everything I have written. Locate the guideposts to solve these codes.
6. There are six gates, two gates and four doors to be precise. Find the key to each and they will open for you.
7. Use the clues to make the journey. A combination of clues, codes, and locations will bring you to the solution. There the prize will present itself to you and change your life forever.

Read, dream, and solve my Friends;

DR. CHARLES B. COOPER III, PHD

ACKNOWLEDGEMENTS

A work such as this is not created without an enormous amount of assistance, guidance, and inspiration. The people who have been this for me are too numerous to name. With that said, there are a few people I want to call out by name:

Charles Cooper IV, Madelyn Cooper, Elizabeth Hill, Ray Hyde, Jared & Kelley Breeden, Dack Axselle, Jared Sims, Terry Conrad, Jay Waitkus, Stella Samuel, Lana Radovich, Becky Kiper, The Footprints Sunday School class, Jane Smith, Charles McCormick, Elizabeth Preston, Nicole Sabbaugh, Dr. Daniel Ford, Dr. Beate Rodewald, Dr. Kostas Matakos, Prof. Amrita Dhillon, Dr. Ferdinand Eibl, Dr. Florian Foos, Dr. Christel Koop, Dr. Gabriel Leon, Dr. Pierre-Louis Vezina, Amy Lloyd, Matthew Mele, Julie Ross, Amy Baird, James B. Owens, Leonard Cohen, Andrea Gibson, Kathryn Penrose, Kelly Jane Torrance, Joy Gibson, Melaney Fischer, Melanie Wilhite, Tammera Cooper, my Mother and Father, The Rhyne Family, Isaac Varner, Stephanie Smith, the staff of the Hunter Holmes McGuire VA Medical Center, The Veterans Writing Project, as well as, the veterans in the support group and all the veterans everywhere.

Each of you have given to this work as you have given to me. I thank you.

Dr. Charles Bradford Cooper III, PhD